THE PRINCIPAL'S GUIDE TO

CURRICULUM LEADERSHIP

THE PRINCIPAL'S GUIDE TO

CURRICULUM LEADERSHIP

RICHARD D. SORENSON
LLOYD MILTON GOLDSMITH
ZULMA Y. MÉNDEZ
KAREN TAYLOR MAXWELL

CORWIN
A SAGE Company

FOR INFORMATION:

Corwin
A SAGE Company
2455 Teller Road
Thousand Oaks, California 91320
(800) 233–9936
Fax: (800) 417–2466
www.corwin.com

SAGE Ltd.
1 Oliver's Yard
55 City Road
London EC1Y 1SP
United Kingdom

SAGE India Pvt. Ltd.
B 1/I 1 Mohan Cooperative Industrial Area
Mathura Road, New Delhi 110 044
India

SAGE Asia-Pacific Pte. Ltd.
33 Pekin Street #02–01
Far East Square
Singapore 048763

Acquisitions Editor: Arnis Burvikovs
Associate Editor: Desirée Bartlett
Editorial Assistant: Kimberly Greenberg
Permissions Editor: Karen Ehrmann
Production Editor: Jane Haenel
Copy Editor: Codi Bowman
Typesetter: Hurix
Proofreader: Susan Schon
Indexer: Terri Corry
Cover Designer: Michael Dubowe

Copyright © 2011 by Corwin

Printed in the United States of America

Library of Congress Cataloging-in-Publication Data

Sorenson, Richard D., author.
The principal's guide to curriculum leadership / Richard D. Sorenson, Lloyd Milton Goldsmith, Zulma Y. Méndez, Karen Taylor Maxwell.

pages; cm
Includes bibliographical references and index.

ISBN 978-1-4129-8080-7 (pbk.)

1. Curriculum planning—United States. 2. School principals—United States. 3. Educational leadership—United States. 4. School management and organization—United States. I. Goldsmith, Lloyd Milton, author. II. Méndez, Zulma Y., author. III. Maxwell, Karen Taylor, author. IV. Title.

LB2806.15.S66 2011

375'.001—dc22   2010041856

This book is printed on acid-free paper.

11 12 13 14 15 10 9 8 7 6 5 4 3 2 1

Contents

List of Tables and Figures

Tables

Figures

Preface

Now that I'm here, where am I?

—Janice Joplin

Pathways to curriculum leadership may be well traversed or newly blazed. However, the curricular trail for many principals is seldom easily trod. Sometimes, principals serving as curriculum leaders wonder if they are on a rocky footpath to a steep mountain grade or in the fast lane of a superhighway or seeking an approaching expressway off-ramp to a safer, more secure, and less traveled frontage road. Such is curriculum leadership—finding the right curricular approach, without detour, in pursuit of organizational excellence, instructional expertise, and academic achievement for all students.

We have purposefully incorporated a "road less traveled" analogy in our Preface as a means of suggesting to the reader that effective curriculum leadership must go beyond traveling the beaten path that continually leads to a curricular destination where far too many principals have tread: The same old place doing the same old thing! We intimate such because it has been said that curriculum is a topic about which just about everyone has extensive knowledge because most have been to school. In reality, few can even define the term. This is not meant to demean. It is simply a fact, and one all too often associated with school principals.

Janice Joplin posed a thought-provoking question so relatable to the topic of curriculum leadership—"Now that I'm here, where am I?" (Echols, 2000). Permit *The Principal's Guide to Curriculum Leadership* to reveal the "where am I" in connection with curricular leadership by forging detectable footprints to be followed, thus directing school leaders to a wide and open roadway where all can clearly see beyond the long shadows of curricular avoidance and organizational mediocrity. Therefore, *The Principal's Guide to Curriculum Leadership* is written to assist principals and prospective principals in understanding the meaning of curriculum as well as curriculum development, integration, evaluation, reform, and renewal.

Principals who desire to enhance their curricular leadership skills will value this book. The book is more than a desk reference or resource. It has been purposefully written to introduce the school leader to effective curricular and instructional techniques and methods and to further allow the leader to apply knowledge gained from the chapter readings directly to the field of practice. *The Principal's Guide to Curriculum Leadership* provides real examples—through practical application, relevant scenarios, and applicable case studies—all designed to better illustrate how principals can become effective curriculum leaders who possess the skills and abilities to guide faculty and students to a new era in curriculum development, instructional initiatives, and programmatic quality and distinction.

To ensure the book's usefulness, it has been purposely organized into brief, single-topic-focused chapters. Each chapter begins with an appropriate quote and general overview and includes numerous visuals, tables, figures, and practical activities of relevance and interest—each related to the field of administrative practice and curriculum leadership:

> Chapter 1, Defining Curriculum Leadership, introduces the reader to Principal Will Wonkermann of Childers School; a character-theme is interweaved throughout the text. This chapter presents three organizational factors that influence curriculum leadership—loose coupling, systems thinking, and collaboration—detailing how each of these factors impacts curriculum leadership.

> Chapter 2, A Curriculum Leadership Journey, investigates the Interstate School Leaders Licensure Consortium (ISLLC) standards relative to the curriculum leadership role. Readers are taken on an imaginary journey through the standards via the imagination of Principal Will Wonkermann. This journey follows a different kind of yellow brick road. So put on your ruby-red Reeboks, tap your heels together three times, and say, "There's no place like an effective school!"

> Chapter 3, Principal Expectations as Curriculum Leader, investigates how high expectations are the key to effective curriculum leadership. High expectations improve instruction, increase faculty performance and student achievement, and equate to overall curricular improvement.

Chapter 4, The Principal's Role in Curriculum Change and Innovation, details how a principal can incorporate curricular change as a means of removing causal factor barriers that inhibit instructional improvement and hinder student achievement.

Chapter 5, Curriculum Leadership in Action, presents an examination of the principal role in curriculum design and development expanding on Walker's Deliberative Model of Curricular Planning. This chapter explores how principals can monitor the curriculum process from the initial development of a curriculum platform, through the deliberation phase of curriculum development, and onto the campus design and implementation stages of successful curriculum revision and reform.

Chapter 6, Where the Action Is: Building Relationships With Teachers, acknowledges how critical it is for principals as curriculum leaders to establish relationships of trust and understanding with faculty and staff. The chapter examines how principals must build a culture free of fear, a teaching/learning arena in which personnel collaborate, and a risk-free environment where meaningful discussions are the norm relative to curriculum development, reform, and revision.

Chapter 7, Systematically Integrating Curriculum and Instruction, examines how principals can lead curricular improvement by integrating curriculum and instruction, which allows faculty to focus on interdisciplinary actions that effectively correlate with student interest, relevant lessons, and meaningful learning.

Chapter 8, Professional Learning and Curriculum Leadership, permits the reader to better understand the leadership role in professional development and how professional learning influences the development, renewal, and delivery of curriculum. Building teacher capacity to best impact effective curriculum leadership and development is also examined.

Chapter 9, The Principal and Legislated Learning: Working the System and the Prospects of Curriculum Renewal, examines the role of legislated or mandated learning and its relationship with curriculum renewal in schools. Readers learn of the process of curriculum renewal and change in an era of shrinking curriculum development and renewal when the demands of corporate America and the mandates of federal and state legislatures dictate public school curriculum. The question to consider throughout this chapter is, What's a principal to do to bring about needed curriculum renewal to our schools?

Chapter 10, Trailblazing Digital Curriculum Leadership 101, introduces the reader to digital curriculum leadership, essential in an era of systemic change. This chapter reminds, if not challenges, the educational leader of the necessity to explore new technologies, analyze technological trends, and confront technical realities as related to curriculum development and reform. In this chapter, the reader will examine curricular methods that correspond to the creation of a digital learning environment. Moreover, the reader will learn of digital procedures as correlated with curriculum implementation via voices from the field of practice.

The Epilogue, the "bow that tops the package," has been designed to connect the 10 chapters of *The Principal's Guide to Curriculum Leadership* and, thus, help the reader conceptually grasp the textual contents. The Epilogue, in the literary world, often details the fate of a book's main character or characters. To some degree, such is true of this book's main character, Will Wonkermann. Now, be patient and wait until you have read the first 10 chapters before turning to the epilogue!

Special features of the book include the following:

- Discussion questions

- Case study applications and problems

- Experiential activities, scenarios, and exercises

- References and resources

Will Wonkermann, Principal of Childers School

A very unique aspect of this book intertwines, from chapter-to-chapter, a lead character by the name of Will Wonkermann, principal at Childers School. Principal Wonkermann helps direct the reader along a continuous and thematic pathway, allowing for a better understanding of the curriculum leadership role. Will Wonkermann is introduced in the book as a relatively new principal at a school with instructional and organizational challenges. He becomes the vehicle throughout the book to represent you the reader. Principal Wonkermann, like you, yearns to be an effective leader. He is eager to learn and explore curriculum leadership processes. Will Wonkermann brings to life a good story, along with interesting characters throughout the text. Who doesn't enjoy a good story? We invite you to actively engage in Principal Wonkermann's embedded story, and the stories of others, as a method of learning more about curriculum leadership. See yourself in these stories. See your colleagues. See how you can change your personal story and the stories of others through effective curriculum leadership.

Finally, *The Principal's Guide to Curriculum Leadership* has been written to provide the principal with essential information and fundamental skills vital to the successful partnering of curriculum and instruction, all designed to benefit our schools' most precious commodity—students—who must always come first and foremost in every curricular decision and instructional effort.

We commend you to the rich and descriptive processes of effectively leading curriculum development, integration, reform, evaluation, and renewal—each of which is depicted in this book for informational reading as well as for content understanding, in-depth analysis, and practical application. May this text lead the reader in the direction of an exciting quest that follows a roadway of proven theory leading to an avenue of essential practice!

We also welcome your feedback as to how we can better enhance the next edition of *The Principal's Guide to Curriculum Leadership*. Your ideas and suggestions can be shared with us by writing or e-mailing Corwin at 2455 Teller Road, Thousand Oaks, California 91320–2218 (Corwin.com).

> *Do not go where the path may lead, go instead where there is no path and leave a trail.*
>
> —Ralph Waldo Emerson

Acknowledgments

To Donna—35 years with my best friend! It's been quite a ride, has it not sweetheart? Donna is "mom" to our two wonderful children, Lisa and Ryan, and to our fine son-in-law, Sam.

My amazing endeavors in the educational profession began 33 years ago with the intervention of my Lord and Savior, Jesus Christ, who worked through a most amazing human being—the now deceased Dr. Buckley Qualls. Donna and I loved this gentle giant of a man. He exemplified what it meant to be an instructional leader and, more important, a servant of God.

I first met Dr. Qualls when I was student teaching. He had the highest of expectations for his students, and I was fortunate that he liked my work. Dr. Qualls directed me toward my first teaching position. He encouraged me to pursue my doctorate in educational leadership. Dr. Qualls was my mentor and remains my hero. I am most indebted, and I do miss you, sir!

—RDS

I would be nothing if it weren't for my family, my friends, and my Lord. Thank you for being patient with me, inspiring me, and growing me.

—LMG

I will always be indebted to my friends and colleagues at The University of Texas at El Paso's Department of Leadership and Foundations. In particular, I am thankful for the unyielding support of Dr. Teresa Cortez, Dr. Rodolfo Rincones, Dr. Kathleen Staudt, Dr. Arturo Pacheco, and Dr. Richard Sorenson. I remain forever grateful to my family. They are a source of endless love and encouragement. *Gracias, papá*, Ramón, and Renato—my life companion and best friend.

—ZYM

Now to him who is able to do immeasurably more than all we ask or imagine, according to his power that is at work within us, to him be glory in the church and in Christ Jesus throughout all generations forever and ever! Amen. (Ephesians 3:20–21)

—*KTM*

Publisher's Acknowledgments

Corwin would like to thank the following individuals for their editorial insight and guidance:

Sean Beggin, Assistant Principal
Andover High School
Andover, MN

Scott Hollinger, Vice President for Talent Development
IDEA Public Schools
Weslaco, TX

Evelyn Robles-Rivas, Principal
Worthington Hooker Elementary School
New Haven, CT

About the Authors

 **Richard D. Sorenson** is an associate professor in the Educational Leadership and Foundations Department at The University of Texas at El Paso (UTEP). He received his EdD from Texas A&M University–Corpus Christi in the area of educational leadership. Dr. Sorenson served public schools for 25 years as a social studies teacher, principal, and associate superintendent for personnel. Currently, Dr. Sorenson serves as director of the Principal Preparation Program at UTEP, and he works with graduate students teaching coursework related to school personnel, school-based budgeting, educational law, and leadership development. He was named the University of Texas at El Paso College of Education Professor of the Year in 2005, is involved with several educational initiatives on the U.S./Mexico border, and is an active writer with numerous professional journal publications. He is coauthor, along with Lloyd Goldsmith, of two Corwin books, *The Principal's Guide to School Budgeting* (2006) and *The Principal's Guide to Managing School Personnel* (2009). Dr. Sorenson has also authored textbooks, teacher resource guides, and workbooks in the area of the elementary and secondary school social studies curricula. He conducts workshops at the state and national levels on topics such as principal preparation, instructional and administrative leadership, and effective teaching practices. He has been actively involved with the Texas Elementary Principals and Supervisors Association, the Texas Association of Secondary School Principals, for which he conducts annual new principal academy seminars, and the Texas Council for the Social Studies. Dr. Sorenson has based his professional life and career on the Biblical principle found in Proverbs 16:3, "Commit your works to the Lord and your plans will be established" (New American Standard Bible). His research interest is linked to the

school leadership role, specifically the examination of conditions and factors that inhibit and discourage lead teachers from pursuing the school principalship as a career option. Dr. Sorenson has been married to his wife Donna, a medical coder, for the past 35 years and has two children: daughter Lisa is a kindergarten teacher who is married to Sam, a petroleum engineer (both Hook 'Em Horns alumni), and son Ryan is a student at UTEP—all of whom are the pride and joy of his life. Of course, the Sorenson family remains a lover of pugs, most notably—One Little Bit and Olive too!

 **Lloyd Milton Goldsmith** is an associate professor in the Graduate Studies in Education Department at Abilene Christian University. He earned his EdD in educational leadership from Baylor University. Dr. Goldsmith has been a leader in transitioning the principal program from a residential program to a quality online program. He teaches courses in school culture, professional development, resource management, and continuous improvement of instruction. He served public schools for 29 years as an elementary science teacher, middle school assistant principal, and elementary school principal. He is coauthor with Richard Sorenson of two Corwin books, *The Principal's Guide to School Budgeting* (2006) and *The Principal's Guide to Managing School Personnel* (2009). He and a fellow chemistry professor Dr. Kim Pamplin codirect a program to facilitate high school chemistry teachers in effective instructional strategies. Recently, he assisted the Texas Education Agency in migrating a state-mandated training on instructional leadership to an online format. Dr. Goldsmith has served as president of the Texas Council of Professor Educational Administration. He is active in the Texas Association of School Administrators. He has presented on educational leadership topics at numerous state, national, and international conferences. Dr. Goldsmith is active in Kiwanas International and Boy Scouts of America. He is active in his church where he teaches Sunday school to lively fourth graders, works with a Boy Scout troop, and leads a life group. Dr. Goldsmith has been married to his wife Mary, a high school science teacher, for 24 years. They have three children. Abigail, a first-year kindergarten teacher, is married to Andrew, a budget analyst. Eleanor, his second daughter, is a student and violinist at Abilene Christian University where she is majoring in elementary and music education. Nelson, his Eagle Scout son, is a junior in high school and a member of its state champion football team. Dr. Goldsmith's favorite activity is hanging around with his family at home playing games.

Zulma Y. Méndez is an assistant professor in the Department of Educational Leadership and Foundations at the University of Texas at El Paso. She earned her PhD from the University of California, Riverside. Her current research and publications explore the relationship between curriculum policy and practice across a number of educational contexts, including the undergraduate curriculum and more recently, at a junior high school in the city of Ciudad Juárez, Mexico. Examining how educational policy is implemented vis-à-vis a standardized curriculum, Professor Méndez continues to probe the limits and possibilities of educational change through curricular reform. She also enjoys teaching and, presently, teaches courses in the area of curriculum studies and qualitative methods of educational research.

Karen Taylor Maxwell is an assistant professor in the Graduate Studies in Education Department at Abilene Christian University (ACU). Her fields of interest include secondary education, behavior management, and campus leadership. Dr. Maxwell holds a Bachelor of Arts degree in English from ACU, master's degrees in curriculum and instruction and educational administration from Texas A&M University–Corpus Christi, and a doctorate in educational leadership from Nova Southeastern University. Before coming to ACU in 2006, Dr. Maxwell worked with the Region 2 Education Service Center in Corpus Christi, Texas, where she codirected a principal certification program and directed the Principal Assessment/Development Center. She also worked extensively with schoolwide discipline programs and behavior management. Dr. Maxwell has taught graduate level courses in educational administration at Texas A&M University–Kingsville, Texas A&M University–Corpus Christi, and Walden University. She has K–12 teaching experience at elementary, middle, and high school levels in public and private schools and has served as a campus principal at the elementary and high school levels. Dr. Maxwell and her husband John met as ACU students and have been married for more than 40 years. Before coming to Abilene, Texas, John served for 15 years as an elder in their local church and managed a medical practice in Corpus Christi, Texas. Karen and John have two children, Marc (Texas Tech 1998), a certified public accountant in Portland, Oregon, and MaryBeth (Lubbock Christian University 1997, Texas Tech 1999), and a son-in-law, Charlton Taylor (Lubbock Christian University 1999, ACU 2004), who ministers the

Golf Course Road Church in Midland, Texas. Charlton and MaryBeth have three sons, Kaden (9), Ashton (6), and Pierson (4). On February 22, 2006, John suffered a massive stroke. He is recovering from paralysis and speech disorders and the whole family continues to adjust to new and challenging circumstances. Dr. Maxwell believes that campus leadership is central to student success, and her goal is to assist with the development of strong, effective campus curriculum leaders.

1

Defining Curriculum Leadership

So much time, and so little to do!

—Willy Wonka in *Willy Wonka and the Chocolate Factory* (Wolper & Stuart, 1971)

Getting Started

We believe it was conceived in 1989. *It* being standards-based reform. The National Council of Teachers of Mathematics (NCTM) developed national standards for "what every student should know and be able to do" (NCTM, 1989, p. 2) in mathematics. Other content areas followed the NCTM's lead and, likewise, created national standards for their fields of study. Not to be left out, states gave birth to state versions. Some state versions were similar to the national standards; others differed. Standards were accompanied by accountability requirements for school districts and individual campuses. These accountability requirements were conjoined with high-stakes testing as well as penalties for those districts and schools that failed to meet the perceived mastery requirements for the standards (Seidel & Short, 2005).

Principals and teachers soon found themselves confronted with what appeared to be an endless list of expectations that their students must meet. Some estimated it would take 22 years for a student to master all the national standards (Marzano & Kendall, 1998). If expectations were not met, dire consequences would be meted out to school districts and individual campuses. Politicians ruled. Creative teaching suffered. Learning fractured. Accountability reigned. Assessment sorted. Teachers mourned. Principals lamented. The system lost its equilibrium.

What is a principal to do?

The opening quote makes it obvious that Willy Wonka never served as a principal, curriculum designer, instructional leader or any other position associated with the design, implementation, alignment, and evaluation of curriculum. If he had served such a role, Willy's quote would have read, "So little time, and so much to do." On the other hand, maybe Willy had been a principal—a principal who didn't understand curriculum leadership.

Willy, a character from Ronald Dahl's book *Charlie and the Chocolate Factory*, was the entrepreneur of Wonka Candy Company and maker of Everlasting Gobstoppers and Wonka Bars. Willy was brought to life in the 1971 film *Willy Wonka and the Chocolate Factory*, starring Gene Wilder. He was reintroduced to another generation in the 2005 film *Charlie and the Chocolate Factory*, starring Johnny Depp.

What separates Willy from other confectioners is his uncanny imagination, which he uses to develop products that connect with children. He makes the impossible possible by creating items such as candy eggs that hatch moving and chirping chocolate chip birds. He even develops a nonmelting ice cream.

Willy cannot operate his unusual candy factory by himself. He needs the assistance of his devoted employees, the Oompa-Loompas. These individuals, although small in stature, possess important skills and unique qualities. For example, Oompa-Loompas have the uncanny ability to always land on their feet, much as a cat does. They communicate primarily through gestures, mime, and song. The Oompa-Loompas sang four songs in the films causing adolescents to pause and think about their behaviors (Ross & Burton, 2005; Wolper & Stuart, 1971).

Just as Willy Wonka used his imagination to connect with children in a meaningful manner, those of us in curriculum leadership must use our uncanny imagination to lead schools where curriculum connects students with learning in a meaningful manner. More than 60 years ago, Gordon Mackenzie, a professor of education at Columbia University, called for curriculum leadership when he opined, "However, the focal point of attention, in any inquiry as to what the school can do, is the curriculum. Viewing the school curriculum in terms of the hazards and the possibilities of life today, the need for leadership here, as in other life is at once clear" (Mackenzie, 1949, p. 264). Mackenzie's call for curriculum leadership 40 years prior to the NCTM standards was broader than one might think. Mackenzie's uncanny imagination envisioned curriculum leadership coming from anyone, yes anyone, who "will think clearly on major problems, and will help to release the leadership in others in solving these problems" (p. 264). Principals have a moral obligation to provide curriculum leadership and, in doing so, involve anyone willing to share in curriculum leadership.

Curriculum leadership involves everyone. Willy needed help from the Oompa-Loompas to successfully operate his chocolate factory, much like campus curriculum leaders need faculty and staff to successfully lead schools. Like the Oompa-Loompas, faculty and staff possess important skills and unique qualities. Some even have the uncanny ability to land on their curriculum feet.

PRINCIPAL WONKERMANN'S LATE AFTERNOON EXPERIENCE

Over the last couple of decades, schools throughout the United States have developed mission statements. Nearly all, if not all, of these statements espouse a belief that all students can learn or that all students will meet with academic success or some variance thereof. For the most part, these are noble and honorable statements. However, mission statements are often developed, framed, and forgotten. But they *were* developed. Stakeholders did encode their mission into written words. These words did capture the heart and purpose of their schools.

Will Wonkermann, principal of Childers School, is standing in his school's foyer reading the school's mission statement prominently displayed on a banner, "All students will meet with academic success." The school is empty except for Mr. Wonkermann. The banner is in the school's colors; the school's mascot stands guard at either end of the statement. Looking at it, he asks himself, "Do I *really* believe this? Do my faculty and staff believe this? Do the parents believe this? Am I blinded by a soft bigotry of low expectations for certain student groups, thus, making me skeptical of the mission statement's practicality?"

The thought of soft bigotry reminded Will of the 1987 film, *Stand and Deliver*, about a teacher whose high expectations for his East Los Angeles barrio students caused great improvement in their academic performance (Maltin, 2007).

(Continued)

(*Continued*)

Will continues examining the banner. It's dusty. For whatever reason, he is compelled to clean it. After a quick trip to the custodian's closet, he returns with a ladder and a rag. He wipes away the dust of time, returns the ladder, comes back, and stands in the hall, and once again, he stares at the banner.

Cleaning the banner somehow cleared some cobwebs from his thoughts about the mission statement. "Yeah, I *do* believe this statement. But am I just some starry-eyed idealist?" he utters aloud causing an echo to reverberate down the deserted hallway.

There is a loud noise outside the building.

Will's reflexes cause him to turn and peer out the front glass doors. He's not sure what caused the noise. But as he looks outside, Will sees the school's neighborhood. He walks the 15 feet to those glass doors passing a trophy case replete with tarnished trophies and plaques, game balls, and dust.

It's been several months since he came to this school although it seems like yesterday. Somehow, this is the first time Will connects the mission statement with the community. Angst appears. How could this be? How could he have missed this? In an attempt to soothe his uneasiness, Will begins rationalizing about the demands of his job.

Several students are mingling around the flagpole. An elderly couple strolls by on the sidewalk holding hands. Will smiles. A car passes by with a stereo blasting so loud Will feels the glass in the school's front doors vibrate. A billboard advertising a local attorney faces the school. It is in English and Spanish. Will wonders how the school's mission statement would sound in Spanish. He purchases a soda, returns to his office, sits down at his desk, and checks his e-mail. Will's body is in his office, but his mind is still in the hall reading the mission statement. Ownership and responsibility for those seven mission words burns inside him. Two Tums should take care of it. They don't.

All students will meet with academic success. *Todos los estudiantes lograrán exito academico.*

A 15th reading of the mission statement does the trick. Will recalls a curriculum workshop he attended last fall. He knows he has the workshop's binder somewhere in his office. The presenter quoted someone named Jacobs, who said it was Will's responsibility to help the school's stakeholders uncover the purpose of schooling (Jacobs, 2004). Maybe this was the source of his sudden discomfort within him.

The more Will reflects on the mission statement, the deeper he sinks into thought.

The mission statement is on the school's website, it's on the stationery, it's in the student handbook, it's in the faculty handbook, and it's in the campus improvement plan. It's even on the district's website. It's in many places, but somehow, one of those places was not his heart. Will doubts it's in the faculty and staff's hearts either. As a matter of fact, he believes it only exists as vinyl words on the formerly dusty vinyl banner. "Why?" he asks himself, as his awakening continues.

Will, like many others, studied educational leadership at Big State University where he earned a master's degree and obtained his principal certification. Will studied organizational theory, school law, resource allocation, special programs, and foundations of administration. However, this mission statement is begging for something more of Will. The mission statement points him toward curriculum leadership.

In the back of his mind, he vaguely recalls some discussion about curriculum leadership. He also knows that he and his colleagues understand the needs of Childers School better than anyone. Will says to himself, "Curriculum leadership must have something to do with the mission statement. It has to because the mission statement is all about academic success."

Avoidance. That's it! Maybe Will is avoiding thinking about the Childers School mission statement because he is uncertain what to do to transform the mission statement from a collection of vinyl letters on a banner to a reality for Childers's innocents. Will calls his students the innocents because of their naïveté of the educational system. It is a term of endearment.

The mission statement crosses his mind again, in no fewer than two languages. All students will meet with academic success. *Todos los estudiantes lograrán exito academico.*

Will reflects silently, "I know a lot more about administrative leadership than I do about curriculum leadership. But curriculum leadership appears to be what is needed to really remove the dust off of the school's mission statement. Curriculum leadership is required to fulfill the Childers School's mission."

Will realizes all students will meet with academic success if and only if curriculum leadership comes to the forefront of his leadership skill set. "But how can I accomplish this?" he ponders.

The more Will wraps his mind around curriculum leadership, the more excited he becomes. Will recognizes that curriculum issues have a tremendous impact on his school. He constructs a list on how curriculum influences Childers School. It influences the following:

- Schedule

- Calendar

- Budget

- Personnel hiring

- Materials purchased

- Grades

- State assessment ranking

(Continued)

(*Continued*)

Will quickly realizes curriculum leadership is not something he can manage alone. Curriculum leadership requires all school stakeholders' help and support.

He peers at his reflection in a mirror and verbalizes his commitment, "I, Will Wonkermann, principal of Childers School, will involve all of Childers's stakeholders as I grow my curriculum leadership skills." Will pops an Everlasting Gobstopper in his mouth, feeling proud of himself and his newfound commitment. Grinning, he leaves his office laughing aloud, "So much time and so little to do."

It did not take long for a little voice from within to start gnawing on him. "You don't have time to do this, Will. You have discipline matters, reports to complete, IEP meetings, ensuring your school complies with state and federal regulations. You work with the teachers and the staff. Don't you get it, Will? There just isn't enough time to add anything else," the little voice said sweetly. The little voice from within continued its gnawing. "Besides, the Feds and the state are mandating you to death with standards. You're really powerless to do anything about the curriculum. Give up this silly curriculum leadership notion, Will," the voice said temptingly.

The little voice from within smiles. Will sighs. He realizes he has unknowingly abdicated his curriculum leadership responsibility. Will starts shaking his head side to side as if awakening from a nightmare. It's time to reclaim the curriculum leadership role. It's my duty he reminds himself. The innocents are depending on me.

Defining Curriculum Leadership

Principal Will Wonkermann's story may not be all that unusual. School leadership's hectic pace makes important things appear unimportant while making unimportant things appear important. Stephen Covey (1989) addresses *important versus unimportant* in the third habit of his seven habits of highly effective people—"Put first things first" (p. 148). Covey asserts that this habit functions in both leadership and management roles. This is of particular importance because principals serve as managers and as leaders (Smith & Piele, 2006, p. 6).

When serving as managers, principals put Covey's (1989) first-things-first habit into practice by efficiently handling the day-to-day matters of running a school. Rudy Giuliani (2002) reported that beginning in 1981, while serving as mayor of New York City, he started every morning with a meeting of his top staff. Rudy proclaimed these meetings as the cornerstone to efficiently managing the city's day-to-day operations. He prided himself in seeing how much work he could get out of the way during the first hour of the day. Rudy realized he would be overwhelmed if he did not have this daily meeting to determine what needed to be done first that day (p. 29). Although principals do not run an organization the size of New York City, similarities exist. Both organizations are social service oriented; taxpayer funded; and regulated by local, state, and national laws and policies.

Besides serving as managers, principals serve as leaders. As leaders, principals use Covey's (1989) first-things-first habit by providing opportunities for all stakeholders to help establish the school's priorities and create a plan for achieving the identified priorities. This happens in campus planning committees, ad hoc committees, department chair meetings, and so on. The first-things-first habit also manifests itself in such leadership activities as casting the school's vision and mission, spending significant time with faculty, and interacting with students (Ferrandino & Tirozzi, 2004).

Like you, Principal Wonkermann is a decent person. He recognizes the necessity for intentionality in curriculum leadership if he truly expects the school's mission statement to become a reality for all school stakeholders. In fact, Will knows it is the principal—not the superintendent—who is key to curriculum leadership (Lunenberg & Ornstein, 2008). Despite his training and experience, Principal Wonkermann remains unsure of all that is involved in curriculum leadership.

What words or concepts are conjured up in your mind when you think about curriculum leadership? Consider these—curriculum, instruction, assessment, evaluation, NCLB, alignment, benchmarking, staff development, learning, teaching, lessons, units, integration, learner outcomes, instructional technology, standards, tracking, essential skills, audit, and enrichment. You probably have other words you would add to this list and some you would strike from it. Nevertheless, defining the obvious is necessary to gain a deeper understanding of what is meant by curriculum leadership. Fortunately or unfortunately, depending on your perspective, no official definition exists for curriculum leadership.

"The Elephant and the Blind Men" story will help us develop a working definition of curriculum leadership. As the story goes, one blind man touches the elephant's leg and declares the elephant is like a pillar. Another touches the elephant's belly and declares the elephant is like a huge wall. Each of the six blind men touch different parts of the elephant and describe it very differently depending on the part of the elephant that was touched.

Defining curriculum leadership is similar to the six blind men's attempt to define an elephant. It depends on what part of curriculum leadership you are touching when you decide to define it. If you are touching national and state curriculum standards, you might define curriculum leadership as "leading school stakeholders toward clear student goals based on national and state curriculum standards." If you are touching curriculum leadership's renewal, then you might define curriculum leadership as "planning and designing continuous improvement of the curriculum." If you are touching curriculum leadership's teaching dimension, then you might define curriculum leadership as "involving faculty and staff in curriculum development to establish faculty and staff needs while acquiring their commitment to the curriculum." All of the blind men defining the elephant were right. Their definition was driven by the part of the elephant they touched. Likewise, we are all correct in defining curriculum leadership. Our definition was also driven by the part of curriculum leadership we touched.

> Curriculum leadership is connecting curriculum, instruction, assessment, and evaluation in an effort to improve learning and understanding.

For discussion purposes, curriculum leadership is defined as connecting curriculum, instruction, assessment, and evaluation in an effort to improve learning and understanding.

Organizational Phenomena Influencing Curriculum Leadership

Curriculum leadership doesn't function in a vacuum. Curriculum leadership exists within a campus that is typically part of a larger system. Principals must consider how the school's organization influences curriculum leadership if they are to be effective in curriculum leadership. Loose coupling, systems thinking, and collaboration are three such phenomena. Adding to the complexity is that these phenomena do not operate independent of one another.

Loose Coupling

Schools can be considered the epitome of what Weick (1976) defines as a loosely coupled organization. Loose coupling referring to the direct control over how work is accomplished. In the case of schools, principals rarely supervise the daily activities of teachers.

This fragments control by making it difficult for principals to know if directives are being followed. For the most part, teaching in K–12 schools is a private act between students and the teacher. Principals typically observe fewer than 0.001% of a teacher's lessons (Sorenson & Goldsmith, 2009, p. 70). Educators, in a loosely coupled environment, have a tendency to resist ideas that are directed at them from higher up the system or from outside organizations that are part of the school's community. Barth (2001) reminds us, "Many teachers find they can exert more power by saying no than by saying yes" (p. 91). This includes saying no to state and federal rules and regulations. This phenomenon is often overlooked or forgotten by school leaders.

Sometimes school leaders lead schools as if they are tightly coupled organizations. They issue decrees expecting them to be followed. But what happens in the classroom is very different from what a principal or any legislative body decrees. If you have been a classroom teacher or are currently a classroom teacher, you know oh-so-well about this phenomenon's existence. Leaders sometime forget in their zeal to affect change that little opportunity exists to actually directly supervise and monitor the implementation of their directives. Schools are loosely coupled organizations.

Principals must consider loose coupling when exhibiting curriculum leadership because the curriculum is typically delivered unsupervised. Never forget this. *Curriculum is typically delivered unsupervised.* Let's repeat this, curriculum-is-typically-delivered-unsupervised. Loose coupling necessitates principals secure faculty buy-in for any curriculum initiative seeking to improve student learning and understanding. Failure to secure faculty buy-in ensures program failure à la loose coupling. Never underestimate loose coupling's impact on curriculum leadership.

Systems Thinking

Peter Senge and his team of education leaders wrote *Schools That Learn* (Senge et al., 2000) as a field guide for educators and parents to teach how systems thinking applies to schools. Senge perceives the school as a social system functioning at the classroom, school, and community level. He observes that these three systems "interact in ways that are sometimes hard to see but that shape the priorities and needs of people at all levels" (Senge et al., p. 11). What happens in the classroom almost always occurs without direct supervision, but it doesn't happen in isolation from other organizational systems.

The classroom is connected to the school that is connected to the community. Not only are these three systems connected but also a host of other forces influences these systems. Among these forces are government, media, businesses, publishers, and community groups (see Figure 1.1). Curriculum leaders must take into consideration systems thinking and the forces beyond the classroom and campus because they impact curriculum leadership.

Figure 1.1   Forces Acting on Schools

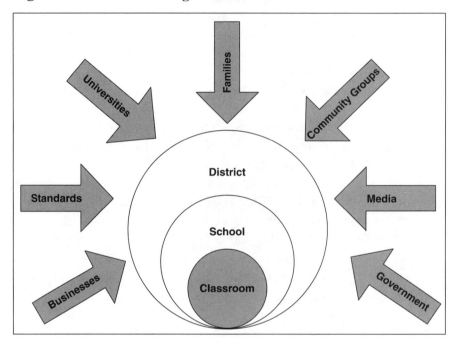

Collaboration

Psychologist Kevin Dunbar's study of groups noted that sparks of collective insight develop during group brainstorming sessions and that the group conversation process actually accelerated the innovative process. In actuality, groups incubated innovation (Sawyer, 2007, p. 128). William J. Gordon's group technique based on creating new analogies using conversation was also found very effective in groups with diverse experiences (Sawyer). Vera John-Steiner, a creativity researcher at the University of New Mexico, identified a form of collaboration she called *integrated collaboration*. This collaboration develops over time with a group. In this collaboration, the work of individuals became less important to the team than the collaboration that created the work. John-Steiner discovered that this collaboration created not only extreme bonding of the group but it also was the most radically innovative (Sawyer, pp. 132, 134).

It's a fatal error not to use collaboration in curriculum matters. Innovation never comes from a single insight; rather, it comes from a series of insights (Sawyer, 2007, p. 7). The 3G iPhone reminds us of this fact. The iPhone is so different from that "brick" cell phone carried in the late 1980s. Even though the 3G iPhone was the latest model when introduced a mere 15 months ago, the 3GS model has already replaced it, and 4G and 5G technology is being developed.

The principal's role as curriculum leader, if done properly, requires involving a wide variety of the school's stakeholders and to do so on a regular basis. As stakeholders collaborate, it's only a matter of time before conflict arises. Some stakeholders resist change; others demand greater and faster change. Public as well as hidden agendas exist. All of this puts stress on the collaborative process and increases the likelihood of conflict.

Collaboration is easier said than done. Humans are social beings, but collaboration remains a challenge for us. For collaboration to exist, conflict must be resolved. In *The Principal's Guide to Managing Personnel* (Sorenson & Goldsmith, 2009), Joe L. Cope introduced the Principal's Peace Primer. Cope reminds us that "it's not all about conflict. Rather it's all about how you *handle* conflict" (p. 101). It's easier to run a school as a dictatorship; the problem with dictatorships and top-down control is people are kept on the bottom. Systems designed to suppress people eventually fail.

Rethinking the Education Hierarchy

The aforementioned loose coupling, systems thinking, and collaboration help us understand phenomena in schools that impact curriculum leadership. Understanding these phenomena is important for curriculum leaders if they are to impact teaching and learning. Could a revision of the education hierarchy make better use of these phenomena, thus improving curriculum, instruction, and achievement?

Adult-Centered Hierarchy Model

State support of education comes with control (Webb, 2006). A typical state education organizational structure begins with the legislature passing education legislation. The state commissioner of education takes this legislation and directs the state education agency in the development of state education and state administrative codes to translate the law and its legislative intent into policy. The policy is distributed to the local education agencies (school districts) where the local school board develops local policies and directs the superintendent in fulfilling state and local policy. In turn, the superintendent directs district- and campus-level administrators in implementing these policies and procedures. The principal, in turn, disseminates the policy to the faculty and staff in a meeting. The faculty, in turn, delivers the curriculum and instruction to the students. Communication is initiated and driven by adults, thus its name—Adult-Centered Hierarchy Model (Figure 1.2).

Figure 1.2   Adult-Centered Hierarchy Model

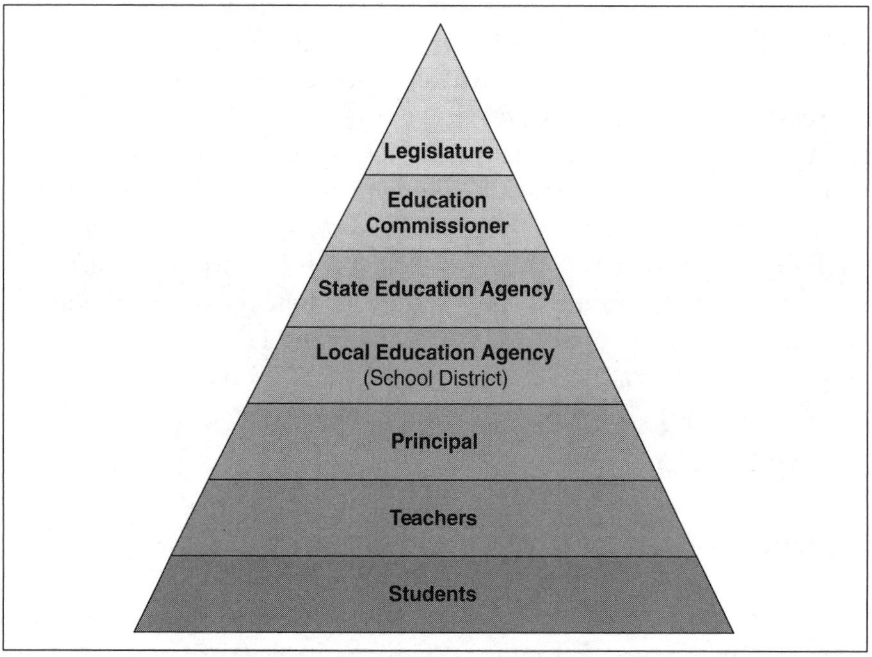

This model implies that the legislature is most important and students are least important, by virtue that the legislature is at the top of the model and students are located at the model's base. Decisions and policies trickle down from the legislature, making their way through five levels before arriving at the student level. The distance from the legislator's desk to the student's desk is great. All types of opportunities exist to bend, misunderstand, or lose the law or policy's intent.

Principals and curriculum leaders must understand this political and educational reality. Understanding it helps school leaders function better in the educational environment. For example, principals and faculty might not resent directives from central office and project negative feelings on these administrators because they understand where central office leaders reside on this model. This knowledge prevents or at least tempers frustration when another mandate is distributed at a central office administrative meeting. It also provides principals with an understanding of why faculty reacts to policies and procedures far removed from the faculty's communication circle. Many district and campus personnel feel they have little or no input into the state curriculum and assessment process.

Student-Centered Hierarchy Model

What would happen if the Adult-Centered Hierarchy Model were turned upside down? Would it make any difference in education? Figure 1.3 illustrates the flipping of the Adult-Centered Hierarchy Model.

Figure 1.3 Student-Centered Hierarchy Model

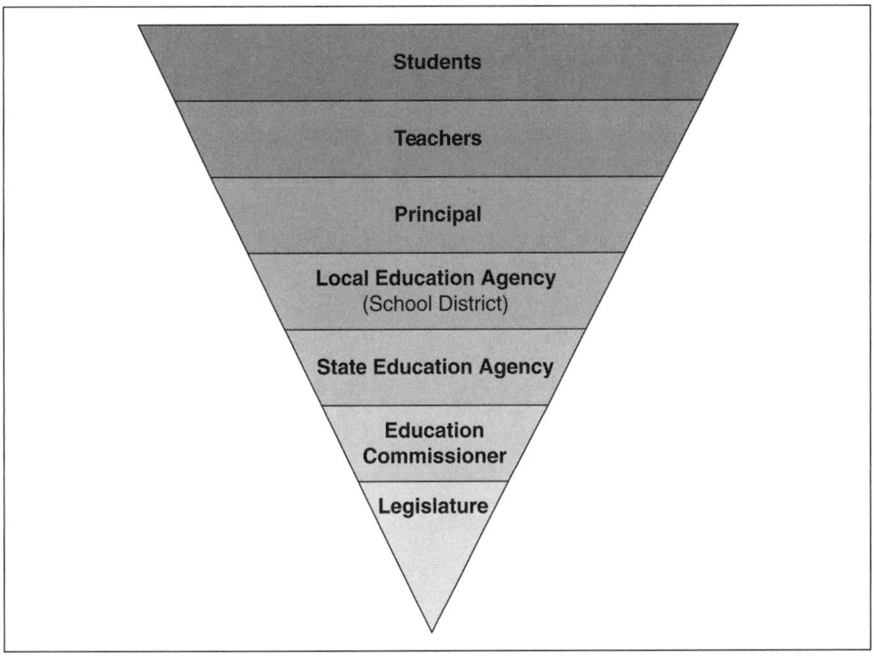

This inversion of the Adult-Centered Hierarchy Model is the Student-Centered Hierarchy Model or the Student-Centered Model for short. In this model, students are at the top and the legislature is at the bottom, reversing the communication structure. Unlike the Adult-Centered Hierarchy Model where actions are done *to*

the students through top-down communication, in the Student-Centered Hierarchy Model actions are done *for* the students.

In the Student-Centered Model, teachers' actions support student learning. Principals and other curriculum leaders provide support for teachers in meeting student needs. Likewise, superintendents' actions facilitate principals' and curriculum leaders' efforts to assist teachers. The local education agency, in turn, supports the superintendents in their efforts to help campus-level curriculum leaders. The state education agency provides support to the local education agency. The state commissioner of education provides guidance to the state education agency in its efforts to assist the local education agency. Finally, the legislature provides the impetus and direction to support the education commissioner.

When compared (Figure 1.4), the Adult-Centered Model and the Student-Centered Model contain the same components. However, the components are reversed.

Figure 1.4   Comparison of the Adult-Centered and Student-Centered Hierarchy Models

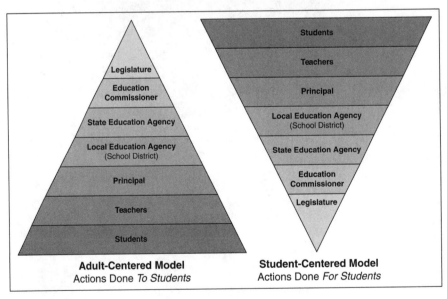

This flipping of the Adult-Centered Hierarchy Model reverses communication intent and focus. In the Adult-Centered Hierarchy Model, the legislature is the focal point and the originator of communication with students being the final recipient of communication. In the Student-Centered Hierarchy Model, students are the focal point and originators of communication with the legislature being the final recipient of communication. This is a powerful shift in communication and organizational emphasis. Students replace adults as the organization's focus. It replaces lip service to student needs with eyes and ear service.

The reader might be thinking this is all well and good, but it's "pie in the sky" thinking that has nothing to help me in my situation. The authors agree. There is little likelihood, at least in our lifetime, that the Adult-Centered Model will be replaced by the Student-Centered Model. However, principals and other campus curriculum leaders are not impotent in their ability to affect curriculum leadership change by changing the communication emphasis at their schools.

> **Serenity Prayer by Elizabeth Sifton**
>
> God give us the grace to accept with serenity the things that cannot be changed, courage to change the things which should be changed, and the wisdom to distinguish the one from the other.
>
> —Ralph Keys, *The Quote Verifier* (2006), p. 190

Principals and campus curriculum leaders must recognize they directly impact three levels of the Student-Centered and Adult-Centered Hierarchy Models—(1) students, (2) parents, and (3) themselves. With this in mind, campus-level versions of the Student-Centered and Adult-Centered Hierarchy Models illustrate their sphere of influence. See Figure 1.5.

Figure 1.5 Campus-Level Adult-Centered and Student-Centered Hierarchy Models

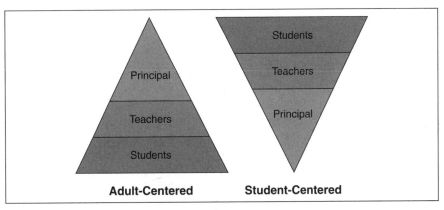

The motto of Alcoholics Anonymous, the Serenity Prayer, might well be a source of wisdom for principals as they strive to improve education in their schools. Principals and other curriculum leaders

are not likely to move their state's hierarchy structure from the Adult-Centered Model to the Student-Centered Model in the near future. This realization is not an excuse to quit; it is a call for realism and serenity. Principals and curriculum leaders *can* recognize the things they cannot change and have the courage to change the things that they can change. In this case, moving their campus hierarchy structure from the Adult-Centered Model to the Student-Centered Model. All journeys begin with a step.

In both truncated models, the same forces are at play as in the comprehensive models. In the Adult-Centered Model, communication still flows from adults toward students. Principals and curriculum leaders direct teachers who, in turn, direct students. In the Student-Centered Model, principals and other curriculum leaders facilitate teachers in implementing the curriculum. Teachers then facilitate students in mastering the curriculum. The Adult-Centered Model has the principal and other curriculum leaders at the top directing downward. In the Student-Centered Model, students are at the top informing teachers who are informing principals and other campus curriculum leaders of their needs. The informing from students to teachers comes in a variety of ways including teacher observation of students, teacher conversations with students, student academic submissions, as well as informal and formal assessment. Teachers inform principals and curriculum leaders through free and open communication in a variety of forums including private conversations, team- or grade-level meetings, and general meetings. Principals gather information through classroom observations, walking the hallways, and visiting with students.

Final Thoughts

Loose coupling, systems thinking, and collaboration are organizational phenomena impacting curriculum leadership (Figure 1.2). National principal standards, principal expectations as curriculum leader, the principal's role in curriculum change and innovation, working with teachers, integrating curriculum and instruction, professional development, digital curriculum leadership, curriculum development, evaluation, and renewal are topics explored in subsequent chapters. These topics and their relationship to the organizational phenomena will enrich our understanding of curriculum leadership (Figure 1.6).

The stage is set for a closer examination of curriculum leadership. Principal Wonkermann puts a face on curriculum leadership. He realizes the things he can change—those things happening on his campus. He knows the things he cannot change (but can influence) that happen off his campus. In the ensuing chapters, Principal Wonkermann will continue helping us explore curriculum leadership.

Figure 1.6   Curriculum Leadership Organizational Phenomena

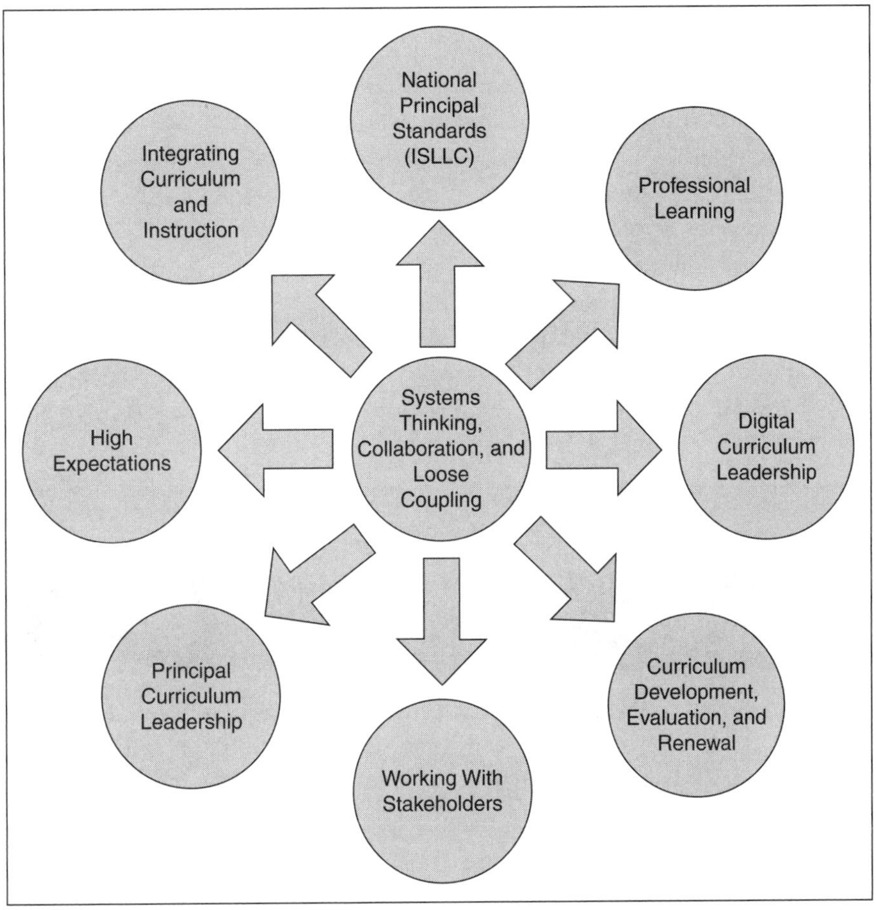

More questions are likely to arise as other questions are answered. But as lifelong learners, the authors are content with provoking thought. We know we do not have all the answers. It will be readers like you who bring life to the text through study groups, graduate coursework, presentations, and self-reflection. And remember, there is so much time and so little to do.

Discussion Questions

1. In 1949, Gordon Mackenzie asserted that five persisting problems must be clarified to achieve success in curriculum leadership: (1) recognize the worth of the individual, (2) improve the quality of social living, (3) maintain freedom to learn, (4) preserve a unified school, and (5) direct education toward goals. Provide clarification for each of Mackenzie's five persisting curriculum leadership problems.

2. Describe your experience with your school's mission statement. How is it perceived at your school? How is it relevant or irrelevant to curriculum leadership at your school?

3. Consider the list of terms on Page 19 on Viewing Tip 6 associated with curriculum leadership. Select any three terms and explain how they help define curriculum leadership.

4. Describe how you have either witnessed or experienced the three organizational phenomena (loose coupling, systems thinking, and collaboration) associated with curriculum leadership.

5. How are the three organizational phenomena (loose coupling, systems thinking, and collaboration) evidenced to the Principal Wonkermann Late Afternoon Experience?

CASE STUDY APPLICATION
Stand and Deliver

This nontraditional case study starts with watching the film *Stand and Deliver*. Put the popcorn in the microwave, turn off the cell phone, find others interested in curriculum leadership, and watch *Stand and Deliver*.

Stand and Deliver *Facts*

- Produced in 1987

- Rated 3 ½ out of 4 stars

- 105 minutes, PG

- Based on fact

- Starring: Ramon Menendez, Edward Olmos, Lou Diamond Phillips, Rosana de Soto, Andy Garcia, Will Gotay, Ingrid Oliu, Virginia Parris, and Mark Eliot

- Olmos plays a tough, demanding teacher who inspires East Los Angeles barrio students to pass an Advanced-Placement Calculus test.

Source: Leonard Maltin's 2007 Movie Guide

Viewing Tips

These tips alert you to issues you should look for while watching the film. Your evidence may be something observed in the film or something *not* observed in the film, a missing piece.

1. Evidence of loose coupling (p. 8)
   - Hint: The scene where the principal gathers faculty (could be the campus planning team) to discuss low test scores.
2. Evidence of systems thinking (p. 9)
3. Evidence of collaboration (p. 10)
4. Evidence of mission issues (p. 3)
5. Evidence of Covey's (1989) third habit of highly effective people: Putting first things first (p. 6)
6. Evidence of matters associated with curriculum leadership (pp. 11–12):

   - Curriculum

   - Instruction

   - Assessment

   - Learning

   - Teaching

   - Standards

   - Tracking

   - Essential skills

   - Audit

   - Technology

   - Enrichment

   - Other concepts you believe might be associated with curriculum leadership

Create six lists, one for each of the major evidence caches. Bulleted lists of your evidence are appropriate, even desirable. If you are reading this with a learning team, you might consider using a WIKI or blog as a convenient learning tool for group collaboration.

Discuss the six evidence caches with others.

Other Resources

DuFour, R., DuFour, R., & Eaker, R. (2008). *Revising professional learning communities at work: New insights for improving schools.* Bloomington, IN: Solution Tree.

Sawyer, K. (2007). *Group genius: The creative power of collaboration.* New York: Basic Books.

Scharmer, C. (2009). *Theory U: Leading from the future as it emerges.* San Francisco: Berrett-Koehler.

Wiles, J. (2009). *Leading curriculum development.* Thousand Oaks, CA: Corwin.

2

A Curriculum Leadership Journey

Close your eyes and tap your heels together three times. And think to yourself, there's no place like home.

—Glinda in *The Wizard of Oz* (LeRoy & Fleming, 1939)

ISLLC Standards and Curriculum Leadership

Principal Will Wonkermann opened our examination of curriculum leadership in Chapter 1 with a solitary moment standing in a hallway musing over his school's mission statement that, in turn, led him to ponder about his role as curriculum leader. This led to his decision to redouble his effort to exhibit curriculum leadership. However, as is the case in many recommitment decisions, self-doubts begin to arise.

Principal Wonkermann is not alone in self-doubts. We all experience them whether we choose to admit it or not. It's one thing to commit to exhibiting curriculum leadership. It's another thing to actually do it. If only a yellow brick road to curriculum leadership existed, school administration would be so much easier Will thought. But like most things in life there is no yellow brick road. We simply can't close our eyes, tap our heels together three times, and say to ourselves, "There's no place like an effective school." We don't have any ruby slippers.

PRINCIPAL WONKERMANN AND THE NATIONAL ISLLC STANDARDS

Will did some Googling and came across the Interstate School Leaders Licensure Consortium Standards (ISLLC). He clicked on the website, www.ccsso.org/content/pdfs/elps_isllc2008.pdf, but did so with skepticism. He was already "standarded" to death. Did he really need another set of standards? To be honest, Will was hoping to find a quick fix, a shortcut to curriculum leadership. In his heart of hearts, he knew that nothing substantial and lasting happened from quick fixes. But his human side still hoped for one. As he read these standards, Will did so through a curriculum leadership lens. He asked himself, "Does a curriculum leadership dimension reside within these national school leader standards or are these standards divorced from curriculum leadership?" Will hadn't yet realized it, but he had struck yellow gold! It wasn't the yellow brick road, but it was pointing him in the right direction for his curriculum leadership journey. Will smiled and laughed to himself, "I have the heart and the courage for this journey—if I only had a brain."

The longer Will examined the ISLLC standards, the more he reaffirmed that these standards were the logical place to begin his exploration of curriculum leadership. It also seemed logical to Will that these standards would contain a curriculum leadership dimension.

The Council of Chief State School Officers (CCSSO), a national organization of state-level education leaders, created the ISLLC in 1996 (Murphy & Shipman, 1998; Shipman, Topps, & Murphy, 1998). The development of the ISLLC standards helped educators define how leaders could positively influence learning. The standards established guidelines to ensure that we do so. Leithwood, Louis, Anderson, and Wahlstrom (2004) confirm 43 states adopted the ISLLC standards or use them as the basis for their standards.

Interstate School Leaders Licensure Consortium Standards (2008)

1. An education leader promotes the success of every student by facilitating the development, articulation, implementation, and stewardship of a vision of learning that is shared and supported by all stakeholders.

2. An education leader promotes the success of every student by advocating, nurturing, and sustaining a school culture and instructional program conducive to student learning and staff professional growth.

3. An education leader promotes the success of every student by ensuring management of the organization, operations, and resources for a safe, efficient, and effective learning environment.

4. An education leader promotes the success of every student by collaborating with faculty and community members, responding to diverse community interests and needs, and by mobilizing community resources.

5. An education leader promotes the success of every student by acting with integrity, fairness, and in an ethical manner.

6. An education leader promotes the success of every student by understanding, responding to, and influencing the larger political, social, economic, legal, and cultural context.

Source: Council of Chief State School Officers, 2008a

The ISLLC standards point curriculum leaders toward their responsibility to improve teaching and learning. It is worth noting that no one leadership theory was franchised as *the* leadership theory for school leaders (National Policy Board for Educational Administration, 2002).

PRINCIPAL WONKERMANN DISCOVERS THE YELLOW BRICK ROAD

Continuing his exploration of the performance expectations and indicators for educational leaders, Will realized ISLLC standards are *policy standards* (Council of Chief State School Officers, 2008a). What he needed in his search for meaningful curriculum guidance was the *Performance Expectations and Indicators for Educational Leaders*, a publication of the Council of Chief State School Officers (A PDF file of this document can be downloaded at http://www.ccsso.org/publications/index.cfm). This companion document to the ISSLC standards was his yellow brick road to curriculum leadership. The performance expectations with their dispositions, elements, and performance indicators made the ISLLC standards operational by portraying the most important actions required by K–12 education

(Continued)

(*Continued*)

leaders to improve teaching and learning (Council of Chief State School Officers, 2008b).

Each ISLLC performance expectation comes with a set of dispositions. Dispositions are our tendency to act on our beliefs, the underpinnings of our individual work, or our moral compass. The dispositions are central to and are reflected in the performance expectations. Each performance expectation is subdivided into three conceptual categories called *elements.* Elements provide organizing themes that help leaders organize conversations with their school's stakeholders in interpreting policies, programs, and practice performance objectives. Finally, *indicators* describe actions that leaders are expected to utilize to breathe life into the performance expectations. See Figure 2.1.

Figure 2.1   *Performance Expectations Structure*

Performance Expectation—based on corresponding ISLLC standard

  ↳ **Dispositions**—central to and reflect the performance expectation

    ↳ **Three Elements**—organizers for the performance indicators

      ↳ **Performance Indicators**—actions and behaviors required to meet the performance expectation

As Will continued his journey toward curriculum leadership, he scheduled six stops, one at each ISLLC performance expectation. At each stop, Principal Wonkermann first reads the plaque containing that performance expectation's dispositions. He then visits the three elements of that performance expectation. While at these elements, he reviews one of that element's indicators to obtain an elementary understanding of that element. Time does not permit examining all 87 indicators. Before embarking on his journey, Will examines his curriculum journey map one final time (Figure 2.2) to be certain he knows where he is headed. He also checks to ensure he hasn't forgotten his moral compass. Without this compass, Will would surely get lost. Will decides to wear his ruby-red Reeboks as his journey might require an extra bounce in his step. Go ahead and put on your ruby-red Reeboks. Let's join Will on his curriculum leadership journey.

Figure 2.2 *Will's Curriculum Leadership Journey*

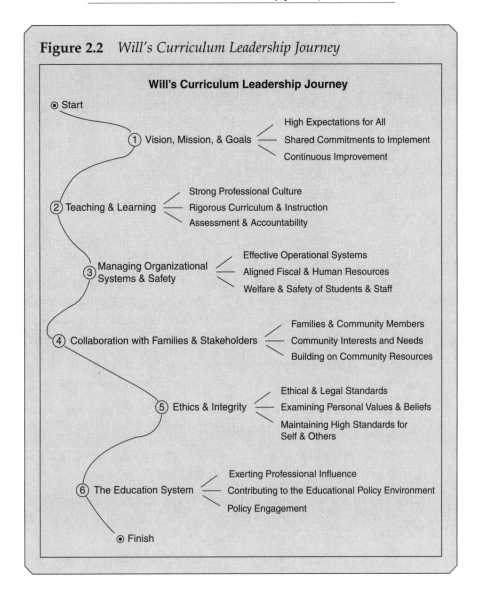

1 Stop → ISLLC Performance Expectation 1: Vision, Mission, and Goals

Education leaders ensure the achievement of all students by guiding the development and implementation of a shared vision of learning, strong organizational mission, and high expectations for every student.

> ### *Performance Expectation 1 Dispositions*
>
> The education leader believes in, values, and is committed to the following:
>
> - Every student learning
> - Collaboration with all stakeholders
> - High expectations for all
> - Examining assumptions and beliefs
> - Continuous improvement using evidence

Developing a vision in an era of rapid change is challenging. The New Media Consortium's Horizon Project (Johnson, Levine, Smith, & Smythe, 2009) identified five critical challenges for schools alone in the area of new technology. These challenges include the following:

1. A growing need exists for formal instruction in key new skills, including literacy, visual literacy, and technology literacy.

2. Students are different, but educational practice and the material that support it are changing only slowly.

3. Learning that incorporates real-life experiences is not occurring enough and is undervalued when it does take place.

4. There is a growing recognition that new technologies must be adopted and used as an everyday part of classroom activities, but effecting this change is difficult.

5. A key challenge is the fundamental structure of the K–12 education establishment.

The New Media Consortium's Horizon Project is but one of many reports with recommendations on where schools need to be planning for the future (Johnson et al., 2009). Other community, private, government, and professional organizations have also issued reports recommending changes in curriculum, instruction, and assessment of student learning.

Society appears to be calling for changes from 20th-century schools to 21st-century schools. These changes include the following:

Passive learning	**To**	Active learning
Teacher centered	**To**	Student centered

Fragmented curriculum	**To**	Integrated curriculum
Low-level curriculum	**To**	High-level curriculum
Irrelevant curriculum	**To**	Relevant curriculum
Little student freedom	**To**	Generous student freedom
Textbook driven	**To**	Research driven
Assessment driven by state and federal testing	**To**	Assessment informed by state and federal testing

The challenge for the principal as curriculum leader is bringing school stakeholders together toward a common vision providing the faculty and staff with a focus and a common language for curriculum and instruction (Glatthorn & Jailall, 2009). If no common vision exists on what needs to be taught, how it will be taught, and how it will be assessed, then how in the world will a school ever meet the needs of its students? Surely, everyone understands this—NOT!

It is quite appropriate that the first performance expectation is about vision. If *you* don't know where *you* are going, then how will *you* know if *you* get there? Furthermore, the "you's" in the previous sentence are not singular but plural. The principal as curriculum leader must bring all stakeholders together with a strategic curriculum plan. Ideally, this plan is part of a comprehensive campus improvement plan connected to the allocation of campus resources. Sorenson and Goldsmith (2006) in *The Principal's Guide to School Budgeting* provide a detailed description of such an integrated process.

This lack of vision is at the root of Principal Will Wonkermann's challenge at Childers School. Childers's mission statement was confined to vinyl letters on a dusty banner. Childers School was devoid of a vision document. Some old-timers remembered someone did something about vision but that was years ago. One teacher vaguely remembered thinking she had received a copy of a vision statement.

Neither the school nor its community owned the mission statement nor were they even aware that a vision statement existed. To add injury to insult, Principal Wonkermann had been at the school for months before even he—the leader—considered Childers School's vision and mission statements. However, to Will's credit he did discover the ignored mission statement. It is this discovery that ignites Childers School's transformation. Childers School's vision and mission challenge is not unlike challenges other schools face, even your school, as educators confront the rapid changes in 21st-century American society.

The question for principals seeking to exert curriculum leadership is how do I guide the development and implementation of a shared vision of learning, strong organizational mission, and high expectations for every student? The answer lies within the campus planning process. Principals must understand curriculum leadership is not a "one-person show." Curriculum leadership is an "us show." In Chapter 1, Principal Wonkermann reacquainted himself with his school's mission statement. He did this alone in an empty hallway and in an empty office. Will knew this time of reflection was only the beginning of the process. He needed to locate the vision statement and reintroduce it to the faculty and staff to determine if it was still a fit or if it needed updating or even scrapped and started from the beginning. Will was certain everyone's input would be needed on such an important matter.

Performance Expectation 1

Vision, mission, and goals, like all performance expectations, contain three elements leaders use in developing and implementing the called for shared vision.

Element A: High Expectations for All

- Element A—The vision and goals establish high, measureable expectations for all students and educators.
  - o Indicator 1—A leader uses varied sources of information and analyzes data about current practices and outcomes to shape a vision, mission, and goals with high, measurable expectations for all students and educators.

A principal leads stakeholders in collecting and analyzing data to identify curriculum goals, assessing the effectiveness of these goals, and promoting them in the school and its community. Bernhardt (2000) purports that schools do not use data well for three reasons: (1) lack of cultural emphasis, (2) lack of training, and (3) fear. Managing data to improve student learning focused on data-driven decision-making skills is necessary to meet the needs of all students and to reach accountability expectations. Bernhardt (1998) reminds curriculum leaders that we must change our process if we expect to obtain different results. Curriculum leaders must go beyond achievement data because the context is missing. Furthermore, Bernhardt believes analyzing achievement data alone keeps educators from meeting student needs.

Element B: Shared Commitments to Implement the Vision, Mission, and Goals

- Element B—The process of creating and sustaining the vision, mission, and goals is inclusive, building common understandings and genuine commitment among all stakeholders.
    - Indicator 1—A leader establishes, conducts, and evaluates processes used to engage staff and community in a shared vision, mission, and goals.

First and foremost, school stakeholders must be led in a collaborative process to develop and implement a shared vision. Vision and mission statements can't be purchased. Vision and mission create the school's soul and must be the result of a vigorous process involving the school's stakeholders. The process is just as important, if not more important than the product. However, once the products (vision and mission statements) are created, they must be sustained. It is the principal's responsibility to ensure these statements are inculcated in the school's culture. The principal melds curriculum matters into these statements by guiding stakeholders to experience ownership and responsibility of the mission and visions statements ensuring that these statements specify a vision of learning that is demanding of every student. If this process is not collaborative, then *shared* should not be expected.

Element C: Continuous Improvement Toward the Vision, Mission, and Goals

- Element C—Education leaders ensure the achievement of all students by guiding the development and implementation of a shared vision of learning, strong organizational mission, and high expectations for every student.
    - Indicator 5—Incorporates the vision and goals into planning (e.g., strategic plan, school improvement plan), change strategies, and instructional programs.

Curriculum leaders ensure that plans include continuous and sustainable curriculum improvement. Continuous improvement means we never arrive; we will never have it just right. We constantly seek avenues to attain high-achievement levels for our students and teachers. Curriculum leaders work with the faculty and staff to establish a continuous improvement cycle where the appropriate stakeholders meet to review data to determine what is working and what isn't and make the necessary course adjustments.

Developing a curriculum plan and distributing it isn't enough. This planning document must be referenced frequently. It should become ragged and marked as the academic year unfolds. The best of plans always requires adjustments. A clean, neat plan at the end of the academic year is indicative of something gone awry.

LEAVING STOP ❶ — VISION, MISSION, AND GOALS

The vision piece of curriculum leadership was coming together for Will. He must engage school and community stakeholders and reach consensus about Childers's vision, mission, and goals if he expected to improve teaching and learning. Will looked at his watch; it was time to head out to the second stop. He wished he could have examined all sixteen indicators of this performance expectation. At least the three he reviewed got him off to a good start. A quick glance at his moral compass affirmed he was on course.

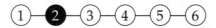

❷ Stop → ISLLC Performance Expectation 2: Teaching and Learning

Education leaders ensure achievement and success of all students by monitoring and continuously improving teaching and learning.

Performance Expectation 2 Dispositions

The education leader believes in, values, and is committed to the following:

- Learning as the fundamental purpose of school

- Diversity as an asset

- Continuous professional growth and development

- Lifelong learning

- Collaboration with all stakeholders

- High expectations for all

- Student learning

The teaching and learning performance expectation is all about student and faculty learning. It recognizes the principal's responsibility as curriculum leader for learning not only of the students but also the faculty and staff too. Leaders must communicate knowledge of the curriculum and instructional strategies as well as expectation for teaching and learning.

Education leaders are responsible for *all* students learning, not *most* students learning. Assisting teachers in using response to intervention is one way leaders help all students learn, not just students covered by Title I and Title III of the No Child Left Behind Act or the Individuals With Disabilities Education Improvement Act. Buffum, Mattos, and Weber (2009) report teachers who ladder teaching service levels with greater intensity meet with greater academic success for students who do not respond to general instructional strategies.

Principals help teachers learn when they facilitate discovery of best practices in teaching and learning and connect those discoveries to current practices and student assessment. Doing so allows teachers to develop shared knowledge that improves decisions and, thus, positively impacts student learning and the learning community (Dufour, Dufour, and Eaker, 2008).

THE JOURNEY CONTINUES

Will was excited arriving at the second of his journey's six stops. He considered the teaching and learning stop the most important stop on his journey. Teaching and learning are at the core of what Will was about and what he wanted Childers School to be about. Performance Expectation 2's seven dispositions oozed teaching and learning. Childers School needed a professional culture. He would share and distribute responsibilities so that other leaders at Childers could assist with curriculum, instruction, and assessment.

Performance Expectation 2

Teaching and learning, like all ISLLC performance expectations, contain three elements leaders use in ensuring the academic success of all students.

Element A: Strong Professional Culture

- Element A—A strong professional culture supports teacher learning and shared commitments to the vision and goals.
  - o Indicator 1—A leader develops shared understanding capacities, commitment to high expectations for all students, and closing achievement gaps. Childers School could definitely benefit from this indicator.

The principal fosters and grows a culture of collaboration, trust, learning, and high expectations on the campus. When a campus like Childers School is under pressure to improve, it is tempting for the principal to switch from a collaborative leadership style to one that is top-down. This tragic error squashes a faculty's ability to improve instruction (Kohm & Nance, 2009). If principals want to receive information from the faculty and staff, they must also share information with the faculty and staff. Communication must be two-way for collaboration to exist. Linda Darling-Hammond (2001) believes it is relationships that influence who shares professional wisdom with whom and who influences the quality of teaching and learning. Principals must express their emotions and ideas freely if they expect the faculty and staff to do likewise. When communication flows freely both ways, then trust takes hold and a culture of collaboration is created. It is in the collaborative culture that learning and high expectations exist.

Element B: Rigorous Curriculum and Instruction

- Element B—Improving achievement of all students requires all educators to know and use rigorous curriculum and effective instructional practices, individualized for success of every student.
  - o Indicator 3—Provides and monitors effects of differentiated teaching strategies, curricular materials, educational technologies, and other resources appropriate to address diverse student populations, including students with disabilities, cultural and linguistic differences, gifted and talented, disadvantaged social economic backgrounds, or other factors affecting learning.

Differentiated teaching strategies reminded Will of a baseball cap he recently purchased. The label tag touted, "One size fits all." The cap's tag is the antithesis of differentiated teaching strategies tag that reads, "One size does not fit all." Will smiled at the quirky association he had just made.

Tomlinson (2005) identified seven characteristics of an effective learning environment for differentiated classrooms. Those characteristics are the following:

- Everyone feels welcomed and contributes to everyone else feeling welcomed.
- Mutual respect is a nonnegotiable.
- Students feel safe in the classroom.
- There is a pervasive expectation of growth.
- The teacher teaches for success.
- A new sort of fairness is evident.
- Teacher and students collaborate for mutual growth and success.

CHARACTERISTICS OF A LEARNING ENVIRONMENT

Will was fascinated by Tomlinson's (2005) learning environment characteristics. He made an immediate connection to Childers's faculty and staff. Were not Tomlinson's characteristics of the differentiated classroom essentially what the adults at Childers School needed to meet with academic success? Will wanted fairness and mutual respect among the adults on the campus. He wanted the faculty to feel safe and meet with success. He wanted the stakeholders to collaborate in planning for the academic success for Childers's students.

Creating a rich learning environment in a differentiated classroom meeting Childers students' needs was virtually identical to the learning environment Will wanted for the faculty and staff. Differentiation must extend beyond the classroom. It must encompass the entire school touching all stakeholders.

Element C: Assessment and Accountability

- Element C—Improving achievement and closing achievement gaps require that leaders make appropriate sound use of assessments, performance management, and accountability strategies to achieve vision, mission, and goals.
  - ○ Indicator 1—Develops and appropriately uses aligned standards-based accountability data to improve the quality of teaching and learning.

Accountability systems determine the effectiveness of schools, teachers, administrators, and curriculum. The principal works with stakeholders in developing assessment and accountability systems to monitor student progress. Frase and English (2000) advocate no room exists for secrecy in this process and that students should not be surprised in instructional situations. Frase and English call this the doctrine of no surprises. Curriculum leaders collaborate with teachers to ensure assessment instruments assess what has been taught. Of course, this requires all students to have equal opportunity to learn what is being assessed. Principal Wonkermann's journey was increasing his understanding of teaching and learning.

LEAVING STOP ❷ — TEACHING AND LEARNING

Will only examined three of the sixteen indicators for this performance expectation. Now more than ever, he realized Childers would need shared leadership to meet all the teaching and learning needs of the teachers and students. It was time to leave for the third stop on his trip.

❸ Stop → ISLLC Performance Expectation 3: Managing Organizational Systems and Safety

Educational leaders ensure the success of all students by managing organizational systems and resources for a safe, high-performing learning environment.

Performance Expectation 3 Dispositions

The education leader believes in, values, and is committed to the following:

- A safe and supportive learning environment

- Collaboration with all stakeholders

- Equitable distribution of resources

- Operating efficiently and effectively

- Management in service of staff and student learning

In the past, many principals focused on managing their schools rather than leading their schools. They found security in buses, facilities, bookrooms, hallways, and flagpoles.

Today's accountability system requires leaders to create a learning environment that goes beyond the maintenance of facilities and buses. Today's leaders must provide a learning environment aligned to the school's vision and mission. Resources, including human, time, financial, technology, the physical plant, and others, must be aligned with the school's vision and mission. Principals must work collaboratively with the school's stakeholders to identify and allocate resources to meet these identified needs. Education leaders promote the learning environment by completing their legal responsibilities, enforcing policies, and supporting due process (CCSSO, 2008b).

REVISITING ABRAHAM MASLOW

Will was intrigued by the nature of this performance expectation. Reading its dispositions whetted his appetite even more.

At first glance, it appeared to Will that a curriculum dimension does not exist for this performance expectation. It seemed to be more of a nonacademic facility and policy performance expectation. "Au contraire!" thought Will. This performance expectation deserved a strong second look, a deeper consideration.

Will decided to consider these questions: Can students learn at their best if they don't feel safe? Can they learn at their best if the building is not well maintained? Can they learn at their best if the faculty and staff are not scheduled efficiently or if they don't have the necessary supplies, instructional tools, and technology? What initially appeared as mundane and not curriculum in nature, in fact, was a must for curriculum leadership. It took Will back to his undergraduate psychology class where he studied Abraham Maslow's hierarchy of needs. Maslow (1999), Will recalled, purports students must have their low-level needs, such as physiological and safety needs, met before they are able to pursue higher-level needs, such as self-actualization.

Performance Expectation 3

Managing organizational systems and safety, like the performance expectations, contains three elements leaders use in developing and maintaining a safe, high-performing learning environment.

Element A: Effective Operational Systems

- Element A—Leaders distribute leadership responsibilities and supervise daily, ongoing management structures and practices to enhance teaching and learning.
  - o Indicator 2—A leader maintains the physical plant for safety, Americans with Disabilities Act of 1990 (ADA) requirements, and other access issues to support learning of every student.

This indicator may not seem academic at all. What is it doing serving as a performance indicator?

The building must be clean and in good repair, as it impacts how people feel about the school. It is important that everyone in the school assumes responsibility for the building maintenance. Nearly everyone can pick up litter on the floors or grounds. Good principals model this behavior.

Many beginning assistant principals find themselves responsible for this indicator. Assistant principals find themselves responsible for constructing custodial schedules around the academic schedule. They also must ensure the proper cleaning supplies are available.

Closely associated with cleaning is building repair. Most assistant principals complete the district's protocol for requesting the maintenance department to make necessary repairs. Principals are also involved in assessing and recommending more involved and costly repairs and remodeling.

Besides being sure the facility meets ADA requirements, principals must be sure the grounds and playgrounds are attractively maintained. It is worth noting that swings and swing sets, climbing bars, and slides account for 87% of student injuries. Ensuring appropriate supervision and keeping the equipment properly maintained are the best actions to prevent injuries (Ubben, Hughes, & Norris, 2007).

Element B: Aligned Fiscal and Human Resources

- Element B—Leaders establish an infrastructure for finance and personnel that operates in support of teaching and learning.
  - o Indicator 3—Aligns resources (such as time, people, space, and money) to achieve visions and goals.

Sorenson and Goldsmith introduced the Sorenson-Goldsmith Integrated Budget Model in *The Principal's Guide to School Budgeting* (2006). This budget model integrates the vision, planning, and budgeting processes. Their budget model is a collaborative process involving all stakeholders. It is designed to integrate with the campus planning process for increased fiscal accountability. The model is data driven (see Chapter 1).

To be properly implemented, the Sorenson-Goldsmith Budget Model requires shared leadership, something Will noticed he needed at the first stop on his curriculum leadership journey. This model brings stakeholders together to regularly examine the allocation and reallocation of resources as needed.

School resources are always scarce. Principals must secure the biggest bang for the buck from fiscal and human resources. Principals have a moral obligation to be good stewards of public funds.

Element C: Protecting the Welfare and Safety of Students and Staff

- Element C—Leaders ensure a safe environment by addressing real and potential challenges to the physical and emotional safety and security of students and staff that interfere with teaching and learning.
  - o Indicator 2—Involves parents, teachers, and students in developing, implementing, and monitoring guidelines and norms for accountable behavior.

The public routinely views discipline in schools as an important challenge (Hoy & Hoy, 2006). In many cases, assistant principals in middle-size and large schools find themselves with discipline management responsibilities. Discipline must be enforced; halls and restrooms must be safe. Everyone must know that bullying is unacceptable. Learning is negatively impacted when people do not feel safe. Leaders must not underestimate the impact of poor discipline management on the school's teaching and learning.

Good discipline does not just happen. A strong discipline plan developed with input from the school's stakeholders, fairly and evenly enforced, goes a long way in creating an effective learning environment. Strong principals use data analysis to help identify weaknesses and strengths in the administration of discipline.

LEAVING STOP ❸ — MANAGING ORGANIZATIONAL SYSTEMS AND SAFETY

As Principal Wonkermann was preparing to leave the third stop on his journey, he committed to promoting a professional working environment. Even though he had only reviewed three of the sixteen indicators at this stop, Will realized this performance expectation possessed an academic dimension, something he questioned upon arriving at this stop.

4 → ISLLC Performance Expectation 4: Collaborating With Families and Stakeholders

Education leaders ensure the success of all students by collaborating with families and stakeholders who represent diverse community interests and needs and mobilizing community resources that improve teaching and learning.

Performance Expectation 4 Dispositions

The education leader believes in, values, and is committed to the following:

- High standards for all

- Including families and the community as partners

- Respect for the diversity of family composition

- Continuous learning and improvement for all

Schools must build positive relationships with their school's community partnerships. All taxpayers pay school taxes, but not all taxpayers have a connection with schools. Only about one-third of U.S. households have children enrolled in public schools (Hilber & Mayer, 2004). This means that two-thirds of households do not have a child in school. Yet when a school sets a levy or wants to pass a bond issue, 50% plus one voter is needed to secure the revenue. Schools must have the support of the community-at-large to serve the community's children.

Hatch (2009) reminds us that the success of our school improvement efforts is dependent on the relationships and opportunities we foster in our school's community. We cannot afford to divorce what is happening inside our schools with what is happening outside in its community. Curriculum leadership must encourage questions and feedback from the community. Developing these relationships not only strengthens the curriculum but it also connects community members who do not have children in school with the school. This, in turn, increases support for public schools from households without children.

> ### *Performance Expectation 4*
>
> Collaborating with families and stakeholders, like all performance expectations, contains three elements leaders use in mobilizing community resources that improve teaching and learning.

Element A: Collaboration With Families and Community Members

- Element A—Leaders extend educational relationships to families and community members to add programs, services, and staff outreach and provide what every student needs to succeed in school and life.
  - o Indicator 2—A leader involves families in decision making about their children's education.

This community function allows stakeholders to know and understand one another. It is only when we know one another that trust can be established; trust must be established for relationships to deepen. By trust we mean that one another's promises, statements, or words can be relied on. Trust grows in our everyday interactions with one another. Bryk and Schneider (2003) reported trust between school stakeholders "improves much of the routine work of schools and is a key resource for reform" (p. 40). Knowing this, principals must lead the adults in making decisions that place the interests of students above their personal interest as well as local politics. Keeping our word and following up on promises builds trust. Acting as curriculum leaders, principals must confront poor teaching, or trust will be lost (Bryk & Schneider, 2003).

It is essential that parents and community members serve on the committee that constructs the campus improvement plan. Having other sets of eyes not involved in the day-to-day operations brings different perspectives, fresh perspectives on how the school can meet the needs of students, families, and community members.

Element B: Community Interests and Needs

- Element B—Leaders respond and contribute to community interests and needs in providing the best possible education for their children.
  - o Indicator 3—A leader seeks out and collaborates with community programs serving students with special needs.

Principal Wonkermann was drawn to Indicator 3. It was of particular interest to him because the father of a student had recently invited him to attend a Kiwanis International club meeting with him. Will knew that Kiwanis clubs were interested in children, so he took advantage of this invitation.

Kiwanis International

Kiwanis is a global organization of volunteers dedicated to changing the world, one child and one community at a time (Kiwanis International, 2010). The majority of the members of this particular Kiwanis club did not have children in a school, yet the club that Will visited had adopted an elementary school campus as its main community project. The club operated a program that rewarded and encouraged struggling students to improve academically. The club also funded Christmas gifts for families in need at the school. Finally, this club joined other Kiwanis clubs in their area to fully fund Camp Courage, a weeklong camp for children in first through twelfth grade who had suffered losses of a loved one through death, divorce, separation, incarceration, or deployment. Campers participated in recreational activities with trained counselors to develop healthy coping skills that ultimately serve to build self-confidence, trust, and an understanding of the grief process (Hendrick Hospice Care, 2010). Nearly all families at their adopted school could not financially provide grief counseling to their children.

Element C: Building on Community Resources

- Element C—Leaders maximize shared resources among schools, districts, and communities that provide key social structures and gathering places in conjunction with other organizations and agencies that provide critical resources for children and families.
  - Indicator 4—A leader secures community support to sustain existing resources and add new resources that address emerging student needs.

One such community resource is Junior Achievement. Junior Achievement is a nationally coordinated community organization involved in schools. Junior Achievement is a partnership between businesses in the community, educators, and volunteers working collaboratively to inspire students to reach their potential. The junior achievers volunteers provide students with hands-on learning experiences on work readiness, entrepreneurship, and financial literacy (Junior Achievement, 2010).

Curriculum leaders can readily tap into community resources like Junior Achievement not only to benefit the children but also to benefit the community members. This type of involvement puts a face on the school for the public.

LEAVING STOP ④ — COLLABORATING WITH FAMILIES AND STAKEHOLDERS

Will had to leave. It was time to go to the next stop.

Will resolved to take collaboration to a higher level even though he had only viewed three of the fourteen indicators for this performance expectation. Curriculum leadership required commitment from everyone if it was to be at its best. Will checked his moral compass. He was on course, but he needed to leave now to stay on schedule.

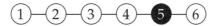

---

⑤ → ISLLC Performance Expectation 5: Ethics and Integrity

Education leaders ensure the success of all students by being ethical and acting with integrity.

Performance Expectation 5 Dispositions

The education leader believes in, values, and is committed to the following:

- The common good over personal interests

- Taking responsibility for actions

- Ethical principles in all relationships and decisions

- Modeling high expectations

- Continuously improving knowledge and skills

This performance expectation quickly evokes strong emotions and opinions, as it gets up close and personal. It is a performance expectation where strong differences in opinion exist and where opposing camps form quickly and become entrenched. "Acting with integrity, fairness, and in an ethical manner" (Council of Chief State School Officers, 2008a, p. 18) is subject to personal interpretation. The emotional intensity of this performance expectation is illustrated in the following brief description of a 2010 incident in a Rhode Island school district.

Central Falls High School

In the spring of 2010, the Central Falls school board, on the recommendation of the superintendent, fired the principal, three assistant principals, and 77 teachers at Central Falls High School (CFHS), the lowest performing high school in Rhode Island. The school is in a community with a median household income of $22,000.

The superintendent using federal guidelines requested teachers to work a longer school day and tutor students after hours for one hour weekly. The superintendent also requested teachers eat lunch often with the students as well as meet 90 minutes every week to discuss teaching and learning. Finally, the superintendent wanted teachers to set aside two weeks in the summer for paid professional development.

The teachers union accepted most of the changes but sought compensation for the additional hours of work. Administration and the union could not reach agreement on this matter.

Federal requirements for school reform of low-performing schools provide two options in cases such as this one. One option is the transformation model that entails a series of changes the faculty agree to adopt. Negotiations on this model failed so the superintendent changed to the turnaround model that allows the firing of every teacher at the school.

Emotions ran high. The president of the teachers union asserted that teachers had been unfairly targeted and noted that teachers had agreed to many concessions requested by the school district. Some lamented the transient nature of and the minority composition of the student body. The superintendent acknowledged that teachers were not solely responsible for the academic situation.

U. S. Secretary of Education Arne Duncan supported the firing of the teachers. Duncan commented that the board had done the right thing for the kids. Secretary Duncan has required that each state's worst performing schools be closed or become charter schools.

Sources: Fletcher & Anderson, 2010; Randi Kaye, 2010; Montopoli, 2010.

Educators are held to a high code of conduct. Schools cannot afford to have educator's conduct harm students. This performance expectation reinforces ethics codes while adding emphasis for educational equality and social justice. A free public education is a unique institution in the American culture in that it provides benefits to a broad and diverse population. Curriculum leaders must remove learning barriers so all students can receive a free and appropriate education. The barriers of discrimination, economics, physical disabilities, gender, and cultural differences must not be allowed to negate high expectations for all students.

Performance Expectation 5

Ethics and integrity, like all performance expectations, contain three elements leaders use in ensuring the success of all students by being ethical and acting with integrity.

Element A: Ethical and Legal Standards

- Element A—Leaders demonstrate appropriate ethical and legal behavior expected by the profession.
  - Indicator 2—A leader protects the rights and appropriate confidentiality of students and staff.

If you were to guess where most student and staff confidentiality is betrayed where would you guess it would be? The classroom? The cafeteria? We propose the teachers' lounge. David Keller (1999) identifies two types of "lounge talk"—caring and toxins. He describes one toxin as when faculty and staff share specifics about a student or the student's family in the lounge. This sharing of information might be done innocently or it could be venting or just plain malicious. Regardless, the student and family's Federal Education Records Privacy Act (FERPA) rights were violated. Teachers and other education professionals are prohibited from discussing confidential information about their students with anyone other than someone with a vested interest in that student.

LOOSE LIPS

Will grimaced as he remembered a situation that happened shortly after his arrival at Childers School. A teacher was venting about a student at a lunch table in the lounge with three colleagues. Unknown to this teacher, a substitute was sitting at the next table overhearing the raised voice of the complaining teacher. The substitute, a neighbor and best friend of the student's mom, had a chance encounter with the student's mom after school at Thelma Lou's Beauty Shop. Will received

(Continued)

> (*Continued*)
>
> an understandably irate phone call from that student's mom. Careless unethical conduct by this teacher created a situation sucking energy from the school's mission.

Element B: Examining Personal Values and Beliefs

- Element B—Leaders demonstrate their commitment to examine personal assumptions, values, beliefs, and practices in service of a shared vision and goals for student learning.
  - o Indicator 4—A leader assesses personal assumptions, values, beliefs, and practices that guide improvement of student learning.

John Maxwell (2003a) reminds us that ethics is never a school issue or a political issue or a social issue; it's always a personal issue. Where would you put yourself on this ethical continuum?

Never ethical————————————————————————Always ethical

Most of us would mark ourselves somewhere between never and always. If you marked "always ethical," do you also walk on water?

Nearly everyone is familiar with the Golden Rule. Because the predominant religion in America is Christianity, we might think this rule is confined to the teachings of Jesus. However, some form of the Golden Rule is found in each of the world's five major religions (Teachingvalues .com, 2010). Eugene Peterson (2007) translated Jesus's statement of the Golden Rule into contemporary English as "Don't pick on people, jump on their failures, criticize their faults—unless, of course, you want the same treatment. That spirit has a way of boomeranging" (p. 21).

Peterson's paraphrasing of the Golden Rule found in Matthew 7 informs curriculum leadership. Consider the following questions:

- Do you pick on students, teachers, parents, and fellow leaders?
- Do you jump on the failures of students, teachers, parents, and fellow leaders?
- Do you criticize the faults of students, teachers, parents, and fellow leaders?
- Do you react when you receive this treatment from students, teachers, parents, and fellow leaders?

These are tough questions, but they must be answered by those in curriculum leadership roles. The Golden Rule could well be one of the directions on Principal Wonkermann's moral compass.

Element C: Maintaining High Standards for Self and Others

- Element C—Leaders perform the work required for high levels of personal and organizational performance, including acquiring new capacities needed to fulfill responsibilities, particularly for high-stakes accountability.
    - ○ Indicator 5—A leader sustains personal motivation, optimism, commitment, energy, and health by balancing professional and personal responsibilities and encouraging similar actions in others.

Did the word *health* catch your attention?

Ray Strand, MD, and Bill Ewing (2006), leading nutrition and preventive medicine authorities, recognized that a common thread connected nearly everyone who came through their offices. This common thread was stress related to minds, emotions, or bodies. When one of these three elements is neglected, it impacts all of them. Recognizing stress is the first step in healing our mind, emotions, and body. Unresolved anger is one of the greatest sources of physical and mental illness.

Strand and Ewing (2006) remind us that our bodies were created for action. Exercising and watching our weight benefits us mentally, emotionally, and relationally. Curriculum leadership and working in schools takes its toll on our body, mind, and emotions. We owe it to ourselves, our families, and our schools to take care of our bodies, so we can function at our best. Exercising and watching our diet is tough to do, but there is more to curriculum leadership than knowledge and leadership skills.

Curriculum leaders must step back regularly and intentionally reflect on their core values. Moral compasses must be checked to ensure they remain pointed in a true direction. How leaders behave with others determines their sphere of influence.

LEAVING STOP ❺ — ETHICS AND INTEGRITY

Will had only visited three of the fourteen indicators for this performance expectation, but he had learned so much about standing up for what is right. Standing up for curriculum leadership was a responsibility of the principal. Rosa Parks crossed Will's mind.

Rosa Parks didn't remain seated on the infamous Montgomery bus in 1955 without a plan. Ms. Parks prepared herself with strategies of nonviolence. Rosa acted only after overcoming her self-doubts. When

(Continued)

(*Continued*)

she remained seated, she had no guarantee that her planning and strategies would work or that others would share in her risk taking. If Rosa Parks had completed a risk assessment to determine her chances of success, she might have gone to the back of the bus. Parker Palmer (2007) postulates that risk takers like Rosa Parks reach a point where they can no longer participate in acts that violate their integrity. Rosa Parks said, "I have learned over the years that when one's mind is made up, this diminishes fear; knowing what must be done does away with fear" (Rosaparksfacts.com, 2010, para 2).

Curriculum leadership, Will thought, must emulate Ms. Parks. Will said to himself, "We know who we are, what we are about, and we follow a moral compass. Sometimes standing up for what is right for students requires curriculum leaders to remain seated."

⑥ → ISLLC Performance Expectation 6: The Education System

Education leaders ensure the success of all students by influencing interrelated systems of political, social, economic, legal, and cultural contexts affecting education to advocate for their teachers' and students' needs.

Performance Expectation 6 Dispositions

The education leader believes in, values, and is committed to the following:

- Advocate for children and education
- Influence policies
- Uphold and improve laws and regulations
- Eliminate barriers to achievement
- Build on diverse social and cultural assets

The world in which today's children reside is radically different from the world in which you spent your childhood. Thomas Friedman (2006) in *The World Is Flat* relayed that his parents would tell him as a boy to finish his dinner because people were starving in

China and India. Friedman now finds himself telling his children to finish their homework because people in China and India are starving for their jobs.

Performance Expectation 6 reminds us that being a curriculum leader requires a principal to provide curriculum and instruction that promotes the success of all students within a global context. Principals, in their role as curriculum leaders, have an obligation to work with all school stakeholders to keep American students competitive in a global community. Considering that students in other industrial countries routinely study a foreign language compared to only one-half of American students points to one weakness in our curriculum (Pufahl, Rhodes, & Christian, 2001). Vivien Stewart (2009), a senior adviser for education at Asia Society where she is leading a national effort to better prepare American students for the 21st century, notes that American students are dismally informed about the issues, languages, and cultures.

Performance Expectation 6

The education system, like all performance expectations, contains three elements for leaders to advocate for their teachers and students' needs.

Element A: Exerting Professional Influence

- Element A—Leaders improve the broader political, social, economic, legal, and cultural context of education for all students and families through active participation and exerting professional influence in the local community and the larger educational policy environment.
  - Indicator 2—A leader actively develops relationships with a range of stakeholders and policymakers to identify, respond to, and influence issues, trends, and potential changes that affect the context of conduct.

A SENATOR'S REQUEST

This indicator reminded Will of an inquiry he received from his state senator's office requesting that he serve on a blue ribbon panel to assess the state's revision of its K–12 technology standards. The

(Continued)

> (*Continued*)
>
> senator relayed to Will that his superintendent and the president of
> the school board had recommended him. Will had been considering
> declining the offer because of the time needed to fulfill this commit-
> ment. Reading this indicator reminded him he had responsibilities
> beyond his campus and district.

Element B: Contributing to the Educational Policy Environment

- Element B—Leaders contribute to policies and political support for excellence and equity in education.
  - Indicator 1—A leader operates consistently to uphold and
    influence federal, state, and local laws, policies, regula-
    tions, and statutory requirements in support of every
    student learning.

Principals must take seriously policy enforcement obligations.
Even if we disagree with a law or policy, we must enforce it.
Educators who disagree with a policy must use the appropriate chan-
nels and strategies to change the policy.

Element C: Policy Engagement

- Element C—Working with policymakers informs and
  improves education policymaking and effectiveness of the
  public's efforts to improve education.
  - Indicator 3—A leader advocates for public policies that
    ensure appropriate and equitable human and fiscal
    resources and improve student learning.

SUPERINTENDENT ANDREWS MENTORS PRINCIPAL WONKERMANN

Dr. Wallace C. Andrews, Will's superintendent, two weeks earlier
had taken Will with him to the state capital to attend a House hearing
on next year's school finance bill. When the hearing broke for lunch,
Dr. Andrews, Will, and a couple of other superintendents discussed
various aspects of the hearing. After the hearing recessed for the day,
Will joined Dr. Andrews and their state representative in her office to
discuss the implications of the proposed changes in the state funding
formula.

This experience significantly changed Will's understanding of how
state politics in the state capital impacted curriculum and instruction.

It inspired Will to seek a committee appointment in his state's principal organization. What happened in his district and state impacted his curriculum leadership at Childers School.

LEAVING STOP ⑥ — THE EDUCATION SYSTEM AND HEADING HOME

Even though he only reviewed three of the eleven indicators for this performance expectation, Principal Will Wonkermann had a greater understanding of public schools interrelatedness to political, social, economic, legal, and cultural systems and how they influence curriculum leadership. He also acquired a greater understanding and appreciation for his superintendent.

This has been quite a journey. Six stops. Eighteen elements. Eighteen indicators examined. Sixty-nine indicators bypassed. Will recognized he had so much more to learn. He removed his ruby-red Reeboks and rubbed his aching feet. He closed his tired eyes and rested his exhausted mind. Principal Wonkermann returned to Childers School a wiser leader, understanding his curriculum leadership journey was just beginning.

Final Thoughts

We completed a quick tour of the ISLLC standards with Principal Will Wonkermann by employing the CCSSO's *Performance Expectations and Indicators for Educational Leaders* as our guide and companion. We briefly reviewed the 18 elements of the performance expectations through a curriculum leadership lens. In an effort to provide a description of the performance expectations, we reviewed one indicator for each of the 18 elements. Our truncated examination of 18 of the 87 indicators provided a peek at the richness of the six performance expectations and their 18 elements.

As we progress through the remaining chapters, we will delve deeper into curriculum leadership and provide a greater understanding of the performance expectations, elements, and indicators. The performance expectations with their elements and indicators inform principals, teachers, curriculum leaders, grade-level chairs, department chairs, lead teachers, or anyone else who yearns to increase their understanding of curriculum leadership to promote teaching and learning.

Discussion Questions

1. Eight areas where society appears to be calling for changes from 20th-century schools to 21st-century schools were identified on Page 26. Have you witnessed any of these calls for change identified by the authors? Which, if any, do you think is the most pressing and why? What, if any, changes would you add to the authors' list?

2. Five dispositions exemplify Performance Expectation 1: Vision, Mission, and Goals. Using these dispositions as a guide, how have you witnessed this performance expectation being implemented? What additional ways do you see this standard being effectively employed?

3. Eight dispositions exemplify Performance Expectation 2: Teaching and Learning. Using these dispositions as a guide, how have you witnessed this performance expectation being implemented?

4. Five dispositions exemplify Performance Expectation 3: Managing Organizational Systems and Safety. Using these dispositions as a guide, how have you witnessed this performance expectation being implemented?

5. Four dispositions exemplify Performance Expectation 4: Collaborating With Families and Stakeholders. Using these dispositions as a guide, how have you witnessed this performance expectation being implemented?

6. Five dispositions exemplify Performance Expectation 5: Ethics and Integrity. Using these dispositions as a guide, how have you witnessed this performance expectation being implemented?

7. Five dispositions exemplify Performance Expectation 6: The Education System. Using these dispositions as a guide, how have you witnessed this performance expectation being implemented?

CASE STUDY APPLICATION

Principal Wonkermann's Late Afternoon Experience: Deja Vu All Over Again

We left Principal Will Wonkermann in Chapter 1 sitting in his office examining self-doubts about his ability to serve as *a* curriculum leader at Childers School. (Yes it's supposed to be "a" and not "the.") Will was beginning to understand curriculum leadership requires shared leadership. He was fighting self-doubts such as "I don't know enough about this" and "Will the faculty roll their eyes when I bring up vision and curriculum leadership?" and "There's not enough time or enough me," and ever so shockingly, "Will they be flying my underwear from the flagpole with me still in it?"

Once again, Will finds himself in his office. This time he's planning a professional learning day just two short weeks away. Will decided it was time for him to share his thoughts about curriculum leadership and vision (Performance Expectation 1) with Childers's stakeholders. He fought off his self-doubts by quoting Civil War Captain David Farragut of the USS Hartford aloud and with strength and emotion, "Damn the torpedoes. Full speed ahead!" (Overton, 2005). Somehow speaking these words gave him renewed courage to share his new-found passion for curriculum leadership. Will knew he, like Captain Farragut, was a calculated risk taker.

As he began planning for the professional learning day, Will pondered Performance Expectation 1 and its three elements.

Performance Expectation 1: Vision, Mission, and Goals

Education leaders ensure the achievement of all students by guiding the development and implementation of a shared vision of learning, strong organizational mission, and setting high expectations for every student.

Elements

- **A—High Expectations for All:** The vision and goals establish high, measurable expectations for all students.

- **B—Shared Commitments to Implement the Vision, Mission, and Goals:** The process of creating and sustaining the vision, mission, and goals is inclusive, building common understandings and genuine commitment among all stakeholders to implement vision and goals.

- **C—Continuous Improvement Toward the Vision, Mission, and Goals:** Education leaders ensure the achievement of all students by guiding the development and implementation of a shared vision of learning, strong organizational mission, and high expectations for every student.

Second, Principal Will Wonkermann considered sharing his understanding of a Student-Centered Hierarchy Model as opposed to an Adult-Centered Model (see Figure 2.3). He wondered how Childers School's stakeholders might react to this paradigm shift.

(Continued)

(*Continued*)

Figure 2.3   *Campus-Level Adult-Centered and Student-Centered Hierarchy Models*

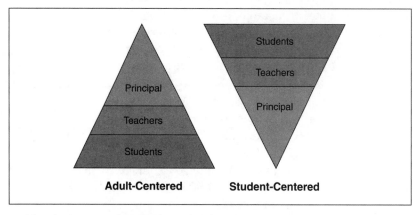

| Adult-Centered | Student-Centered |

Third, he pondered the Childers School mission statement in English and in Spanish:

> All students will meet with academic success.
>
> *Todos los estudiantes lograrán exito academico.*

Finally, he thought about changes from 20th-century schools to 21st-century schools and how they applied to Childers School. Could he use this information in bringing the school together in a common vision?

Passive learning	**To**	Active learning
Teacher centered	**To**	Student centered
Fragmented curriculum	**To**	Integrated curriculum
Low-level curriculum	**To**	High-level curriculum
Irrelevant curriculum	**To**	Relevant curriculum
Little student freedom	**To**	Generous student freedom
Textbook driven	**To**	Research driven
Assessment driven by state and federal testing	**To**	Assessment informed by state and federal testing

Will realized other ideas would come to mind as he planned what he hoped would be a pivotal moment in Childers School's history. Will was glad to see you, his faithful assistant principal enter his office. You will help plan and deliver this important professional learning day.

Application

Plan the professional learning day on ISLLC Performance Expectation 1 for the employees as well as eight parents and four community members at Childers School. The professional learning day starts at 8:30 a.m. and concludes at 4:00 p.m. The school district requires the professional learning day use the entire allotted time. You are to provide a 15-minute break in the morning and a 15-minute break in the afternoon. You must allow 60 to 75 minutes for lunch.

The professional learning will occur in the library where the faculty, staff, parents, and community members will sit at round tables with a capacity of four adults per table. The library contains an interactive whiteboard and has WIFI service. A mobile lab of 30 wireless laptop computers is available for use. Sixty teachers, paraprofessionals, and other staff members as well as 12 parents and community members will be present. One-thousand dollars in professional learning funds are available for the training. These funds cannot be used to purchase lunch. However, you can use up to $150 for snacks.

The learning outcome for the session is to collaboratively develop vision and mission statements for Childers School supported by all stakeholders. The existing statements may be reaffirmed, modified, or replaced.

Using this information and other resources of your choosing develop the agenda and action plan for this day to allow participants to master the learning outcome.

You and Principal Wonkermann will meet the following week with Dr. Wallace Andrews, superintendent, sharing the results of this professional learning day.

Other Resources

Glatthorn, A., Bosche, F., & Whitehead, B. (2009). *Curriculum leadership: Strategies for development and implementation* (2nd ed.). Thousand Oaks, CA: Sage.

Tileston, D. (2005). *10 best teaching practices: How brain research, learning styles, and standards define teaching competencies* (2nd ed.). Thousand Oaks, CA: Corwin.

3

Principal Expectations as Curriculum Leader

Shoot low, Sheriff, I think she's ridin' a Shetland!

—Bob Wills (Country Music Television Inc., 2008)

Shoot Low, Expect Less

Bob Wills, the King of Western Swing, humorously verbalized—as an intro to the musical number *Deep in the Heart of Texas*—what some principals may be tempted to do when working with curriculum. That is, "shoot low" to minimize potential instructional repercussions. In other words, a principal may intentionally, or unintentionally, lower curricular expectations in anticipation that teacher leaders will maximize the difference with effective classroom instruction, as a method of increasing student achievement and, thus, concealing a principal's ineptitude relative to curricular leadership.

Does this leadership approach accurately epitomize how many principals initiate curriculum leadership? Such is a relevant question with a possible and revealing answer. The late Allan Glatthorn, noted author and curriculum specialist, once acknowledged, "When I told a friend that the title of one of my books was *Principal as Curriculum Leader* (Glatthorn & Jailall, 2009), she responded, 'That's an oxymoron if I ever heard one'" (Glatthorn quoted in Cunningham & Corderio, 2006, p. 228).

The "shoot low" principal expectation can only generate an "expect less" curricular leadership model. Principals who lead with this mindset commit an academic injustice to their students. They know better. Research over the decades strongly supports the precept that principals have a profound effect on student achievement if high curricular and instructional expectations are the norm (Cennamo & Kalk, 2005; Reeves, 2006; Schmoker, 2006; Tanner & Tanner, 2006; Wiles, 2009). Additionally, principals must be directly involved in the planning, design, evaluation, and renewal of curriculum, instruction, and assessment practices (Fullan, 2008; Marzano, Waters, & McNulty, 2005). Any less of a principal expectation asserts an age-old adage— "Boys, we're getting nowhere fast!"

Understanding Principal Expectations in Curriculum Development

Principals must establish curricular expectations based on personal content knowledge, an understanding of instruction and instructional strategies and activities, and an awareness of how to properly evaluate curriculum design. Content knowledge includes research methods, data analysis, and skill mastery. Instructional understanding includes a comprehension of methods, materials, strategies, and techniques essential to effectively implementing curricular approaches at the school-site level. The evaluative piece of curriculum leadership relates to the principal being cognizant of differing assessment tools such as diagnostic, placement, formative, summative, and accreditation.

Curricular leadership demands high principal expectations. High expectations propel every individual in a school to greater levels of efficiency and excellence. High expectations nourish a "yes we can" attitude and build organizational confidence for student academic excellence. High curricular expectations correlate with data-driven analysis, research-based decision-making, student-centered initiatives, and best-practice results. High expectations create accelerated curricular and instructional approaches that, in turn, increase student achievement and success. Effective principals establish and follow through with the highest of curricular and instructional expectations: expectations that are appropriate, positive, and realistic. High expectations hold all members of the learning community accountable for providing effective instruction. When personnel and students are motivated, challenged, and provided opportunities to excel, the result is curricular excellence that equates to relevant instruction, interesting content, meaningful learning, and increased student achievement. High expectations are an essential, if not a critical, aspect of the curriculum development process. Low expectations, on the other hand, fulfill a dead-end prophecy. Consider the following account.

Why Waste Our Time, Part I

Elvin Bealittle served as principal at Union Elementary School and had, for many years, been a strong proponent of ability grouping and tracking. This was Mr. Bealittle's expectation and all followed his lead. This less-than-stellar expectation resulted in a dismal instructional setting. Teachers decided which students were in a particular ability group. Students who were generally poor, minorities, from broken homes, or whose parents were labeled "druggies" were placed in the low-ability groups. Teachers had minimal expectations for these students. These students weren't expected to do much more than the simplest of instructional tasks—worksheets and independent seatwork focusing on the most basic of skill orientations. The expectation was implicit: Remain in your seat, do your work, be quiet, read the assigned text—if you can—and answer the questions at the conclusion of each chapter. The principal had a demeaning term that he used to describe these students—lazy!

To further exacerbate the problem, the teachers did nothing to facilitate higher-order thinking, let alone teach at a challenging level. The teachers knew many of the students' families, as they had taught either their parents, siblings, or both. The teachers had long since determined that these particular kids, like the students' family members, would most certainly drop out of school. "Why waste our time" was a familiar line of reasoning as voiced by many of the faculty at Union Elementary School. Mr. Bealittle often stated, "These kids won't amount to a hill of beans. Do we really expect they'll contribute to our community?"

A culture of low expectations creates low achievement. Whose fault was it that the students in the "low groups" at Union Elementary School were far from successful? Can the students be blamed? Certainly not! The fault lands squarely on the desk of the curriculum leader——Mr. Bealittle.

Why Waste Our Time, Part II

Now, for the rest of the story! A new superintendent arrived at Union Consolidated School District, and Mr. Elvin Bealittle soon found himself reassigned to a menial job at central office (sound familiar?). Alvina Gogetter was named the new principal at Union Elementary School. The new principal, working in collaboration with faculty, dismantled ability grouping as an instructional technique. Initially, the teachers were reticent in adopting the new curricular approach and some were even resistant in following the new principal's directives. However, with time, the faculty at Union Elementary School recognized that an emotionally supportive curricular process, which provided an emphasis on quality instruction for *all* students, was a win-win situation. Even the campus naysayers, with significant collaborative and facilitative efforts by the principal, eventually warmed to the changes. It took a serious commitment by all parties, but ultimately, Ms. Gogetter and team learned to work together, recognizing the importance of respecting the ideas of one another. In fact, the principal and team began incorporating minority students' culture into the teaching process. The teachers even agreed to guide and facilitate—rather than control—student learning. It was not an easy process, as early on, the new principal found the faculty far from persuadable. However, prior to the conclusion of the first semester, Ms. Gogetter and team were able to structure a curricular approach emphasizing teaching of meaningful and interesting content. Ms. Gogetter also ensured that teachers developed learning activities that encouraged student participation.

Within the course of a single school year, learning increased as evidenced by improved test scores. Teachers learned to appreciate collaborating with the principal in the design and implementation of a new integrated curriculum. The onetime low-group students began to enjoy school, and their parents soon felt welcome at Union Elementary School.

The moral of this story is that principals will ultimately develop a learning environment where knowledge acquisition is no longer for an elite few if they are willing to work hard, are deliberative in their efforts to collaborate and facilitate, are willing to interact with a sometimes unreceptive faculty and staff, and are ready to maintain the highest of expectations, even in an adverse situation. Then and only then will principals reap the reward of an instructional program that emphasizes the acquisition of knowledge and skills as a right for *all* students, regardless of their background, race or ethnicity, social setting, or future aspirations.

Principal Expectations in the Curriculum Leadership Role

The principal, as curriculum leader, must engage all members of the learning community in curriculum planning, assessment, and renewal processes. Never underestimate the value of a principal's involvement and interaction in the curricular process. Such involvement and interaction relate to what Méndez and Sorenson (2010) propose as stages to assist principals in understanding how to effectively plan, assess, and renew curriculum. These four guiding stages are identified as (1) *membership inclusion*, (2) *assessment prioritization*, (3) *instructional enhancements*, and (4) *conflict polarization*. We have purposefully adapted and further developed these four stages into seven curricular expectations that are critical to a principal understanding how to effectively and collaboratively lead a curriculum team (see Figure 3.1).

Expectation 1: Team Identification and Inclusion

The curriculum team, as previously noted in Chapter 1, must include teachers, parents, principals, and other members of the school community. The principal-led curriculum team identifies the purpose of the curricular process and ensures that it is aligned with the campus vision, as well as the goals and objectives established in the campus improvement plan.

Marsh and Willis (2007) in their classic text *Curriculum: Alternative Approaches, Ongoing Issues* remind us that beyond the teaching role itself, curriculum development is the most important professional activity in which educators are involved. We further believe that the effective principal must acknowledge this fact and be prepared to lead the curriculum team in the development of an exceptional instructional program. To do so, the team must consist, at various times and for various reasons, of resource individuals and entities (see Table 3.1). For example, when serving as the curriculum leader, a principal must consider which participants, and from what levels, will serve in curricular processes. Levels are identified as (1) *district office leaders*, (2) *school-site leaders*, (3) *school-site personnel*, (4) *school-community clientele*, (5) *professional facilitators*, and (6) *local entities*. A more in-depth examination of these participant levels follows.

Figure 3.1 Seven Principal Expectations in the Curriculum Leadership Role

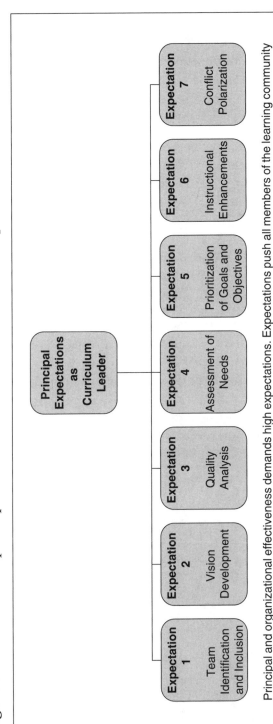

Principal and organizational effectiveness demands high expectations. Expectations push all members of the learning community to excel and succeed. High expectations promote a level of excellence and build confidence in the school leader, faculty, and students. High expectations correlate with data-driven analysis and decision making. Principals who exert the highest of expectations lead others in efforts to increase student achievement (Lezotte, 1997).

High expectations in the school organization, as attributed to curricular leadership, supports and enhances creativeness, self-confidence, energy enhancement, achievement orientation, assertiveness, quality orientation, an instructionally focused learning environment, and visionary leadership where all members of the learning community are goal directed, change oriented, and task driven (Sorenson & Goldsmith, 2009).

Curriculum leaders who lead with the highest of expectations motivate others, maintain priorities, develop potential, empower others, and regularly evaluate progress (Maxwell, 2003b).

Table 3.1   Proposed Members of the Curriculum Planning Team

District Office Leaders	Superintendent, associate and/or assistant superintendents, curriculum director, director of curriculum research, director of professional development, director of technology, director of media services, media specialists, and director of federal programs
School-Site Leaders	Principal, assistant or vice principals, site specialists (curriculum, instruction, technology), and lead or master teachers
School-Site Personnel	Librarians and paraprofessionals
School Community Clientele	Students, parents, business leaders, friends of education, adopt-a-school organizations, and partners in education
Professional Facilitators	University professors, educational experts (authors, trainers, researchers, consultants), teacher organization/union representatives, state or national teacher/principal association officials, education service center consultants, state department of education officials, testing corporation representatives, and regional educational laboratory researchers
Local Entities	News media (print journalists/radio-television professionals), service organizations (American Red Cross, civic clubs, etc.), special interest groups, concerned citizens, commercial/corporate organizations, political groups, and church/religious groups

District Office Leaders

Typically, external facilitators, such as district office leaders, are called on to ensure that the curricular processes are maintained relative to national and state standards, as well as district policies. Curriculum-oriented processes rarely proceed in a smooth and less-than-ambiguous manner. When circumstances dictate, external facilitators such as district office leaders (see Chapter 7 scenario *Curriculum Integration, Are You Kidding Me?*) must be called on to serve as part of a curriculum team. District office leaders, as team members, might include the following:

- Superintendent, associate and/or assistant superintendent(s)
- Curriculum director
- Director of curriculum research
- Director of professional development
- Director of technology
- Director of media services
- Media specialists
- Director of federal programs (special education, bilingual education, Title I, etc.)

Each district office leader brings specific levels of expertise to the curriculum team and assists principals in overcoming unexpected problems and unforeseen issues.

School-Site Leaders

Lunenburg and Irby (2006) assert there is a critical relationship role for school-site leaders in curriculum projects. School-site leaders serve as the impetus for effective curriculum development and a successful instructional program. What we do know, and what research continues to support, is an educational constant: Principals who are actively involved in curricular and instructional processes lead schools where students excel, on average, 5% to 15% higher on standardized testing than other schools where principals are less active (March & Peters, 2002). School-site leaders include the following:

- Principal
- Assistant- or vice-principals
- Site-specialists or coaches in areas of
  - Curriculum
  - Instruction (Math, Science, Applied Arts, etc.)
  - Technology
- Lead or master teachers

Site-level specialists must be experts in leading teachers in curriculum processes by affecting how teachers teach, how teachers utilize curriculum guides, and how teachers professionally interact with students. These specialists are important players in curriculum planning, instruction, and assessment. School-site specialists help teachers understand and value the importance of student perspectives, structure lessons that challenge student understanding of the content areas, ensure that lessons are relevant and of interest to students, aid teachers in the design of lessons that incorporate key aspects of curriculum guides and scope and sequence charts and help teachers properly assess student ability and mastery of predetermined classroom investigations (Holt-Reynolds, 2000; Rainer, Guyton, & Bowen, 2000; Wiggins, 1999).

School-Site Personnel

Teaching has been defined in the literature as an art (Stenhouse, 1988), a science (Lifsey, 2008), and a moral craft (Fullan & Hargreaves, 1991). However defined, teaching and the role of teachers is critical to a school's success. Just as important, the role of teachers in curricular processes is essential because teachers are planners, decision makers, and experienced in the practice of effective instructional techniques, strategies, and methodologies. As a result, the best teachers know *what* to teach, *when* to teach, and *how* to teach—all designed to ensure student academic success.

Beyond teachers, who else should serve as school-site personnel in the design, assessment, and renewal of curriculum? Librarians should be included because of their knowledge base and expertise relative to important resources, along with other research and reading materials. Additionally, paraprofessionals should serve on the curriculum team, most notably when certain "paras" are actively involved in the instructional process or serve in roles such as overseers of instructional resource or material or media centers.

School Community Clientele

School community clientele often express interest in numerous school-related issues, and as a result, they can be active participants in curriculum processes. Any list of clientele must include, first and foremost, students. Students have a vested interested in their learning, and given the opportunity, they *can* and *should* participate in curriculum planning. The list must also include parents who yield a variety of skills and levels of expertise that can enrich the curriculum planning and renewal process (Lee & Smith, 1996). Listed next are several clientele of the school community who can be incorporated within the curriculum team.

- Students (especially at the secondary level)
- Parents
- Business leaders
- Friends of education
- Adopt-a-school organizations
- Partners in education

Ornstein and Hunkins (2004) recommend that valuable resource clientele are often available outside a school system. Principals, working in collaboration with the curriculum team, can overcome certain curricular problems by calling on these valuable sources to effectively serve as an additional set of eyes relative to mediating instructionally oriented circumstances and situations.

Professional Facilitators

Professional facilitators include those from outside the school who have specialized knowledge, skill, or expertise that can be utilized to enhance curriculum planning. Such individuals typically have earned state, national, or international reputations and are often hired on a contractual basis by schools or school districts. A list of professional facilitators might include the following:

- University professors
- Educational experts (authors, trainers, researchers, consultants)
- Teacher organization/union representatives
- State or national teacher/principal association officials
- Education service center consultants
- State department of education officials
- Testing corporation representatives
- Regional educational laboratory researchers

Fullan (1999; 2001) suggests that professional facilitators who effectively assist schools and school systems, relative to curriculum planning, instruction, and assessment, are frequently described as receiving intrinsic satisfaction from working with others. These facilitators are candid and straightforward in their assessment of curricular issues. They are motivated and enthusiastic in working with others to solve curricular problems, and they are often able to cope with the frustrations faced by many principals, teachers, and other team members who are inundated with curricular concerns.

Local Entities

There are times when a principal and the curriculum team wish to involve what Marsh and Willis (2007, p. 204) call "linkers" in curriculum planning, assessment, and renewal. Linkers are those entities that can be of assistance to a school or school system or may be politically expedient to involve in the curricular process. Local entities might include the following:

- News media (print journalist/radio-television professionals)
- Service organizations (American Red Cross, civic clubs, etc.)
- Special interest groups
- Concerned citizens
- Commercial/corporate organizations
- Political groups
- Church/religious groups

Expectation 1 Fulfilled

When a principal-led curriculum team initiates a curriculum-oriented process, a need for outside assistance often becomes an expectation. Knowing where to seek critical expertise, advice, and monetary assistance can be a daunting task. The authors propose that the previously noted lists of potential curriculum team members can help alleviate probable stress when conducting curricular and instructional planning and renewal efforts.

Recall the words from Ecclesiastes:

> Two can accomplish more than twice as much as one, for the results can be much better. If one falls, the other pulls him up; but if a man falls when he is alone, he's in trouble. . . . And one standing alone can be attacked and defeated, but two can stand back-to-back and conquer; three is even better, for a triple-braided cord is not easily broken. (Ecclesiastes 4: 9–12, *The Living Bible*)

Expectation 2: Vision Development

What is "vision" from a curriculum leadership perspective? Conger (1989) noted two decades ago that vision is a leadership ability to see beyond current realities. Bennis and Nanus (1985) suggested that vision is a collaborative and team development effort. Berlew (1992) attributes vision to unifying an organization. Finally, Ubben, Hughes, and Norris (2007) equate vision to "four Cs"—(1) creative, (2) communicative, (3) compelling, and (4) committed leadership. The authors of this text personally appreciate the definition of vision as described by Lunenburg and Irby (2006): A vision is an attempt by a principal to explain to others what a school hopes to create and achieve. Let's examine the term "vision" from a research-based perspective and then apply the noted theory, with a series of tips, to the field of practice.

The Northwest Regional Educational Laboratory (2005) relates that vision is a method of merging common possibilities into great

Meet the needs of students [handwritten]

potential. This research foundation further relates that visionary principals imagine the potential for a great curricular future simply because they are able to obtain and analyze data and then utilize this data to conceive new and unforeseen curricular and instructional phenomena.

The Charles A. Dana Research Center (2003) reveals there are certain frameworks for visionary leadership. For example, principals must have a vision for the following:

1. Learners and how students learn, along with a vision for the role of the curriculum leader in promoting student learning.

2. Teachers and what it means to be a teacher. What is the teacher role relative to students, instruction, and curriculum development? How does the principal envision the empowerment of teachers?

3. Curriculum development and how the curriculum leader envisions quality instruction, student diversity, integrated lesson content, teaching methodologies, instructional strategies, and student achievement.

4. Professional development as related to curriculum design, assessment, and renewal. How does the lead learner envision professional growth impacting curricular improvement, programmatic change, instructional delivery, student learning, and overall achievement?

Examining the research and then applying the theory to practice is a complicated venture unless principals are visionaries who develop goals to achieve instructional enhancement by means of curriculum planning, assessment, and renewal. A commitment to goal development, objective adaptation, and strategy or action implementation are all essential components of what must be accomplished by the visionary principal in the field of curricular practice.

A seven-step approach to creating a campus vision, as defined by Sorenson and Goldsmith (2009) and oriented to the curriculum development process, should be considered by the school principal, in collaboration with the curriculum team, when applying theory to practice. The seven steps are (1) identify the traditional or historical curriculum of the school, (2) conduct an in-depth analysis of current curriculum trends, (3) examine what the school curriculum can become for student achievement to increase, (4) assess the campus curricular strengths and further identify areas to target for growth and development, (5) identify campus curriculum problems and inhibiting factors that are interfering with student achievement, (6) develop a plan of action focusing on research-based, best-practice

Developing a vision [handwritten]

instructional techniques, along with alternative approaches to curriculum design and development (see Chapter 7), and (7) monitor, evaluate, and adjust campus action plans (to include newly revised curriculum guides) through frequent meetings and brainstorming sessions with various members of the learning community.

We offer 10 practitioner-oriented tips for developing a vision for curriculum improvement.

1. **Challenge yourself and your team.** Pursue curricular risks. Remember, there is no failure in any risk attempted—only the potential for gain. Risk can open the eyes of an organization to new, different, and endless opportunities for curriculum advancement and instructional success.

2. **Envision the unimaginable.** Look at where you are today and where you and your team would like to be tomorrow, next week, next month, next year, and so on. Remember this: If the mind can conceive it, you can achieve it!

3. **Exhibit courage.** Never hesitate to take a major step forward. When you lead with courage, you attract people. When you attract people, they will follow. When people follow, the results will be phenomenal.

4. **Lead with integrity.** Principals become effective curriculum leaders by the quality of their actions and the integrity of their intent (see the Chapter 7 section titled Ethical Leadership). Joan Bruster, a friend and former colleague of the authors, often stated that integrity could be summed up in two sentences: "We make a living by what we get. We make a life by what we give" (2001). Give all you can to the students in your care.

5. **Practice makes perfect.** If you truly desire to become an effective curriculum leader, work at the task. Delve into the daily practice of curriculum planning, assessment, evaluation, and renewal. Only when we commit ourselves to hands-on experiences are we truly capable of learning and experiencing effective curriculum leadership.

6. **Implement high expectations.** Effective principals who lead curriculum development and renewal efforts utilize each of the seven expectations to curricular success as noted in this chapter. What principals are able to obtain from others is largely dependent on established expectations. High expectations are related to principal support; the empowerment of others; fixed boundaries; constructive use of time; commitment to achievement, positive values, and ethical conduct; strong interpersonal skills; and a genuine sense of purpose (Search Institute, 2003).

7. **Initiate change.** Change is the single most important element in successful curriculum leadership (see Chapter 4). Curricular change equates to organizational growth, which ensures increased student achievement.

8. **Apply curriculum design, assessment, and renewal processes.** If you don't know how or are at the very least unsure as to how to initiate the processes, examine the details as noted in Chapters 7, 9, and 10.

9. **Believe it can be done.** Lead with confidence and know actions speak louder than words. Consider our personal belief system that is based on a clear and direct command: "Commit your works to the Lord and your plans will be established" (Proverbs 16:3, *New American Standard Bible*).

10. **Celebrate success.** When a principal works in collaboration with the curriculum team, numerous opportunities for establishing a culture of appreciation will manifest themselves. Sorenson and Goldsmith (2006) relate that principals who lead effective organizations experience success and celebrate often. Opportunities to celebrate success will increase when curriculum and instruction are integrated, when teaching supports learning, when learning is differentiated, and when increased student achievement is an organizational norm.

Expectation 2 Fulfilled

When a principal and curriculum team is visionary in their approaches to curriculum development and renewal practices, a striving for quality will be apparent. Quality efforts in curriculum design and instructional implementation are closely associated with a leader's expectation to instill a campus vision, along with an ability to analyze pertinent data and relevant information.

Expectation 3: Quality Analysis

Quality analysis, often referred to as information analysis, is a thorough examination of a campus improvement or action plan from a curricular perspective. Quality analysis is a method of determining problematic causal factors as a means of (1) establishing performance objectives, (2) conducting a needs assessment, and (3) scrutinizing a curricular issue or problem (Sorenson, 2006). Quality analysis does not simply rest with the gathering of information. The principal and the curriculum team must conduct a quality analysis of patterns and trends within and across multiple sources of data. A quality analysis of a curricular problem entails one very important step: the examination of data and the advancement of appropriate strategies to address the development of effective curricular and instructional processes.

Quality analysis is a principal-oriented, practice-based recommended method of data scrutiny that permits a school leader and the curriculum planning team to decipher probable causal factors that may be contributing to low performance in particular subject areas for specific student populations. For example, consider the following situation faced by principals.

WHAT'S A PRINCIPAL TO DO?

Will Wonkermann, principal at Childers School, had a problem. A significant percentage of students in two grade levels were struggling academically. Some were failing multiple classes. Struggling students were unable to read with comprehension or write with clarity. These students were testing as English learners and barely passing the English achievement test. Each student had, again barely, received passing grades in previous grades. These students seemed bored, were often disengaged, and were uninterested in school. Principal Wonkermann kept asking himself, "What's a principal to do?"

Great question! What is a principal to do in a circumstance akin to the situation noted? The answer requires a quality analysis. Let's begin an investigation relative to incorporating and utilizing such an analysis. Two types of quality analyses are required to begin working through the problem at Childers School. First, the principal, working with the curriculum team, must seek "soft" data and information. Second, the principal and curriculum team must seek "hard" data and information. Both sets of information can come from inside or outside the school or district. Soft data or information is often considered more "gray in concept" or qualitative in nature. Hard data is typically considered more black and white or quantitative, relative to the analysis process. We will use a four-quadrant quality analysis model as a means of understanding how to conduct a more in-depth examination of the quality analysis approach to curriculum development and renewal.

Quadrant 1: Quality Outside/Soft Data and Information

When conducting a quality analysis, a principal and curriculum team must examine the research literature along with best-practice approaches. This process necessitates enlisting the support of district and school-site leaders, as well as professional facilitators who have

a firm understanding of practice-based frameworks as related to a curricular problem. In the previous Childers School scenario, students were disengaged, uninterested, and failing classes. What is the root of this problem? What will the research reveal? To answer these questions, as well as others, a principal and curriculum team must understand and be receptive to delving into the research literature and the associated best practices. This process includes examining research-based journal articles relative to the subject, seeking the advice and recommendations of professional facilitators, consulting with educational research laboratories, and providing release time for teacher leaders to make site visits to those schools (local and distant) that are effectively implementing best practices associated with the curricular issue and instructional problem.

Quadrant 2: Quality Outside/Hard Data and Information

Outside sources of data essential to a quality analysis include information typically derived from federal and state entities and statutes. Federal entities might include the United States Department of Education or the Office of Civil Rights. Federal statutes to possibly consider include the No Child Left Behind (NCLB) Act of 2001, and the Individuals with Disabilities Act (IDEA). State entities could include the state board for educator certification, the state board of education, the state education agency, and the state attorney general's office, for opinions rendered. Appropriate statutes to consider would be State Education Code, State Administrative Code, and Commissioner of Education rulings.

Quadrant 3: Quality Inside/Soft Data and Information

Quality information that can be found within a school and/or school system includes conducted survey results, focus group queries and associated information, interviews, school-site visits, observations of effective teaching practices, surveys of organizational climate and culture, student profiles, teacher opinions, and brainstorming sessions. These sources of quality information can provide pertinent data to a principal and curriculum team relative to initiating curriculum change and improving the instructional program.

Quadrant 4: Quality Inside/Hard Data and Information

Inside or hard data from within a school and/or school system can be the basis for tangible/hands-on information. This inside/hard data might include the following records:

- Student academic records to include cumulative folders
- State assessment/accountability records
- Fiscal education information management system (FEIMS) records
- School board policies
- Administrative regulations and procedures
- School district attorney opinions
- Attendance records of school meetings
- Classroom assessments and other benchmarking records

These are a few examples of information from within a school or school system that a principal can utilize when conducting a quality analysis of a curriculum issue and/or an instructional problem.

As a final note, it is important to recognize that in the field of administrative practice, many principals can effectively utilize the quality analysis approach in two important and distinctive ways:

1. To confirm what they are noting in Quadrant 4 (*Quality Inside/ Hard Data and Information*)

2. To confirm a barrier-based hunch they have formed because of the Quadrant 3 (*Quality Inside/Soft Data and Information*) analysis of data and information

Take an opportunity to initiate the quality analysis approach in your school. You will be pleasantly surprised with the results. More important, the curriculum planning and assessment process will improve, the instructional program will enhance, and student achievement will increase.

Expectation 3 Fulfilled

When a principal and curriculum team implements a quality analysis relative to curriculum planning, assessment, evaluation, and renewal, such an expectation will lead to a closer scrutiny of barriers affecting the curriculum process and the instructional program. This scrutiny will lead the principal and team to recognize that certain academic areas targeted for improvement must be assessed and prioritized.

Expectation 4: Assessment of Needs

A needs assessment and prioritized listing of campus essentials must be conducted prior to any curriculum improvement efforts.

This course of action ensures that team members recognize how curriculum planning benefits teaching and learning. Along with an assessment of instructional needs, the effective principal is expected to lead the curriculum team in prioritizing school needs to positively affect the instructional program.

Sorenson and Goldsmith (2006), in their text *The Principal's Guide to School Budgeting*, note that a major expectation of an effective principal is to analyze the school improvement or action plan. This plan is the vehicle that drives the curricular processes and instructional program of any school. In conducting a needs assessment, the authors identify four important phases essential to understanding the performance of a school. These phases include (1) *initiating the inquiry process*; (2) *deriving consensus on the issues to be addressed*; (3) *developing and implementing processes of collecting, organizing, and interpreting relevant data*; and (4) *focusing on the needs of highest priority*. Let's examine each of these phases in more detail.

Initiating the Inquiry Process

When initiating the inquiry process, an expectation of effective principals is to review the district and school's mission statement (recall Principal Will Wonkermann in Chapter 1). The mission of a school, as described by Maxwell (2003b), is a method for initiating victory in an organization. Heller (1999) defines mission as setting sights on future developments. Effective principals establish a school's mission by seeking the unattainable. How? Simply, intensify ordinary efforts into extraordinary achievements. One might wonder by what means this can be accomplished. Begin by recognizing the following: There are transformational leaders—those who see the benefits of change and initiate alternative or even revolutionary aims or acts. There are pragmatic leaders—those who regrettably accept change only after it has been proven successful. Then there are habitual leaders—those who are in the habit of resisting change and who would rather seek an excuse for rejecting solutions for curriculum renewal. What type of leader are you? Have you actually identified a mission for your school? Do you understand and instructionally incorporate the mission statement of your school? Have you initiated the inquiry process at your school? Let's delve further into the needs assessment topic.

Deriving Consensus

Reaching consensus relative to the needs assessment process occurs when a principal has ensured that (1) all pertinent sources of data have been reviewed and analyzed; (2) all curricular and instructional issues have been identified, examined, and discussed; and (3) a determination of areas of substantive schoolwide improvement initiatives have been identified by the principal and curriculum team. To actually seek and derive consensus, a method of decision making includes more input rather than less. Recall the axiom from Chapter 1: *All of us are smarter than any one of us!* Debating a topic and arguing the pros and cons of an issue must be encouraged by the principal if problems are to be solved and decisions to be made. Otherwise, school personnel will feel they have had a less than participative voice.

Effective principals recognize that some decisions make themselves. Other decisions come with an either/or choice. Others have multiple options for consideration and approval. For the later decisions, a consensus must be derived, and this takes a systematic approach. Such an approach is initiated when a principal and curriculum team generate ideas, gather relevant information, and, thus, decide on a course of action.

Collecting and Interpreting Data

Effective principals, working in collaboration with the curriculum team, collect, organize, and interpret all relevant data as a method of determining which issues impair the overall improvement of a school. This process includes examining the data as noted in the Initiating the Inquiry Process section of this chapter. Next, a principal discusses with personnel what the data reveals and how such will positively or negatively impact the clientele of the learning community. Finally, this information is compiled for effective action and implementation but not before a needs prioritization list is developed.

Prioritizing Needs

When focusing on the curricular and instructional needs of the highest priority in a school, principals must work with the curriculum team and review the research literature as related to the problem at hand. Then, the principal and team conduct a full examination of the needs and present a recommendation with a priority ranking of each identified need. However, three important questions must first be answered:

1. What is the potential for effecting curricular change and overall school improvement?

2. What human, fiscal, and/or material resources (including release time) are required to implement curricular change?

3. What expertise (internal and/or external) is available to bring about necessary change and overall curricular improvement?

The prioritization of needs is realized and further accomplished when the curriculum team and the school principal work together in a collaborative manner. This process also involves ethical decision making, which will be examined in Chapter 7.

Expectation 4 Fulfilled

When a principal and curriculum team establish the expectation of completing a needs assessment, the development of instructional goals and objectives becomes an essential component of any curricular review and assessment process. As goals and objectives are developed, each must be carefully prioritized in an effort to ensure that student achievement, as opposed to personal or private advancements, is the focus of a principal and/or curriculum team.

Expectation 5: Prioritization of Goals and Objectives

Goals and objectives in a campus improvement plan or a curriculum plan must be developed and prioritized utilizing a collaborative process. The school's campus planning committee is a logical choice for this task. This committee reviews the pertinent research literature and other available data before reaching a consensus on the priority of needs as a means of fulfilling the mission of the school. The committee, working in tandem with the principal, reallocates resources to ensure that the curricular concern is fiscally addressed. This is accomplished by allocating dollars to priority goal number one, then to priority goal number two, and so on, as funding is available. Successful schools prioritize their needs and fund them as budget allocations permit (Sorenson & Goldsmith, 2006).

Finally, a principal leads the prioritization process by ensuring that the curriculum team remains nonpartisan, free from bias, honest in their endeavors, and careful to avoid any outright injustices. Fairness is always the appropriate model when leading. School and other professional interests must prevail over any private or personal agendas. The bottom line, what is in the best interest of the students?

Expectation 5 Fulfilled

When a principal and curriculum team prioritize goals and objectives as an expectation of the curriculum review and assessment process, it becomes apparent that certain instructional enhancements are necessary to build a strong academic program. These enhancements must focus on specified curricular-oriented formats that further ensure overall programmatic improvement and student success.

Expectation 6: Instructional Enhancements

Newly designed curriculum must be developed and written to reveal cognitive and affective skills, concepts, and learning outcomes. Various formats are utilized when developing and writing curriculum. Glickman, Gordon, and Ross-Gordon (2009) suggest three formats worthy of serious consideration. These formats are (1) *behavioral-objective*, (2) *webbing*, and (3) *results-only*. Each format serves as a useful construct when establishing the principal expectation of curriculum enhancement, instructional improvement, and increased student achievement.

The behavioral-objective format is one in which the developers of curriculum determine what aspects of instruction need to be learned, then state the learning outcomes by means of behavioral objectives and actions or strategies that specify teaching techniques and learning activities. For example, consider the following two behavioral objectives. One is an effective objective and the other ineffective.

Objective 1: One-hundred percent of the bilingual-program teachers (PreK–6), the principal, and two assistant principals will participate in an average of 10 hours of professional development designed to build educator capacity to effectively articulate and implement a two-way bilingual program.

Objective 2: Parents of English learners will participate in parent outreach/training sessions.

Can you explain why one of the behavioral objectives is more effective than the other? To assist in answering the noted question, recall that all behavioral objectives must be SMART (to use an acronym)—**S**pecific, **M**easurable, **A**chievable, **R**ealistic, and **T**imebound. Now, analyze the two objectives previously listed and determine which one is SMART and why.

Effective behavioral objectives are performance oriented. In other words, a behavioral objective must include numbers, percentages for summative and cumulative evaluations, and targets (reachable in one year) with at least one or more strategies or actions for completion. This format will be examined in greater detail in Chapter 6. Such a curricular approach includes pre- and posttest methods to better determine which aspects of the objectives need to be skill enhanced and which have been successfully mastered by the students.

The webbing format is one in which curriculum developers and writers determine initially—prior to predetermining any knowledge of skill development—the major themes, potential student learning activities, and probable learning outcomes. Learning is based on what Groundwater-Smith (1996) describes as multiple-modalities of learning, to include reading, writing, listening, constructing, and integration of fields of knowledge (content areas) within the specified themes. Consider the following example.

Learning Outcomes

1. Students will be able to identify three types of automobile engines: (1) internal combustion, (2) electrical charged, and (3) solar operated.

2. Students will distinguish between the advantages and disadvantages of the differing automobile engines and the impact of pollutants on the environment.

3. Students will support one set of findings as to which of the three automotive engines least pollutes the environment.

Learning Methods

Students will utilize multiple modalities to initiate learning (i.e., research reading, process writing, active listening, and collaborative constructing).

Webbing Integration

Students—through the integration of fields of knowledge in the subject areas of science (physics), history, mathematics, language arts, and economics—will successfully master the learning objectives/outcomes.

The webbing integration format is examined in greater detail in Chapter 7. This particular format is considered within the research literature as one of the better methods of initiating and implementing effective curricular change that will positively impact student interest, coursework relevance, and thus, increase student achievement.

The results-only format is one in which the developers and writers of curriculum provide teachers the widest latitude for utilization of instructional materials, learning activities, and teaching techniques. For example, those assessing a course curriculum might propose certain goals along with general learning objectives related to a subject area or lesson unit, along with instructional methods to evaluate student learning. This particular format permits the teacher to determine when and how to teach certain skills. Therefore, the teacher is held accountable for the results only.

Expectation 6 Fulfilled

When a principal and curriculum team initiate instructional enhancements, positive change along with organizational improvement and increased student achievement will occur. An optimal instructional enhancement to any curricular process is the incorporation of the webbing format. This particular enhancement provides for specific learning outcomes and instructional methods along with a meaningful integration of content or subject areas. As previously noted, the webbing format increases student interest, provides for coursework relevance, and better ensures student achievement (see Chapter 7).

However, conflict can be expected while fulfilling this particular expectation. While conflict is inevitable within any organization, it can be minimized when a principal and curriculum team communicate, cooperate, and construct curriculum and instructional plans in a civil manner. However, a principal must understand how to handle conflict polarization at the campus level if organizational success is a priority.

Expectation 7: Conflict Polarization

Conflict within any organization occurs when two opposing parties have interests or goals that are incompatible (Robbins, 2006). Conflict within a curriculum development group can occur when team members: (a) have strong differences in values, beliefs, or goals; (b) are competing for resources; (c) are experiencing high levels of pressure or stress; or (d) face uncertain futures or incompatible demands (i.e., raise test scores or look elsewhere for another teaching position!) (Yukl, 2001).

Finally, conflict can occur within the curriculum team when a principal acts in a manner that is either unethical or inconsistent with the mission and/or vision of a school. However, in many instances, the consistent source of conflict within an organization is simply a lack of communication. A principal can significantly minimize conflict within a group by enhancing his or her communication and listening skills, as well as spending time with team members (Sorenson & Goldsmith, 2009).

Meaningful dialogue between the principal—the steward of the campus academic vision—teachers, parents, and other members of the learning community must be initiated to overcome any potential for polarizing conflict that can obscure the curriculum process and instructional improvement efforts. When conflict polarizes an organization, disharmony ensues and opportunities for improvement degenerate into disorder and confusion. Consider the case where

Principal Will Wonkermann and the curriculum team at Childers School meet for the first time and begin to work collaboratively to alleviate any potential for ensuing conflict.

THE THREE Cs OF SCHOOL MANAGEMENT: A RETURN TO WILL WONKERMANN, PRINCIPAL OF CHILDERS SCHOOL

Will Wonkermann was sitting in his office late one afternoon contemplating the events of the day. New curricular initiatives were being piloted at Childers School, with significant success and positive personnel reception, thanks in great part to his conflict management skills. Will vividly recalled beginning his first year as principal at Childers School. Prior to his arrival, the school had been beset by low student test scores, and the basis for the school's low accountability ratings was a lack of curricular leadership. The previous principal had invested most of her time handling student discipline issues and parental complaints. The previous principal, as Will recalled, often stated to campus personnel, "I've no time for working with the curriculum or the instructional program. I've got campus facilitators to handle those issues." Although it was true that campus facilitators were available and several were competent in their role, none had ever been properly trained in effective curricular change processes, until the arrival of Mr. Wonkermann as campus principal.

Will had recognized this problem at once, and not long after being named the new principal of Childers School, he initiated a first meeting with the curriculum team. He promptly asked the following: "What will it take for me to work with this group?" Several members of the team responded that the principal needed to listen to their concerns and be open to suggestions and feedback. Additionally, other members noted it was important that they know up front what the principal expected of them, the quantity and quality of group work, and how often group meetings would occur. Fred Mertz, a crusty algebra teacher, stated emphatically, "You need to respect us and we need to respect you!" Mr. Wonkermann responded with a "no problem there, Fred." Then, Laurie Gatlin, the head volleyball coach, and never one to remain silent for long, stated, "We need encouraging engagement. Don't talk down to us. We're here to solve a problem, not create another one." Finally, Donna Arnold, chair of the business department, spoke up noting, "We need some leadership 'withitness'—I mean you, Mr. Wonkermann, need to get with it and lead us in the right direction so we can dig ourselves out of this accountability hole!"

In those early days of his principalship, the curriculum group began to slowly but deliberatively function. Will fondly recalled being quite amazed as to how committee expectations began to overlap with his expectations.

(Continued)

(*Continued*)

Will also remembered being pleased with the level of cooperation from the curriculum team, on a member-by-member basis. At the time, progress had been slow in the design of new curriculum guides for the differing school departments. At first, the curriculum meetings had been somewhat combative but eventually evolved into once-a-week sessions where civility prevailed and team members, working collaboratively with their new principal, made essential curricular and instructional adjustments.

Will inwardly smiled as he thought about how conflicting some of those initial meetings had been, but now, he was impressed with the level of maturity and responsibility exhibited by the curriculum team. As he reflected on those early days in his curricular leadership role, he was genuinely satisfied that conflict polarization over the curricular and instructional changes made had been minimal. He was even more impressed with his willingness to not only initiate curricular change but also make the necessary changes collaboratively.

Thinking back, Will had to credit the initial success of the curriculum team and their efforts to a research article he had read while attending Union State University. The article was titled "The Three Cs of School Management," coauthored by David W. Johnson and Roger T. Johnson (1999). The "three Cs" were (1) *cooperative community*, (2) *constructive conflict resolution*, and (3) *civic values*. Will had recognized from reading the article that conflict is inevitable and often necessary for groups to work effectively in achieving mutual goals. Additionally, he recalled an important lesson he had learned early in his administrative career: When conflict is handled well, leader support and group respect are eventual outcomes.

At that time and even more so today, Will thought to himself, when conflict within the curriculum team arose, he always focused the team on research positions and how advocating said positions would help rather than hinder student achievement. To this day, he also welcomed reverse perspectives, listening carefully to each position presented. He had learned to respectfully refute, if appropriate, an opposing position or attack by presenting and advocating what the research revealed. Such best-practice evidence enhanced reasoning on all sides and allowed for a formalized agreement. Often, as a means of further reducing conflict, Will learned to remind the team, "We must do what is in the best interest of the students and not necessarily what's in the best interest of any one of us!"

Pause and Consider

- To avoid conflict polarization, how would you, as principal or prospective principal, initiate a cooperative community?
- What did Will Wonkermann do to develop a cooperative community?

- How can conflict be resolved when working with groups—most notably curriculum teams—who are opposed to change?
- How can conflict resolution be constructive?
- What civic values were displayed or utilized by Mr. Wonkermann and the curriculum development team at Childers School?

Expectation 7 Fulfilled

When a principal and curriculum team provide optimal influence on any curricular process, an open and positive teaching and learning climate is the outcome. A positive climate, based on collaborative leadership, creates an environment in which all parties feel secure, sense their voices will be heard, and believe that their ideas will be seriously considered. Such a climate creates an organizational culture where conflict is expected but is seldom polarizing.

Final Thoughts

Expectations! Do you, as a leader, really want to "shoot low" and "expect less" from your team when it comes to curriculum planning, assessment, evaluation, and renewal? We expect not. Nonetheless, one cannot help but be reminded of a quote from Buckley Qualls (1981), a former university professor. One day in class, Dr. Qualls told a group of students the following:

> The first thing a new principal must do is fight the battle of expectations. This is a battle for the hearts and minds of the campus team. If the principal wins this battle, the expectation is simple: The team will follow the principal anywhere. If the principal loses this battle, the expectation is simple: The principal will never do any real good.

High expectations are the key to effective curriculum leadership. High expectations result in instructional improvement. High expectations increase faculty performance and student achievement. High expectations equate to school improvement. However, high expectations come with a price: Curriculum leaders and team members will never again be satisfied with the status quo. They will be ever diligent in seeking organizational excellence. They will be ever reaching for the next standard—going even higher in their commitment to quality than could possibly have been predicted. Are you ready to reach? Are you ready to lead? What are your expectations?

Discussion Questions

1. Why are high principal expectations critical to curriculum leadership, a culture of academic excellence, and increased student achievement? Provide examples to support your answers.

2. Which of the principal expectations in the curriculum leadership role were ignored by Elvin Bealittle in the Why Waste Our Time—Part I scenario? Which principal expectations were incorporated by Alvina Gogetter in Part II of the scenario?

3. Consider the curriculum development and renewal processes at your school. Do such exist? Why or why not? Can your answer be related to any of the seven curricular expectations for principal leadership? Be specific in your answer.

4. Which of the 10 practitioner-oriented tips for developing a vision for curriculum improvement are incorporated, implemented, or encouraged at your school? Which of the 10 tips need to be used by your curriculum leader? Provide detailed explanations in your answers.

5. Which quadrant(s) of the Quality Analysis expectation is/are the most important to determining causal factors negatively affecting curricular enhancement and instructional improvement at your school? Explain why.

6. Has conflict ever been a polarizing factor at a school where you were employed? How can a principal lead a team in overcoming conflict polarization, most notably when working to enhance the curriculum design, assessment, and renewal processes?

CASE STUDY APPLICATION
Who's the Turkey This Thanksgiving?

Lisa Nihcan was a kindergarten teacher at Red Greene Elementary School in the suburban community of Sunset Bluff. Lisa worked diligently like most first-year teachers in preparing her students for the required learning. She spent countless hours at school developing lessons, creating instructional materials, and encouraging her students to excel academically, behaviorally, and socially. Lisa had been described by her principal, in an evaluation appraisal, as being a "first-year, first-rate teacher who exhibits the highest of professional efforts and teaching initiatives." Lisa loved her work and the students in her charge. The students, in turn, loved Ms. Nihcan!

However, Lisa recently told a former university professor, who she had seen at the Sunset Bluff Mall, that teaching would be so much better if "administration would just let us teach!" The professor smiled and replied, "Yep, I hear that a lot." Then the professor asked a relevant question: "Lisa, what's the problem?" Lisa laughed and stated, "Don't get me wrong, I love my principal, but she just gets in the way when it comes to teaching." The professor then asked, "What do you mean?" Lisa began a most interesting story.

The kindergarten team at Red Greene Elementary School was preparing lessons for the upcoming Thanksgiving week. It would be a short week, just three days in length, but it was a great time of year. The kids were already excited and talking nonstop about roasted turkey and grandmas and grandpas coming to their homes. The students undoubtedly needed some free time away from school to play—to just be kids. Naturally, the kindergarten teachers were just as excited. They were anxious for a much-needed respite from their daily teaching routines. As the team met on the Wednesday before Thanksgiving week, Lisa and two of her colleagues, Abbi Rahmon and Brenda Hiccon, suggested to the two other kindergarten team members that their students engage in some Thanksgiving-oriented learning activities correlated with the state-mandated curriculum and district-adopted essential knowledge and skills. The two other team members agreed. Erika, the team leader, said to Lisa, Abbi, and Brenda, "Great idea! You girls run with it and develop lesson plans and activities that relate to the Thanksgiving theme and to our curriculum guide." The team agreed.

Lisa, Abbi, and Brenda spent all day Saturday and half of Sunday, after church, preparing lessons for the upcoming Thanksgiving week. The Thanksgiving three-day week was fully accounted for from a curriculum-oriented and instructionally focused perspective. Every lesson related to the kindergarten curriculum objectives. The lessons included the students making pilgrim vests and hats and using "t" words in five sentences to be written on a turkey cutout. The students would also read a Thanksgiving story, collaboratively write a Thanksgiving poem, and engage in other Thanksgiving-related/integrated-learning activities. When Lisa, Abbi, and Brenda presented the lessons to the two other members of the kindergarten team, the response was positive. Later, Lisa electronically forwarded the lesson plans to their principal.

On Monday, the first day of Thanksgiving week, all of the daily learning activities were laid out on the students' desks before the beginning of the school day. The bell sounded and the kindergarten students eagerly entered their classrooms. The teachers smiled at the students' enthusiasm as the kids saw the "Turkey-day stuff" (as one

(*Continued*)

(*Continued*)

student noted) on their desks. Abbi shouted down the hall to Lisa: "Way to go, Lisa! Our kids are going to love this week!" Lisa grinned. At the same time, Lisa noticed their principal, Dr. Ainslee Mogford, purposefully walking down the kindergarten hallway.

"Good morning, Dr. Mogford. Happy Thanksgiving week," Lisa exclaimed! With a frown and in a stern voice, Dr. Mogford replied, "We need to talk about the kindergarten lesson plans for this week." Lisa said, "Sure, now or later?" The principal grimly replied, "Have the team meet with me during planning time." Lisa walked down the hallway toward Abbi and said, "Well, so much for starting off on a positive note this week."

Later in the morning, the kindergarten teachers met with Dr. Mogford. The principal began the conversation with a frown stating, "Ladies, your plans won't work. You know that our test scores in third grade have dropped significantly, and we need everyone in kindergarten, first, and second grades to strictly stress preparing our students for the state accountability exam. We don't have time nor do I have the patience for the coloring of pilgrims and Indians." Erika, never one to keep her mouth shut when she should, said aloud, "I think they're called Native Americans." Dr. Mogford responded, "Don't patronize me, young lady!" Erika blushed and said no more.

Lisa decided to take a chance and spoke up noting that the designed lessons followed the kindergarten curriculum guide. Abbi added, "Our lesson plans certainly correlate with the district's essential knowledge and skills." The principal responded, "I'm talking about getting our students ready for the state exam, and I need your students focused on that—understood?" Rather than argue any further, Lisa, Abbi, and Brenda looked at one another and realized the whole issue was a moot point. The kindergarten team agreed to change the lesson plans and learning activities. Dr. Mogford concluded the meeting with a smile and said, "Good, let's get back to work!"

That evening, Lisa, Abbi, and Brenda——along with the other two kindergarten teachers—worked until ten o'clock changing the Thanksgiving-week lesson plans. The teachers focused on developing assessment activities for their students that modeled the format of the State Assessment of Knowledge and Skills (SAKS) exam. Later that evening, as they were preparing to leave the school, Lisa looked at Abbi and Brenda and just shrugged her shoulders. Abbi shook her head and exclaimed, "What kind of expectation does our principal have?" Brenda sighed and said, "Come on now, who's the turkey this Thanksgiving?"

Application Questions

1. Which of the seven principal expectations in the curriculum leadership role did Dr. Ainslee Mogford, principal at Red Greene Elementary School, fail to incorporate while interacting with the kindergarten team? Explain your answer by providing concrete examples as to how the principal could rectify the situation.

2. Quality analysis has been defined by the authors of the text as being "a method of determining problematic causal factors as a means of scrutinizing a curricular issue or problem" (p. 67). What do you perceive to be the curricular issue or problem at Red Greene Elementary School? What's a principal to do? Be specific.

3. Which aspects of the four-quadrant quality analysis model described in the chapter could best be utilized to better scrutinize the curricular problem(s) faced by Principal Mogford? Support your answer.

4. What specific format, as identified in Principal Expectation 6: Instructional Enhancements, could Dr. Mogford incorporate as curriculum leader to improve the Who's the Turkey This Thanksgiving? curricular/instructional situation? Provide a detailed explanation.

5. Joe L. Cope, contributing author to the Sorenson and Goldsmith text *The Principal's Guide to Managing School Personnel* (2009), writes of The Principal's Peace Primer to include (1) preserve purpose, (2) protect process, (3) practice patience, (4) promote people, (5) prize perceptions, (6) praise progress, (7) produce a plan, and (8) perfect peace. Consider the potential for conflict polarization at Red Greene Elementary School and determine which of the eight platforms from the Principal's Peace Primer could be used by Dr. Mogford to remedy the curricular/instructional problem exposed in the case study? Be specific in your answer.

6. Which of Johnson and Johnson's (1999) "Three Cs of School Management" did the principal at Red Greene Elementary School fail to embrace as curriculum leader relative to the situation presented in the case study? Explain.

Other Resources

Brubaker, D. L. (2004). *Revitalizing curriculum leadership: Inspiring and empowering your school community*. Thousand Oaks, CA: Corwin.

Holcomb, E. L. (2008). *Asking the right questions: Tools for collaboration and school change*. Thousand Oaks, CA: Corwin.

Schmoker, M. (1999). *Results: Key to continuous school improvement* (2nd ed.). Alexandria, VA: Association for Supervision and Curriculum Development (ASCD).

4

The Principal's Role in Curriculum Change and Innovation

One change leaves the way open for the introduction of others!

—Niccolò Machiavelli

Constructive Change = Positive Growth

The Apostle Paul wrote, in the year AD 57, "Be transformed by the renewing of your mind" (Romans 12:2, *New International Bible*). Consider the terms change, transformation, alteration, renewal, revitalization, innovation, growth, development, and achievement. Do these terms and their order of listing lead one to think or believe that each term actually builds upon the other? Can a simple term like "change" equate to personal as well as professional and organizational growth, development, and achievement? Or is the term "change" more complicated in meaning? Is change actually equivalent to the precept that people perceive change as either a positive or a negative depending on the actual outcome of the change, along with the degree of change-oriented influence initiated by the leader?

Should a principal's role in curricular change be summed up with a second series of questions: Is it better for me *not* to be an instrument of change, *not* to make a decision relative to change, *not* to take a stand for innovation? Is it better for me, my students, and my school to do *none* of the above?

We all know the correct answer to each of those questions! We recognize that the answer is so simple, so straightforward, yet so very complex. We *must* be the instrument of change at school. We *must* initiate innovative curricular approaches to improve the instructional program. It is our mission. It is our calling. It is what we are *required* to do if we desire to be successful as curriculum leaders and effective school principals.

However, in the back of our minds we are thinking, "It isn't easy!" That's true, but we do understand that leading is never easy—it's hard work! Mindful of our limitations, we *must* take comfort in the fact that although change is difficult, it is a constant in life. Therefore, it is a principal's responsibility to effectively lead the change process if the expectation is an enhanced curriculum, continued organizational improvement, and increased student achievement.

Machiavelli was right, as was the Apostle Paul. Change necessitates more change, and with more change, comes a renewal of the mind. In the case of the school principal, a renewal of the mind creates the potential for the revitalization of the leadership role, which equates to the leadership charge of ensuring an innovative campus curriculum. How, might you ask?

The Basis for Change and Why It Is So Necessary

Lazear (1992) suggests that leaders can change *today* what needs to be changed. Concomitantly, Marshall McLuhan (McLuhan & Fiore, 2005), Canadian educator, philosopher, and scholar, recognized that it is human nature to avoid change. Consider the adage: Most people hate any change that doesn't jingle in their pocket! Probably true. In fact, Lunenburg and Ornstein (2008) suggest that the greatest barrier to change, from a curricular perspective, is apathy among leaders. Why change when it is easier to maintain the status quo? Many principals are more than delighted to keep things as they have always been. This attitude breeds contentment, which, in turn, fosters a certain sentiment that becomes institutionalized: Change is unwise, it is unproductive, and it is nothing more than an unwarranted attempt to jump on a new curricular or instructional bandwagon. Change has occurred far too many times in the past, so why change when the effect will result in the same dismal outcome? This line of reasoning relates to a somewhat dated study, yet regrettably, applicable in far too many instances today. Bacharach (1981) found that only 17% of a principal's time is allocated to what is most important in our schools—curriculum, instruction, and student achievement. Sadly, little has changed in 30 years as documented in a study conducted by Grigsby, Schumacher, Decman, and Simieou (2010), although elementary school principals appear to be more attuned to the curricular and instructional leadership role. Secondary school principals have yet to fully transition into the role of curriculum and instructional leaders.

Marshall McLuhan (McLuhan & Fiore, 2005) understood and emphasized that leaders who move from a zone of comfort into the role of change initiator create for an organization a pathway to greater individual satisfaction and collective success. Such an acknowledgment should inspire school principals, as curriculum leaders, to become courageous in changing what really needs to be changed. In reality, change is vital because most people are satisfied with the status quo—the same old way of doing something, usually the same something that has been less than beneficial for everyone in the organization. Without change, the following happens:

1. Faculty and staff move in the same curricular and instructional direction, continuing to impede student learning.

2. Status quo permeates a school and allows teachers to think only of their self-interests.

3. People value their needs at the expense of the vision, mission, and goals of the school.

4. Teamwork, organizational collaboration, and genuine cooperation will be nothing more than lip service.

5. Directive, authoritative, and/or dictatorial decision making becomes a constant, and collaborative leadership will not be achieved.

6. Effective curriculum leadership along with intrinsic organizational motivation toward school improvement and increased student achievement will never occur.

7. The creation and maintenance of an effective and productive workplace—where challenging efforts and opportunities for professional growth and development and a student-centered learning environment are valued—will never be the norm.

Change requires great effort. Change will always be met with resistance. The greatest challenge for a principal is to help personnel overcome change barriers by anticipating and understanding the reasons for resistance.

Why We Resist Change

The only constant in life is change. Change is inevitable. Yet we remain so resistant to the unavoidable. W. Edwards Deming once stated, "It is not necessary to change. Survival is not mandatory" (The Quote Garden, 2010). What a declaration! To understand why we resist change and to recognize the need to survive organizationally, the curriculum leader must first recognize the reasons.

   1. *We are creatures of habit.* We are comfortable doing what we've always done in the same old way we've always done it! Think about incorporating technology into curriculum. Curriculum development and the delivery of instructional techniques and strategies over the last few years have changed dramatically, for the better in most instances. When the authors first began teaching in the 1970s, the methods of instruction were via the "sage on stage" and the chalkboard. Then, we learned to utilize the overhead transparency projector. What a technological leap forward! Next, we adapted the desktop computer into our curriculum utilizing PowerPoint software as a method of instructional delivery. Then, we were able to gain the use of the laptop and further change the curriculum through instructional delivery with Internet connectivity. Now, we interact with students through online and distant learning, both of which incorporate the use of hand-held PDAs, which are servers for a multitude of electronic transmissions, expanding curricular opportunities that further serve to enhance instructional methods, teaching techniques, and student achievement. These changes have occurred within the last 20 years. In fact, the rapidity of change correlates, if not accelerates, with the pace of technology. It is amazing how these technological advancements have impacted and changed curricular leadership, the curriculum of schools, the instructional program, and student learning and achievement (see Chapter 10). In some schools, these technological changes have only occurred in the last 10 or less years. In some schools, certain technological changes have yet to occur. Why? Easy answer—lack of funding. Correct answer—resistance to change!

   2. *We fear the unknown.* Faculty and staff members often resist change because they do not understand the new in their lives. Change can create uncertainties. The curriculum leader who initiates change must provide training and, with training, care and concern—a little handholding—for those who fear the unknown.

3. *We have a high need for security.* Everyone has insecurities. Some more than others and for differing reasons. However, the curriculum leader must assure all members of the learning community that change relative to the curriculum or the instructional program does not threaten their livelihood. Change must be intended for personal as well as professional benefit. It cannot be used as a tool for the loss of position, power, or prestige. Change cannot limit participative decision making or collaborative problem solving. Change must be seen as a better method of accessing information, improving productivity, enhancing learning, and increasing achievement. Change must be revealed by the curriculum leader to be a win-win proposition. Insecurity threatens expertise.

4. *We are threatened in areas of expertise.* Faculty and staff often resist change because they *do* recognize current problems in the curriculum and instructional program. Change often threatens to expose instructional weaknesses, curricular shortcomings, or, in some cases, general ineptitude. Consider the following curricular circumstance.

TECHNOLOGICAL CHANGE COMES TO CHILDERS SCHOOL
Arlene, What's the Real Problem? Can Will Wonkermann Help?

Arlene Zarsky had been a longtime teacher at Childers School. The school, under the direction of Principal Will Wonkermann had implemented a new curriculum program that revolved around technological expertise. The newly designed curriculum guides were online and were downloaded into instructional formats for use in daily lesson planning. All curricular objectives were accessed via the electronic system. Grades were to be electronically generated and inputted into the system. Student assessments, quarterly progress reports, and all grade reporting were to be done electronically. Regular reports to parents were sent via e-mail. PDAs had been issued to all faculty and staff for curricular, instructional, and professional use. The incorporation of iPods, iPhones, iPads, interactive smart boards, USB tablets, Prometheanworld ActivSlate touchboards, LCD projectors, digital cameras, as well as the instructional use of Tokbox, CloudLinux, Facebook, Twitter, MySpace, and eduphoria!SchoolObjects:forethough into all content areas were just a few of the numerous technological advances and changes at Childers School.

Arlene often sat silently in faculty meetings with her arms crossed while the differing and innovative technological changes were being teacher generated and approved. Arlene was in panic mode as Principal Will Wonkermann and the curriculum team initiated the new changes. With her less-than-enthusiastic demeanor being noticed by others, Arlene was regularly asked if she was ready to implement the changes. She eagerly replied, "You bet!" However, Arlene was passive-aggressive in her real attitude and behavior. In actuality, Arlene was genuinely threatened in her area of expertise.

One day after school, Arlene was asked by her principal, Will Wonkermann, if he could be of any assistance to Arlene when it came to the technological changes being advocated. Arlene lowered her head and sheepishly admitted that she couldn't adjust to nor could she implement the new changes. Arlene told Mr. Wonkermann that she needed two more years before she could retire and she didn't know what to do. "I can't quit my teaching job. I'm too close to retirement," confided Arlene. "I'm an excellent teacher. Can't I do things the way I've always done them?" asked Arlene.

Principal Wonkermann knew it was important to be empathetic with Arlene, but it was essential that he maintain a high level of expectation when it came to the proposed changes. He matter-of-factly asked, "Arlene, what's the real problem? Why are you bothered by these changes? We have on-campus experts who can assist you with the technological changes." Arlene looked her principal straight in the eye and then admitted, "I never learned to type! I've never used a typewriter, let alone a computer. I'm a techno-dummy. My daughter-in-law designs all of my teacher-generated lessons on her computer. My colleagues at the grade-level help me with all of my grade reporting and e-mails. I'm too old for technological advances. It scares me to death! It's a phobia and it's about to drive me crazy!"

Then, Arlene explained, "When I was in ninth-grade and took typing class, my fingers were never nimble enough for my teacher, Mr. Townsend. He was forever on my case, constantly belittling me about my lack of typing skills. He regularly whacked my hands with a ruler when I made keyboarding mistakes! He also humiliated me in front of my peers by making snide remarks about my performance. Mr. Wonkermann, I'm afraid of all of these changes. I'm afraid I will fail!"

Pause and Consider

- Why did Arlene Zarsky feel threatened by the proposed curriculum and instructional changes at Childers School?

- What can Principal Will Wonkermann do to assist Arlene, beyond asking, "What's the real problem?"

- Reflect on each of the seven reasons why change is necessary. Which of the reasons, beyond Number 4, might apply to Arlene and Will Wonkermann at Childers School?

The previous scenario is not farfetched. In fact, from a technology into the curriculum into the classroom perspective, we still have teachers in the workforce who do not know how to utilize e-mail, let alone electronic links, related educational software, and essential hardware (Anderson & Dexter, 2005; Brooks-Young, 2006; Wenglinsky, 2005). So what does it all mean? Recall the Bob Dylan song, "The Times They Are A-Changin'" (Dylan, 1964). Changing times, in this context, means we are living in exponential times. Consider the works of Fisch, McLeod, & Bronman (2009), *Did you know?*

- The top 10 in-demand jobs currently available in the United States did not exist five years ago.
- We are currently preparing our students for jobs that do not exist, using technologies that have yet to be invented.
- The United States Department of Labor estimates that today's learners will have 10 to 14 jobs by the time they reach the age of 38.
- There are over 200 million registered users on MySpace.
- There are 31 billion searches on Google every month.
- Today, the number of text messages sent and received each day exceeds the total population of the planet.
- The number of Internet devices today exceeds 1,000,000,000.
- The amount of new technological information is doubling every two years. For students beginning high school, this means that half of what they learn in their freshman year of study will be outdated by their junior year of study.
- During the time you read these nine bulleted statements, 694,000 songs were downloaded by your students—illegally.

An article in *The Washington Post* (St. George, 2009) further provides us with an idea as to how technology has impacted and changed communication and learning relative to the students we serve. A 15-year-old Rockville, Maryland girl sent and received 6,473 cell phone text messages in a single month. The teen revealed the following about her constant communication with others and indirectly suggested how technological advances must be addressed in the curriculum and the classroom: "I would die without it" (para. 2), she says of her text life. She is not alone. Researchers stipulate that teens in the United States with cell phones average more than 2,200 text messages a month. Educators must grapple with this and similar technological concerns as text messaging as a form of communication and learning has exploded across the formative years of our next generation of learners (St. George).

Now, consider the following questions: (1) Are you changing the way you develop and implement curriculum? (2) Are you changing the way you teach to meet the technological needs of today's learners who will be our future workers and citizens? (3) Are you leading students today to meet the challenges of tomorrow? (4) Are you threatened in the area of technological expertise?

1. *We dread potential challenges.* We have already recognized that leading is hard work. So is teaching, learning, adapting, and changing. With any change, large or small, comes the necessity for additional work, extended hours, extra duties, essential learning opportunities, and more responsibilities. Teachers often think of change as another obligation to be placed on top of an already full agenda. Packed agendas, additional tasks, and more accountability equate to a dreaded workplace where group resistance can quickly escalate. When a principal initiates change, even in collaboration with the curriculum team, and the remainder of the learning community is not ready for the awaiting challenges associated with the change, such is a sign that proper planning and preparation has not occurred. Was it not Jorge Descamps (2009), recognized scholar, who said, "The prepared mind favors change"? Remember, when we fail to prepare, we prepare to fail!

2. *We don't trust or respect the leader.* Principals must earn the trust and respect of the members of the learning community if change is to be accepted. Group resistance will intensify manyfold if the curriculum leader is not trusted or respected by faculty and staff. Sorenson and Goldsmith (2009) remind leaders that "trust and respect enable personnel to adopt innovation and risk-taking as part of the school's culture" (p. 35). When school personnel feel secure in examining new ideas to improve student learning, they are much more receptive to change. Trustworthy principals create conditions that enable personnel to take a chance on change. Trustworthy principals exude confidence, ability, knowledge, and expertise. Trustworthy principals are committed to the well-being of individual faculty who may be dreading the challenge of another potential change. Robbins (2006) suggests a lower level of trust often results in a higher level of illegitimate political behaviors, which frequently lead to conflict (i.e., group resistance, if not out-and-out sabotage).

3. *We sense our power status is threatened.* In all areas of our lives certain levels of status exist, especially in our relationships with others. This is most notable from a power perspective. No person is ready to incorporate a change if it is perceived to threaten an individual's

power or status within the organization. We treasure our levels of authority and control, no matter how insignificant. Consider the situation at Childers School.

MY WAY OR THE HIGHWAY

L. Hermann Seeger, chairperson of the English department, had served in his departmental leadership role for 27 years. Recently, Will Wonkermann, the new principal at Childers School, had incorporated several curriculum changes—one of which directly affected the power status of L. Hermann Seeger. Professor Seeger, as he expected students and faculty alike to call him, took great pride in being the senior member of the English department. He wielded tremendous power over curricular and other departmental decisions. In fact, no decision was made in the English department without Professor Seeger's approval. Hermann was the department power broker, and everyone knew their role and place, including previous principals at Childers School.

Recent changes instituted by Principal Wonkermann related specifically to participative decision making. These changes involved all stakeholders and impacted curriculum design and instructional delivery. Hermann was of the old-school and believed in the philosophy of "my way or the highway." He also taught strictly by lecture since he believed he knew the most about Shakespearian literature. He liked to share what he believed to be an iconic truism: "When L. Hermann Seeger speaks, everyone listens!" Students were expected to sit attentively in class and listen as Professor Seeger spoke of sonnets, alliterations, and often in an unfamiliar English of centuries past. There would, in fact, be no cooperative learning, no differentiated instruction, or any other "new and improved" curricular approach or instructional method incorporated into *his* department. His way worked best, just ask Professor L. Hermann Seeger!

However, Will Wonkermann, as new principal, had different ideas and presented changes for the better (at least the other members of the English department thought so). Will was creating quite a following of faculty, staff, and students—all of whom supported the new curricular approaches and the participative decision-making model. Mr. Seeger strongly disagreed with such changes, and since he was not one to sit idly by while his power status was threatened, he became most vocal in his antagonism toward the notion of change at Childers School.

Pause and Consider

- By what means did L. Hermann Seeger sense that the new principal at Childers School was a threat to his power status? Why?

- What must Will Wonkermann, as a new principal, do to assuage "Professor" Seeger's concerns relative to the change process at Childers School?

- Do any of the other seven reasons for resisting change apply to this particular scenario? How and by what means?

How to Overcome Resistance to Change

Overcoming resistance to change is not an easy chore. Research over the decades has suggested that resistance to change can be alleviated through communication, participation, facilitation, support, negotiation, professional development, empowerment, motivation, and the elimination of nonnegotiable aspects of curriculum and instruction (Chin & Benne, 1969; Fullan, 2002; Heller, 1998; Lunenburg & Irby, 2006; Lunenburg & Ornstein, 2008; Sarason, 1994). From a negative or detrimental perspective, resistance to change can be overcome by a leader who utilizes coercion and manipulation (Carrell, Kuzmits, & Elbert, 1997), neither of which the authors would recommend.

Effective curriculum leaders manage to overcome faculty resistance to change by (1) respecting people, (2) establishing high levels of trust in a supportive climate, (3) enacting power equalization (participative leadership), (4) confronting the status quo (typically a causal factor in change resistance), and (5) creating an environment of team ownership (i.e., buy-in).

Robbins and Hunsaker (2005), Robbins and Judge (2008), and Sorenson, Cortez, and Negrete (2010) assert that resistance to change can be overcome by a leader who incorporates influential methods. These methods include the following:

1. *The establishment of integrity.* School personnel and other members of the learning community will never listen to nor respond to a curriculum leader who they believe is dishonest, incompetent, nonobjective, unethical, or immoral.

2. *The use of positive approaches.* When initiating change, curriculum leaders must incorporate positive approaches by working with the curriculum team and other members of the learning community. Such approaches include being respectful, genuine, caring, and recognizing of the accomplishments of individuals and groups. Other

positive approaches to change initiation include being sincere, direct, and tactful in all forms of communication.

3. *The articulation of a clear vision and mission.* Faculty and staff will never be convinced of the need for change unless the principal can effectively establish a vision as to how the curricular program needs to be improved. To do so, the curriculum leader must carefully articulate the need for change through the medium of a clear and precise message, which must be in concert with the mission of the school.

4. *The use of data-based decision making.* Logical and reasoned arguments for change can be readily presented to members of the learning community when a principal incorporates data into decision-making processes. However, any decision for change will have limited impact unless the need for change is supported with research and data from which a factual assessment can be ascertained relative to how the curriculum must be transformed.

Alex Cornell, as cited in Hughes, Ginnett, and Curphy (2009) suggested that our world today is a chaotic place—however, such a muddled world must be confronted methodically. Data-based analysis and decision making is the basis for a systematic critique within any organization. This is especially true when change must be of the highest quality. High-quality change, based on data analysis, will have a direct and measurable impact on curricular decisions. Curriculum leaders must determine if there is a quality (data-driven) component to any change decision and subsequent modifying initiative. To do so, simply ask, does this change and initiative seek to improve services to our students? If the answer is yes, it is imperative that the principal collect the necessary data, with appropriate analysis, to ensure that the highest quality decisions are made in the best interest of students (Sorenson, 2005).

5. *The use of persuasion.* Effective principals, who initiate curricular change, articulate a clear vision and mission. They also persuade others with the presentation of rational and objective evidence (research- and data-based information) that supports the planned curriculum change. Principals who are exceptional persuaders possess a leadership skill that builds trust among followers (Sorenson, 2004). Susan Gerhards (2008), former educator and conservative commentator, has remarked, "How a faculty perceives change, whether positively or negatively, seldom depends on the outcome of

the change itself, but rather on the degree of influence and the use of persuasive skills by the principal."

The Change Process in Curriculum Development

Effective principals recognize faculty and staff will publicly state the need for change, but in their hearts, they remain reticent. We understand the reasons for restraint. As a matter of fact, we have learned how to overcome resistance to change. By what means does the curriculum leader successfully initiate the change process in curriculum development?

For starters, begin slowly but purposefully! Research has consistently revealed that effective curricular change begins with the principal who listens carefully to the team and moves cautiously yet deliberately when it comes to the curriculum change process. This pace requires frequent face-to-face meetings and person-to-person interactions to ensure that teacher buy-in is actually occurring (Glatthorn & Jailall, 2009; Méndez & Sorenson, in press; Tomlinson & McTighe, 2006; Wiles, 2009).

Next, effective curriculum leaders utilize the group process. Lunenburg and Ornstein (2008) relate that curricular change must be a group effort. We absolutely agree! Question—What permits the group process to readily influence curricular change? Cannon and Griffith (2007) assert effective groups develop shared goals and vision, structure strategies for change through interactive communication, establish collaborative leadership, exercise power and influence relative to organizational change, manage conflict, and initiate professional development to ensure that any change is understood and implemented. Effective leaders need effective groups to initiate curricular change. Therefore, curriculum development teams must assume numerous roles and responsibilities in the curricular change process. These roles and responsibilities include the following:

- Understanding the research that supports the practice
- Recognizing the need for change in curriculum development and design
- Noting that the instructional program must be improved to ensure increased student learning and achievement
- Balancing the needs of the students with the goals of state and federal mandates

- Being open to research-based, student-centered, and best-practice curricular and instructional approaches
- Acknowledging the need for parental, community, and professional clientele in the curriculum development and planning processes
- Encouraging faculty and staff members to be receptive to the essential improvements to curriculum and instruction
- Appreciating the fact that the integration of curriculum and instruction includes what Tomlinson and McTighe (2006) call an essential four-way partnership between: (1) differentiated instruction, (2) diversified learning, (3) cultural inclusionary activities, and (4) understanding by design

Additionally, curriculum development teams and the curriculum leader must concede that time is of the essence.

Subsequently, any change in the curriculum development process must include leadership that is driven by a knowledge and understanding of curricular matters. Principals can no longer accept the notion that someone else is responsible for curriculum development. Principals *must* be experts in curriculum development. Regrettably, the role of curriculum expert is what intimidates many school leaders and relates to the Glatthorn quote previously incorporated in Chapter 3: "When I told a friend that the title of one of my books was *Principal as Curriculum Leader* [Glatthorn & Jailall, 2009], she responded, 'That's an oxymoron if I ever heard one'" (Glatthorn quoted in Cunningham & Corderio, 2006, p. 228).

In recent years, curriculum leadership in relation to the principal role has been sidestepped and delegated to others in what has been described by McNeil (2000) as a contradiction of school reform. McNeil argues that when a high-standards curriculum is linked to a coercive accountability system, the result is standardization, reduction of curriculum to that which is tested, a decline of innovation, a centralization of control in state and federal policymakers, and an abdication of the curriculum leadership role by school principals. Now, more than ever, principals and curriculum teams must retake the curricular initiative. Principals must be curriculum experts. The question remains: What is curriculum expertise relative to the principal role?

Curriculum expertise for the principal begins with an understanding of two terms: *curriculum* and *instruction*. Curriculum is frequently defined as *what* is taught in the school. Instruction is the *how*—the methods, techniques, and strategies that assist students in the learning process. We will further examine the meanings of curriculum and instruction in Chapter 7. However, in effective schools and classrooms the two terms merge into what Marsh and Willis (2007) call an interrelated set of plans, experiences, and activities (both planned and unplanned) that a student undertakes with guidance from curriculum experts and other educators in the field of practice.

Curriculum expertise for the principal effectively correlates with the theoretical works of Bruner (1960) whose idea of a spiraling effect serves as a foundational model, which stipulates that previous learning is the basis for subsequent learning. In other words, learning must be continuous, and the subject matter content must be built on an escalating ladder that extends from grade level to grade level. Bruner, as a curriculum theorist and expert, believed that curriculum leaders must possess the knowledge and concepts of subject areas, understanding how learning relates to the structure of a particular subject area. That said, a principal must acknowledge that subject areas be interconnected. A principal does not have to know everything about every subject taught in a school. However, a principal must know that subjects must be connected by an interwoven thread that ties all the subjects together in the learning process. This thread is the curriculum, and it has a profound impact on the instructional program.

What makes a principal a curriculum expert? To begin with, principals must understand the enduring value of Taba's (1962) work that reveals a correlating connection between curriculum research and instructional practice:

1. **Knowledge complexity:** Curriculum must embed basic principles within course content to include abstract ideas, complex systems, causal relationships, and methods of inquiry, discovery, and problem solving.

2. **Essential acquisition:** Curriculum must be regularly evaluated and revised to include new content to be learned and mastered.

3. **Scope and sequence:** Curriculum must be extensive in its concentration and coverage across a range of content areas. Curriculum must differentiate levels of knowledge and learning. Curriculum must be cumulative and continuous.

4. **Integrative approaches:** Curriculum must be integrated, emphasizing a variety of content themes, lesson topics, and instructional units. Integrative approaches in curriculum development ensure that one content area relates to another.

5. **Valid considerations:** Curriculum must be relevant and practical to the learner. Instructional content must be sound and relate to the mission, goals, objectives, and strategies of a school's improvement or action plan.

6. **Interest and significance:** Curriculum must be meaningful, consequential, and of significance to the learner. Why must I learn algebra? How will I ever use English literature in my profession? What role will world history play in my work as a landscape architect? Questions of interest and significance, such as these posed, as well as a host of others, must be addressed and assessed when developing curriculum.

7. **Useful endeavors:** Curriculum must be applicable beyond the school walls. Principals, as curriculum experts, must be able to ask the following questions of faculty when developing curriculum: (1) What will our students learn that can provide them opportunities to place curricular initiatives and instruction into real-world practice? (2) Will our students gain intrinsic satisfaction from their learning experiences? (3) How will the learning our students acquire help them attain their personal and professional goals? (4) Which of the learning experiences our students acquire are repetitive in coursework and is the repetition necessary? (5) Will our students gain knowledge in one subject area that will be beneficial in another subject area?

Next, principals, as curriculum experts, must recognize that certain philosophical, social, and/or moral implications be addressed when developing and/or changing curriculum. Glanz (2006) reveals that the key to curriculum leadership and change is the school principal, not the superintendent, not the director of curriculum, not the chief financial officer, and not any other district-level personnel. Principals face, on a daily basis, a litany of curricular issues, which must be addressed, evaluated, and often changed. The one individual who must serve as the leader of curriculum in a school is the principal.

Finally, let's examine a listing of curricular issues, as identified by Lunenburg and Ornstein (2008), Marsh and Willis (2007), and Tanner and Tanner (2006), that must be confronted by the curriculum leader.

- Student-centered curriculum versus subject content- and/or teacher-centered curriculum

- Generalized versus specialized curriculum and/or instructional content
- Homogeneous versus heterogeneous grouping
- Tracking versus individualized needs—gifted and talented, regular, at-risk, and disabled learners
- Academic tracking versus vocational tracking
- Essential knowledge skills versus abstract skills
- Excellence in learning and teaching versus equality versus equity
- Needs of society versus needs of learner
- Didactic knowledge versus moral character
- Cognitive versus affective learning
- Traditional versus progressive instructional methods

Compare this listing to the societal changes identified in Chapter 2, the section titled: ISLLC Performance Expectation 1: Vision, Mission, and Goals. How are the lists similar? In what ways are the lists different? What do the lists reveal about change in our schools, change in society, change in curriculum and curriculum leadership?

Curriculum change begins with principal expertise in the curriculum development process. Principals must understand that their expertise in curriculum and curriculum development is the first step to initiating change, managing change, and overcoming learning community resistance to change.

Final Thoughts

Curricular change begins with the curriculum leader—the school principal. Curricular change is the basis for instructional growth, teacher development, and student achievement. Curricular change is an absolute, a constant, and a necessity. Without change, we become stagnant, stuck in a rut, doing the same old thing——the same old way. It is essential that curriculum leaders recognize that change brings out the worst and the very best in people. The worst because we are creatures of habit and fear the unknown—especially when the unknown relates to potential change. The best because change equates to higher levels of trust, more supportive and open cultures, power equalization, and team ownership.

Curricular changes occur when schools are led by principals who articulate a clear vision, examine the research literature relative to curriculum issues, analyze the data, solve problems, stay abreast of technological advances and changes, and make decisions through group processes. Curricular enhancement, school improvement, and student achievement result when the school principal recognizes the causes for change, analyzes the need for change, identifies the demand for change, evaluates the complexity of change, anticipates the resistance to change, cautiously and deliberately implements change, and understands the ramifications of initiating and, just as important, failing to initiate change.

What are the ramifications for a principal who fails to lead, who neglects to bring about essential, if not critical, curricular and instructional change? The ramifications are staggering, as exemplified in the following account reported in *Our Daily Bread* (Williams, 2007):

> A 12-year-old boy on a school field trip to a museum stuck a wad of chewing gum on a painting worth $1.5 million. The gum left a stain about the size of a quarter on Helen Frankenthaler's landmark abstract, *The Bay*. Officials at the Detroit Institute of Arts were unsure whether they could remove the gum. The boy was suspended from school. "I don't think he understood the ramifications of what he did," said a school official.

Unlike the 12-year-old boy, principals must understand the ramifications of their actions and their inactions, relative to their role and responsibility as a change agent when it comes to curriculum leadership. Principals can ill afford to "gum-up" curriculum leadership, as the resulting "stain" will be long lasting.

As a concluding consideration, contemplate the message of leadership change found within the lyrics of "I'm Just an Old Chunk of Coal But I'm Gonna Be a Diamond Some Day," a Billy Joe Shaver song popularized in recordings, concerts, and crusades by the late Johnny Cash (Cachet Records, 1979). The message, in both title and song, is simple yet revealing: Successful change will not occur until "someone" changes. That someone is us!

To move an individual or organization from "an old chunk of coal" to "a diamond someday," the principal, as curriculum leader and agent of change, must build a vision; create a positive teaching and learning climate; mobilize personnel by engaging support from all members in the learning community; provide essential professional development; ensure fiscal, human, and material resources are available; and then remove any causal factor barriers that may exist and inhibit curricular change, instructional innovation, technological advances, or programmatic renewal. Students are depending on leadership for a change—change that is for the better. Remember, constructive change = positive growth!

> *After you've done a thing the same way for two years, look it over*
>   *carefully.*
> *After five years, look at it with suspicion.*
> *After ten years, throw it away and start all over!*

> —Alfred Edward Perlman (Random Quotes, 2010)

Discussion Questions

1. Leadership is about positive change. Marzano, Waters, and McNulty (2005) suggest that a responsibility of any leader is to believe in or relate to any change initiative or innovation required. Otherwise, such a change will fail, no matter its merits, or the change will be a victim of faculty sabotage. This statement relates to the fact that the curriculum leader must be an agent of change. Are you ready to lead change? Can you tolerate change? Take an opportunity to self-administer the Managing Change Tolerance Test found at the conclusion of this chapter. Determine if you are change oriented or simply one of those individuals who loathe change, unless of course, it jingles in your pocket. Discuss in groups how you, the curriculum leader, plan to manage and/ or tolerate change.

2. Consider each of the seven reasons why we resist change as detailed in the chapter. Which of the seven relates to you personally? Which of the seven relates to your school? What can you, as an individual, do to help yourself and your school overcome resistance to change?

3. Reflect on the five methods for overcoming resistance to change that are identified in the chapter. When curricular innovation has failed at your school, which of the five methods were not incorporated or utilized by the curriculum leader? How would you, as a practicing or prospective curriculum/principal leader, help overcome resistance to change at the campus level? Be specific in your response.

4. Identify definite areas of curricular expertise that you, from a professional growth and development perspective, need to precisely

(Continued)

(*Continued*)

focus on for improvement purposes. Examine the seven connections between curriculum theory and instructional practice, as identified by Hilda Taba (1962) in the chapter, as the basis for initial consideration. Next, discuss in group format how you might work to improve your curricular weaknesses, turning them into areas of expertise. Then, further consider how to improve in your role as curriculum leader, specifically as you continue to read and analyze the text.

5. How would you, as a new or future leader of curriculum improvement, help members of the learning community overcome the greatest barrier to change—apathy? What would you do *first* to help a team in overcoming apathy, thus bringing about curricular change at your school?

6. Sam Wineburg (2006), in his article "A Sobering Big Idea," surmises a school's curriculum will positively change when principal and faculty bravely initiate the process of change. Do you concur? If yes, explain how and by what means. If no, what is holding principals and teachers back from making necessary curricular change? Explain.

CASE STUDY APPLICATION
It's a Real Puzzle to Me!

Reven High School, a campus located in a large urban center, employing slightly over 200 faculty and staff, was encountering faculty and staff turnover and absenteeism problems. The school, located in the southwest, produced average to below-average test scores on the state accountability exam.

Two years ago, the school district initiated curriculum and instructional changes in an effort to improve student test scores. The changes were mandated by the new superintendent of schools and were further imposed by Tom Cartusi, the curriculum director for secondary schools, and Ellen Fong, the Title I district facilitator. Both Tom and Ellen came to Reven High School with the district dictates and chartered new territory in an attempt to change the curriculum and, thus, improve the instructional program. Both were met with strong resistance by the high school's faculty and staff. Nevertheless, Tom and Ellen moved forward. Change had arrived!

Adriana Sanchez, principal at Reven High School, was very concerned about the impact of the curriculum changes brought by Tom and Ellen. Although the changes had been made, subsequent and unforeseen problems materialized: Faculty absenteeism and high turn-over rates were greatly affecting campus morale. Additionally, student test scores continued to decline. Now, halfway into the third year, following the mandated curriculum changes, Principal Sanchez asked Tom Cartusi and Ellen Fong to meet with her to discuss the situation.

Principal Sanchez: At first I thought the high levels of absenteeism and faculty turnover were only temporary—just some faculty and staff having trouble adjusting to the new curricular changes. But my word, after two years and now going on three, we've got to figure this one out! Come on, what's the real problem here?

Tom Cartusi: Well, your staff is knowledgeable and dedicated, no doubt. They live in the area, so commuting a long distance across the city doesn't seem to be the problem. They seem loyal to you, Adriana. I'm not certain what the problem could be, unless it's related to all the curriculum changes. But that can't be. As you know, these are excellent changes—research based and all.

Ellen Fong: I really don't get it. It's a real puzzle to me. Like Tom noted, your staff is really good. It's not as if they don't want to teach or that they don't like the kids or they have trouble with you, the principal. They come to work, but after a while they start taking days off. Then, low and behold, when spring arrives, they either request a transfer to another campus or simply quit. This just beats the heck out of me!

Principal Sanchez: Well, we've had a 45% turnover rate each of the last two years and the superintendent is on my case. He wants the bleeding stopped, and stopped now! Tom, do you have any suggestions?

Tom Cartusi: None that I can think of. It's January, and if the trend continues Adriana, I suspect you can expect another rash of transfer requests or resignations.

Principal Sanchez: Tom, don't tell me something I already know! Come on now, I need some advice! Ellen, what are your thoughts?

(Continued)

(Continued)

Ellen Fong: Well, I hate to admit it, but the faculty and staff keep telling me that we're the problem.

Tom Cartusi: Ellen, give me a break! We've been over this before. You and I have worked all over this district and never had this type of problem. Don't lay this predicament at our doorstep. Adriana, you wanted our help and you got it. We've done our job. It seems to me that this is your problem now. We made the changes, now you have to implement them. Maybe your staff needs a little motivation. Maybe you're not the right person for the principalship here at Reven High School.

Principal Sanchez: Tom, this problem is bigger than any one of us. Now, don't get me wrong, I'll take full responsibility because I am the principal, but this is a deeper issue than we think. I believe we are only scratching at the surface of the problem.

Tom Cartusi: Well, the two of you can work it out because this is my last day here at Reven High. I'm off to Elgin Middle School for another round of curricular change. I'm certain things will eventually work out for the best. They always do, right? Good luck!

Application Questions

1. Gordon (2004) suggests that school culture is an obstacle to curriculum change. Gordon further asserts that in many schools the primary purpose of culture is to resist change. Consider this perspective and then articulate in writing how these assertions are correct or incorrect. Relate your answer to The Basis for Change and Why It Is Necessary and the Why We Resist Change sections in this chapter.

2. Reeves (2006) challenges a series of educational myths, one of which suggests that people are content with the status quo. Many principals and teachers in low-performing schools are willing to continue with their minimal efforts as opposed to bringing about curricular change that could lead to organizational improvement and increased student achievement. Based on your experiences and the information revealed in this chapter, do you agree or disagree with this assessment as proposed by Douglas B. Reeves, chairman and founder of the Center for Performance Assessment? Support your answer.

3. Wolfgang von Goethe (1749–1832), famous German writer and thinker, wrote, "To act is easy; to think is hard" (*The Columbia World of Quotations*, 1996). Contemplate the case study scenario. What do you *think* is the problem at Reven High School and what *actions* are necessary for Principal Adriana Sanchez to remedy the situation? Respond in detail and relate your answer to the research relative to organizational change and curriculum leadership.

4. Bass (1985) believed that those leaders who transform organizations through curriculum change possess visioning, rhetorical, and persuasive skills. What must Principal Sanchez do to transform faculty thinking and the overall culture at Reven High School to ensure curricular change positively impacts student success and achievement? Be specific in your answer.

5. In the case study scenario, Principal Sanchez states to Ellen Fong, "Come on now, I need some advice! Ellen, what are your thoughts?" Ellen Fong replies, "Well, I hate to admit it, but the faculty and staff keep telling me that we're the problem." What does Ellen mean by suggesting that "we're the problem"? What do you believe is the real problem at Reven High School relative to curriculum change? What is the principal, as the curriculum expert, to do in this situation?

6. Robert Heller (1998) in his essential manager book *Managing Change* relates productive and positive change requires planning. What planning initiatives and curriculum expertise efforts were ignored by Principal Sanchez and district officials, Tom Cartusi, and Ellen Fong? Explain your answer.

MANAGING CHANGE TOLERANCE TEST

INSTRUCTIONS: Listed here are several statements related to the curriculum leadership role in a successful organization. Place yourself in the curricular role and determine how you would react to each of the statements presented.

Next to each statement are five letters, A to E. Circle the letter that best describes how you would react according to the following scale:

A. This statement is completely acceptable.

B. This statement is acceptable most of the time.

C. This statement causes me to have no reaction one way or another.

(Continued)

(*Continued*)

  D. This statement is somewhat unpleasant for me.

  E. This statement is very unpleasant for me.

REMEMBER: Think and respond as if you are in the curriculum leadership role now!

1. I regularly spend 30% to 40% of my time in curriculum and/or instructional meetings.   A B C D E

2. A year and a half ago, my position did not exist, and I have been essentially inventing my role and responsibilities as I go along.   A B C D E

3. The curricular responsibilities I either assume or am assigned consistently exceed the authority I have for discharging them.   A B C D E

4. At any given moment in my curriculum leadership role, I have on the average about a dozen telephone calls to return.   A B C D E

5. About two weeks a year of formal professional development training is needed relative to my position.   A B C D E

6. There is no objective method to measure my effectiveness in my curriculum leadership role.   A B C D E

7. I report to different supervisors for differing aspects as related to my curriculum leadership role, and each supervisor has input with regard to my performance appraisal.   A B C D E

8. On average, about one-third of my day is spent dealing with unexpected situations that require all scheduled work to be postponed.   A B C D E

9. My curriculum leadership position requires that I daily read and absorb a significant number of e-mails.   A B C D E

10. I must be out of the office for curriculum and/or instructional meetings at least three times each day.   A B C D E

11. My chances of promotion depend on how I play the political game in my organization.   A B C D E

12. During the time that I have been employed, my organization has been reorganized about every two to three years with the arrival of a new school superintendent.   A B C D E

13. While there are several possible promotion opportunities for me, I really have no realistic chance of moving up in my organization.   A B C D E

14. While I have several excellent ideas about how to make serious and productive curricular improvements, I have no direct influence on the policies in my organization.   A B C D E

15. My organization has recently developed a "Center for Administrative Assessment and Improvement" where I, along with other leaders, will be required to go through a series of extensive batteries of psychological tests to assess my leadership potential.   A B C D E

16. My organization is a defendant in a lawsuit, and if the case goes to court, I will be required to testify about some decisions I have made.   A B C D E

17. Advanced technological software and hardware is continually being introduced in my organization, necessitating regular training that I must attend.   A B C D E

18. My computer is regularly monitored by the technology department and their staff without my knowledge as to when such oversight is occurring.   A B C D E

19. The vast majority of my decisions are reviewed by my superiors.   A B C D E

20. I can expect anywhere from two to five programmatic changes each day.   A B C D E

21. I was strongly supported in my curriculum leadership role by my direct supervisor who has since left the organization for another similar position elsewhere.   A B C D E

22. Personnel that I work with and supervise are no longer supportive of the curricular changes that were instituted by upper management in my organization.   A B C D E

23. Three of the seven members of the board of trustees are no longer supportive of the necessary changes that I instituted last year.   A B C D E

SCORE

Scoring Key

Use the following scale for calculating your score:

    A = 4 points

    B = 3 points

    C = 2 points

(Continued)

(*Continued*)

D = 1 point

E = 0 points

Compute your total, divide by 23, and round to one decimal place.

Although the results are not intended to be more than suggestive, the higher your score, the more comfortable you may be with change.

It is suggested that you analyze your score as if it were a grade-point average. In this way, a 4.0 average is an A, a 3.0 is a B, a 2.0 is a C, and scores below 1.0, well, are considered failures in managing change.

Using replies from nearly 500 new leaders, the range of scores was found to be quite narrow—between 1.0 and 2.2. The average score was between 1.5 and 1.6—equivalent to a D+/C- grade!

If such scores are to be generalized, clearly people are not very tolerant of change in organizations!

So are you change oriented, or are you one of those individuals who despise change, unless it jingles in your pocket?

Source: Vaill, P. B. (1989). *Managing as a performing art: New ideas for a world of chaotic change.* San Francisco: Jossey-Bass. Adapted with modifications and reproduced with permission of publisher. All rights reserved.

Other Resources

Brubaker, D. L. (2004). *Revitalizing curriculum leadership: Inspiring and empowering your school community.* Thousand Oaks, CA: Corwin.

Cherniss, C. (2006). *School change and the microsociety program.* Thousand Oaks, CA: Corwin.

McEwan, E. K. (2003). *Seven steps to effective instructional leadership.* Thousand Oaks, CA: Corwin.

Senge, P., Kleiner, A., Roberts, C., Ross, R., Roth, G., & Smith, B. (1999). *The dance of change: The challenges to sustaining momentum in learning organizations.* New York: Doubleday.

Smith, L. (2008). *Schools that change: Evidence-based improvement and effective change leadership.* Thousand Oaks, CA: Corwin.

Williams, R. B. (2008). *Twelve roles of facilitators for school change.* Thousand Oaks, CA: Corwin.

5

Curriculum Leadership in Action

If you want to build a ship, don't drum up people together to collect wood and don't assign them tasks and work, but rather teach them to long for the endless immensity of the sea.

—Antoine de Saint-Exupery (2003)

In Chapter 1, we described the principal's role as one that involves managing the everydayness of school life. Specifically, we discussed the principal's role as one involving the exercise of curriculum leadership. The principal as a leader of curriculum development, revision, and implementation is one who constantly seeks to formulate and reformulate the purpose of schooling. In this chapter, we explore the process of formulating and revising a school's curriculum. We will describe curriculum leadership in action.

The Role of the Principal in Curriculum Design and Development

Curriculum leadership is a verb. It signals to the delicate task of connecting the matter of which schooling is made: curriculum, instruction, assessment, and evaluation. The task is delicate because its linkage calls for high skill and because the quality of students' scholastic or academic lives depend on a principal's ability to understand their interconnectedness and to act on such an understanding. Curriculum leadership as a verb requires a deliberate focus on curricular matters resulting in the improvement of students' educative experiences and learning.

Though curriculum leadership should be of utmost importance to principals and as such it should be nurtured and practiced, principals often find themselves unable or unwilling to engage in the curriculum leadership process. In an era of accountability, curriculum leadership is an equally cherished yet elusive pursuit. In fact, as you recall from Chapter 1, Will Wonkermann's initial conception of his school's mission statement as being unattainable is characteristic of principals. His frustration and fear of whether and how he could accomplish the school mission parallels the complexity of his responsibility: To maintain the daily administrative operations of the school and to actively ensure that students are exposed to a rigorous and well-rounded curriculum.

Will Wonkermann, like most principals, is expected to make certain that *no child is left behind*. As such, he struggles with an accountability system that seems to regiment much of what he does; yet it expects him to find creative ways of fulfilling his school's mission. Caught in this dilemma, Principal Wonkermann is frustrated. Though he would hardly admit it, Will is afraid. He has mistakenly placed the entire weight of the school's mission and its attainment on his shoulders. Will is forgetting that fulfilling the school's mission involves everyone.

RETHINKING THE ROLE OF THE PRINCIPAL

In the quiet of a late afternoon at Childers School, Principal Wonkermann's memories of his last—and secretly his only—workshop on curriculum revision are now fragmented and, thus, incomplete. What a luxury and how critical, he realizes, it is that future school leaders are now better prepared, than ever before, on matters of curriculum. Will recalls his intern is taking a course, Curriculum Renewal, at the local university. Yet for Will the workshop he recently conducted was, in fact, the first time he was asked to really think about curriculum and curriculum leadership. During the workshop, facilitators insisted on the redefinition of the principalship. From being conceived as a campus manager or administrator, principals, he had heard, and now learned, were to lead in determining the very stuff that schooling is about: curriculum and instruction.

The Challenges of Leading

How is a principal to lead on matters of curriculum? How is a principal to lead a school in achieving the mission to which a principal is committed? Multiple meetings, discipline matters, personnel issues, and budgeting are a prominent part of every principal's daily routine. High-stakes testing and accountability are the stuff a principal and faculty live and breathe. And now, a new demand called curriculum leadership threatens to populate an already exhausting schedule.

The struggles of Will Wonkermann evoke the challenges that other principals increasingly face in schools around the nation, large and small. The enormity of the challenge is only exacerbated by principals' conception of what it means to lead and what can and should reasonably be done about curriculum matters. Like other principals, Will Wonkermann knows he is accountable for the education students receive at Childers School. He also knows there is a mandated curriculum that sets the minimum educational standards students must meet. Contingent on how schooling is organized by a principal and team, a leader and team will meet and exceed (or not) the educative experiences that the school community legitimately expects to be delivered.

To be certain, the role of a principal is even more demanding and the expectations are increasingly higher (Sergiovanni, Kelleher, McCarthy, & Fowler, 2009). However, we know that it is every principal's desire to fulfill a school's mission and provide students with the best education. Principals must recognize they are not alone. Other stakeholders share responsibility for a school's mission

> **Educational brokers** are leaders who readily negotiate and mediate divergent positions by propitiating frank, respectful, and, in most cases, essential exchanges.

and should be engaged in nurturing and sustaining a curriculum to fulfill it. Curriculum leadership demands that all principals act as **educational brokers.**

A principal is, first and foremost, to broker the expertise, talent, aspirations, and the collective effort of the school community including teachers, parents, and students.

> **Cultural translators** are leaders who serve as interpreters of the language, culture, and values of a school community and who translate said language and values to the school's constituency.

Moreover, because a school and its curriculum are always shaped by and accountable to its surrounding local community, a principal's role as an educational broker expands to one of **cultural translator**.

Cultural translation is an essential element of curriculum leadership. This is especially true as effective principals, if they are to realize their schools' mission, are expected to foster and maintain open lines of communication between schools and communities.

Our conception of principals as able educational brokers and cultural translators suggests a notion of curriculum leadership as a collective endeavor. An endeavor carefully and closely orchestrated and guided by the school principal, a leader with sharply refined managerial and curricular skills. This principal is one who is knowledgeable about the intricate functioning of school organizations, committed and respected not just inside the school building but in the surrounding community, and confident to procure and engage the knowledge, insight, and support of those interested in the school curriculum.

WHAT'S A PRINCIPAL TO DO?

In his office, as he prepared to leave after a long day at Childers School, Principal Will Wonkermann experienced mixed emotions. His initial fear was associated with the recognition that staying committed to the school mission would require an enormous amount of work and effort. However, this fear quickly turned to excitement—and even a kind of relief—with the realization that the school and its community possess the essential resources for curriculum innovation, renewal, and change. Childers School, Will thought, can no longer wait.

Will was reassured by the ideas in that dusty binder that he had collected at the recent curriculum workshop. In his binder, Will examined a brief description of Walker's (1971) *Deliberative Model of Curriculum Development*. This model, a classic and indispensible work in the field of curriculum studies, really caught his attention. Avidly, he read the two and a half pages associated with the model and its deliberative process. Each word resonated with what he believed. Childers needed help, especially in the area of curriculum leadership, development, and revision. Realizing it was getting late in the evening, Will marked the pages, closed the binder, grabbed his keys, and walked toward the school parking lot. The last glimpses of daylight found him enthusiastically thinking about his next steps.

Systematic as he was, Will knew he would need to put in place a process that allowed all stakeholders to participate in curriculum deliberations. He was convinced a process was necessary as he attempted to guide his fellow educators from the abstractness of curriculum theory toward a sphere of relevant practice that would be equally valued and supported by stakeholders outside the school's halls and classrooms.

Thus, while he deliberately would seek to engage the instrumentalities that curricular theory afforded his teachers and specialists, he must be attentive to parents, students, and other stakeholders' ideas when it came to sound educational practice. Will, as he started his car to drive home, was confident that, however complex curricular deliberations could become, collective work could potentially produce the academic excellence all aspired to and strongly desired for all students at Childers School.

Curriculum Leadership Through Walker's Deliberative Model of Curriculum Development

Few theories of curriculum advance an open framework to engage educators and communities in the collaboration of curriculum development. Walker's (1971) *Deliberative Model of Curriculum Development* is a model that specifies a process for the deliberation of curriculum development. The model is useful because it identifies the various stages or "phases" that the work of curriculum development entails. Walker's model offers principals a structure that makes curriculum leadership less abstract as it guides them in understanding, reconsidering, and organizing the enormous yet collective task of developing and improving the school curriculum. (Examine the Expectation 1: Team Identification and Inclusion section of Chapter 3 and the Building Block 6: A Learning Culture for All section in Chapter 6.)

Moreover, Walker's (1971) model assumes that involving the entire school community in the planning process by utilizing and bringing their unique experiences and skills to the curriculum development table will enrich the school's curricular program. Thus, if the model calls for collective work and communication among school personnel and other stakeholders, it also requires principals who are capable educational brokers and cultural translators—curriculum leaders—to actualize the deliberative process.

Enacting the Deliberative Model of Curriculum Development

In the deliberative model of curriculum development, three phases are critical. Walker (1971) identifies the three moments or phases as

(1) *platform*, (2) *deliberation*, and (3) *design*. In each phase of the model, the principal's curriculum leadership as an educational broker and cultural translator plays a central role.

Platform

The platform phase of Walker's (1971) deliberative model of curriculum development involves deep conversations about the plans, visions, and goals that should be a part of a school curriculum. The dialogue and expected argumentation serves as an opportunity to share and ponder each participant's perspectives and beliefs regarding a school curriculum. Thus, assuming that stakeholders bring diverse and, at times, competing values and orientations, the principal's role as a curriculum leader is to broker the divergent positions by propitiating a frank but respectful exchange.

During the platform phase of the deliberative process, Walker (1971) contends that a common language to approach concepts, theories, aims, vision, and programmatic issues should be achieved. If articulating perspectives on what is and what can be the school curriculum is a complex task, formulating those ideas with terms and concepts that all understand and agree on is just as challenging. Thus, in the identification of a potential course of action toward the achievement of what is desirable and possible, the principal's skills as a cultural translator are invaluable. Brokering between school personnel and community members, the principal paves the way for the articulation of a common language that describes and specifies the educational goals of the school community.

Curriculum leadership is, thus, about contributing to the establishment of a process that nurtures and preserves the collective nature of articulating a school curriculum. As an educational broker and a cultural translator, the principal leadership role is critical if full membership participation and inclusion are to be achieved and sustained. Moreover, because the principal is and should be a steward of the campus curricular vision, his or her job is to elicit, facilitate, clarify, and enrich stakeholders' articulation of their unique vision of school knowledge, teaching, and learning.

As the platform phase unfolds, participants bring their particular ideas, visions, and interests to the deliberation table where viewpoints may very well diverge. When clashing viewpoints emerge, the principal's role is to mediate and guide participants in overcoming any polarization and conflict that can obfuscate the collective effort. Conflict, if not dealt with constructively, may hinder the school community's efforts as it can distract and discourage stakeholders from the critical work of fulfilling the school mission.

In sum, a principal's curriculum leadership role, as we conceive it, should contribute and guide the process of planning and executing the school curriculum. Such leadership invites open discussion and exchange during the platform stage. It provides a structure that fosters collaboration and camaraderie so everyone's voices are considered and heard. It also provides a structure by which all ideas can be seriously considered and acted on.

Deliberation

Having established a set of understandings and a common language with which to pursue a school curriculum, a school community is ready to enter the deliberation phase. In this phase, Walker (1971) calls attention to the process by which all stakeholders move from the conceptual work of negotiating and finding a common language for curriculum to the programmatic dimension that outlining a plan demands. The move toward the programmatic involves a factual assessment of the material conditions of a school.

Equally critical are campus needs assessments and listings of campus resource materials as elements that guide the identification of a school curriculum. Data sources, such as quantitative information (student records, state assessment records, classroom assessments, and other relevant benchmarks), as well as qualitative records (surveys, focus group information, interviews, school-site visits, student profiles, and brainstorming initiatives) are invaluable resources that a principal can share and make accessible to stakeholders. Both quantitative and qualitative data—obtained from within the district or school and from sources outside the school system—should also be made available by the principal (refer to Chapter 3). By using these varied data sets, the principal, as a cultural translator, ensures that stakeholders understand the school data, do not lose sight of campus needs, and outline what is desirable and possible during the development of a school curriculum.

Design

In this phase of Walker's (1971) deliberative approach, school personnel and stakeholders have established a common language and have negotiated clear goals for their school curriculum. As a result, they are ready to engage in the work of producing a school curriculum. The principal's role is to oversee that its design and development is brought to fruition by all stakeholders. The outcome of this phase is the production of curriculum plans as well as their instrumentation for adequate assessment.

WILL WONKERMANN IMPLEMENTS WALKER'S (1971) DELIBERATIVE MODEL OF CURRICULUM DEVELOPMENT

Though Principal Wonkermann was initially concerned about revisiting the school mission and about discussing the role each member of the school community played in achieving it, he paused after returning to school the next morning and decided he would engage in another quick yet careful reading of his workshop materials. He felt both excited and uncertain about engaging the school community in a discussion of the school's mission and its implications for Childers's curriculum. But as he reflected on the mixture of feelings he was experiencing, Wonkermann discovered that it was the *how* to engage his school community in a conversation rather than the resulting outcomes that caused his worries.

Principal Wonkermann knew that most members of the school community had much to contribute to a conversation about the school mission. However, he also knew that there were various perspectives and views about what needed to be included in the mission. The possibility of engaging diverse ideas and perspectives made the task an opportunity and a challenge. He knew this because he had witnessed the sense of frustration and further alienation that previous attempts at discussing the school's mission had brought about in members of the school community. This time around, he wanted to approach the discussion in a different way. He was ready to implement Walker's (1971) deliberative model of curriculum development at Childers School.

A Systematic Approach

Curriculum leadership requires a vision and a methodical approach to achieve it. Thus, principals must possess a clear idea of what schooling is about. The latter is necessary, as principals are expected to delineate the direction in which all efforts must focus. Equally important, principals must know how to provide and carry out a method toward the achievement of their vision. Hence, the need for principals to familiarize themselves and others with various curriculum approaches and theories that aid in the development of a systematic approach to guide the school community in the articulation of a school mission and curriculum. Without such a systematic approach, a principal's and the school community's work, regardless of the level of commitment and enthusiasm, is doomed to fail.

In the forthcoming scenario, consider how, at the conclusion of the spring semester and in preparation for the following school year, Principal Wonkermann introduces and models, in a faculty meeting setting, the three phases of Walker's (1971) deliberative model. Although the model is typically used to engage education professionals outside the school community, Principal Wonkermann decides to implement the model with faculty at Childers School. At the conclusion of the scenario, read and respond to the Pause and Consider questions.

PRINCIPAL WONKERMANN MEETS WITH THE FACULTY AT CHILDERS SCHOOL

Hello everybody. As I have previously communicated, I would like to invite you to engage in a conversation about our school's mission and curriculum. As the school year comes to a close, we are now ready to begin our planning efforts for next year. First, we want to revisit our school mission in light of our successes along with the common goals we have yet to accomplish. I know that these discussions are fraught with difficulty, and they will demand much from all of us. These discussions will require time in an already busy schedule, and I will call on you during this period when we are all feeling overextended. More than anything, this time of discussion will require creativity and innovation in a context of standardization and prescriptive approaches to schooling. I suspect that revisiting our school mission will mean that we will have to look at our curriculum and determine whether and how it aligns with our vision of what schooling at Childers must be.

The work ahead of us is significant, challenging, and necessary. As your principal, I know that moving forward with this task will be impossible unless we are willing to work collectively. Collective work is difficult to achieve if trust and adequate support from the school leadership team is nonexistent. I pledge to you my strongest support as we begin to move forward in this process. At Childers School we have worked together to build a strong school community. Amid both our common and divergent views, it is our commitment to excellence that has brought us together and keeps us working as a team. It is this same commitment that motivates us to continue searching for ways to improve. It is this commitment that should encourage us to take on the task of revisiting our school mission.

Commitment is a crucial element in the work that is ahead of us. But as a pragmatist, I know that commitment can quickly fade if the

(Continued)

(Continued)

structures that support collective work and innovation are not in place at the school level. I want to be certain that our commitment is an ingredient that guides our efforts even at those junctures when the going gets tough. But in addition to commitment, part of what I believe is required for us to move on systematically relative to the work I am proposing is a framework or model that permits us to collectively complete the curriculum work that we, as a school community, have outlined. Though the notion of searching for a model or framework that helps us to carry out our task effectively might come across as intimidating, I want to propose to you the use of what I believe to be a promising approach to the task at hand.

This task, this new approach, the work at hand is known as Walker's (1971) deliberative model of curriculum development. It is the model that was discussed at the last leadership academy I attended. I am confident that implementing this model will be of great value, especially as we revisit our school mission. I am particularly interested in us incorporating this particular model here at Childers School because it captures the spirit of collaboration to which we are committed.

Pause and Consider

- What are the most common concerns teachers have with regard to collectively working on the school mission and curriculum?

- As a principal or prospective principal, are you convinced that Principal Wonkermann's implementation of Walker's deliberative model will nurture the inclusion of all ideas and views as the work of revising the school mission and curriculum unfold? Why? Why not? What would you need to hear or see to be convinced?

- What are the opportunities and limitations of the model as presented by Principal Wonkermann?

Now consider the next scenario that illustrates a level of skepticism that might ensue while seeking to deliberate about the school mission and curriculum. This scenario also illustrates that although deliberation might not be an imperative to everyone, a common commitment to student learning is the very issue that principals, as curriculum leaders, insist on as they seek to anchor the deliberation of what the school mission is and must be, along with what the school curriculum is and must become.

PONDERING THE LONG-STANDING TENSION BETWEEN ACCOUNTABILITY AND EXCELLENCE: THE PLATFORM PHASE

Alma Cortinas is a well-respected mathematics teacher. Her commitment to her students is unquestionable. At Childers School, almost everyone agrees with one of Alma's colleagues: "No one knows her mathematics curriculum better than Alma Cortinas." Alma follows the scope and sequence established by the school district, and it is to that regimented approach that Alma attributes her instructional success. Hence, as she listens to Principal Wonkermann, she is uncertain that deliberating about the school's mission and curriculum is a necessary task. To this young but experienced teacher, schooling is about incorporating the state-mandated curriculum. Schooling, for Alma, is also about helping students master the lesson content in a way that is reflected on the state accountability exam. Conversations that are not focused on the accountability process seem, at least to Alma, to be irrelevant.

Therefore, Alma has mixed reactions as she listens to Mr. Wonkermann's call to revisit Childers's school mission through a deliberation model. Suddenly, Alma thinks to herself, "What is most important, meeting the state accountability standards and performing well on the state exam or focusing on the high-minded goals posed in a school mission statement? And since when do those high-minded goals matter given the increased pressure to perform well on the state accountability exam?" Then, Alma did it—she really did it! She blurted out, in the form of a series of questions, what she was really thinking! "Mr. Wonkermann, do you really expect us to put aside the state standards, the accountability process, and the practice of testing to focus on a few words posted above the office entry door and read each morning during the announcements? Who are you kidding? Is it more important to set aside what keeps us all employed, ensuring that our students master the state exam, or play around with a mission statement that reads, 'Childers School is committed to providing the best possible education to *all* students?' Excuse me sir. I don't mean to be disrespectful but have we lost our minds?"

First, there was silence as the rest of the faculty starred in amazement at Alma. Second, a small round of applause occurred. Finally, a low murmuring spread across the room.

To establish a common language toward the achievement of common goals, deep conversations are critically important in the platform phase of the deliberative model. Though the questions that teachers and administrators raise might appear seemingly basic or even at odds with mandated curriculum, their articulation is necessary because considering those questions allows for an opportunity to engage in deep conversations about vision, goals, and plans. The platform phase, although at times unnerving, is a valuable opportunity for leaders to engage with those who agree with them but also with others who might be skeptical. Working through the tension that divergent ideas might pose is an intimate part of the platform phase. Will Wonkermann knows his role, understands the task, and is facilitating an essential aspect of curriculum reform.

A DETERMINED RETURN TO THE FACULTY MEETING DISCUSSION

Principal Wonkermann patiently and purposefully waited for a few seconds until the faculty murmuring dissipated. Determined in mind and action, he genuinely thanked Alma for initiating "a serious discussion of his proposal" and for helping to "establish the platform" from which to begin a long needed and most essential discussion. Then Will, in a cordial tone, asked whether anyone else shared the view expressed by Alma or whether anyone wanted to elaborate further relative to the expressed view. In a split second, another teacher stated that revisiting and revising the school mission statement was an important task, however, as the teacher put it, "Our plates are already full with all of the accountability stuff." Nodding, Principal Wonkermann said, "Sure, accountability is certainly an issue of concern for all of us." Determined, he plodded further and asked, "What other issues or concerns can you identify that might challenge our work relative to the school mission?" Responding to his question, a third teacher asked, "Wouldn't focusing on the school mission distract us too much from the real demands of our district, which are mainly on increasing test scores?" The inquiry elicited another round of applause and even more murmuring from the group.

As teachers continued to express their concerns, one of the assistant principals, Bill Stempson, listed each concern on the electronic smart board. Seeing such a listing on the board conveyed the idea that teachers' views were being acknowledged, not avoided or ignored. The listing of concerns helped everyone to stay on task and avoided redundancy. Thus, as the conversation continued for the next few minutes, participants elaborated on the stated concerns or identified even more.

When it seemed as if everyone had had a chance to speak, a new round of discussions ensued. Teresa López, a second assistant principal, who had remained silent but attentively listening asked, "It seems to me that we are assuming that the school mission and the accountability and testing processes are separate items, and I am wondering if that indeed is the case?" Mrs. López had just posed the question, when a teacher, rather intrigued, asked for clarification, "What do you mean?" Mrs. López then said, "Well, as I sit here listening to what is being said, I am of the opinion that it makes perfect sense to have doubts or to be concerned about losing focus. That is, it seems reasonable to want to concentrate our efforts on the very thing that apparently counts: accountability. However, I am also thinking that the school mission as it stands, or at least as I interpret it, does not divorce questions of accountability from a commitment to excellence." She paused for a couple of seconds and then continued: "So the question for me is whether and how accountability and excellence are commitments that we willingly express but recognize as inseparable from our school mission? My sense is that at Childers School we do not just care about increasing test scores but that we also strive for instructional and curricular excellence." As Mrs. López finished talking, the other assistant principal, Bill Stempson, who was writing on the electronic smart board, included the main idea of what his colleague had just publicly shared: "Accountability matters; we strive for excellence."

The faculty and staff gradually became more engaged. A few other teachers raised their hands to participate and Principal Wonkermann looking at them, then at the board, and then at the clock, asked for another round of active discussion. Trying to keep the conversation focused, he said, "I see that some of you want to contribute to the discussion, and I will just ask, given our time constraints and the fact that this is only the beginning of our many conversations, that this next round of participation addresses the issues that have been raised." Another teacher then said, "Yes, I want to respond to some of what Mrs. López has just noted. Here at our table, we were saying, accountability is important, it's mandated, it's the law, and we want to meet the standards. However, excellence is our calling but we need support, we need help. Help and support is what we need from the district and from our school leadership team."

It is important to recognize that Principal Will Wonkermann's initial elicitation during the faculty meeting served to exemplify the platform phase of Walker's (1971) deliberative model. That is, as curriculum leaders, we must invite deep and frank conversations about the direction we propose for our schools. By doing so, we seek to establish common ground when we elicit teachers' perspectives on the invitation to work together when revising the school mission statement and when revising or reforming curriculum. Perspectives must be voiced and made visible in writing. Thus, as perspectives are written, effective principals signal a commitment to propitiate that all perspectives are acknowledged and considered rather than avoided or averted. Those perspectives and issues that are raised by school personnel will constitute the platform from which we can collectively move forward to the deliberation phase.

LET THE DELIBERATIONS BEGIN!

During the early part of the summer, the Childers School faculty and staff set aside a couple of dates to meet and continue the earlier conversation. Minutes from the previous meeting were distributed and some additional time was provided so everyone could review the document. As people read quietly through it, someone in the crowd teasingly said, "Oh boy, we were on a roll last month." The comment produced laughter and it served as an aperture for Principal Wonkermann to reiterate his commitment to facilitate the effort they had initiated just a few weeks ago.

Principal Wonkermann began the conversation: "We wanted to be certain each of you had a copy of the minutes from our last meeting to help us stay on task with our deliberations today. The minutes, if you will, render testimony to our concerns and to the issues we have previously identified. Reviewing these minutes, these concerns, and these issues also helps us to not lose sight of the progress we have made. However, before we move ahead, does anybody have any questions, doubts, or suggestions? If not, then I'll proceed but please let me know if you want to share anything as we move forward."

Principal Wonkermann then noted, "From our last meeting, we came to agreement about the importance of working on the school mission statement and how it interrelates with our curriculum. But as your school principal, I am aware that some of you are more convinced than others about the task at hand. That's fine. We are a community of professionals, and as such, I know each of you have various convictions and ways of looking at the complex task of schooling. However, I want to say that I appreciate your being present today despite the fact that you might have more questions than answers at this point. As some of you expressed last time, you are committed to the students and to instructional excellence at Childers School, and that, I suspect, is what keeps you engaged."

Principal Wonkermann then asked Mrs. López to present to the faculty a number of documents for consideration. One document in particular was the campus needs assessment, along with a listing of various campus resource materials, and of course, other documents that included, for example, state assessment records. The idea behind sharing these materials was to provide the faculty with data necessary to make informed programmatic decisions with regard to the direction the team wished to take and how such a venture could best be represented in the school's mission statement and revised curriculum.

Principal Wonkermann proceeded: "I have also asked Ms. Alma Cortinas, one of our math teachers, to help us examine each of the documents and especially to help us make sense of the data."

Ms. Cortinas then took the lead and stated, "Yes, thank you, Mr. Wonkermann and Mrs. López. A couple of weeks ago, when I was asked to take a look at the documents in front of you, in preparation for today's meeting, I was, at first, overwhelmed. Too much information! Then as I took my time and reviewed each of the documents, I became aware of certain areas of concern, certain causal barriers. I must also say that I was able to gain some appreciation for the often modest but significant gains we have made. That aside, as I finished looking at the various documents and data, I was left with this question: What does this mean for the present and future of our school, and how does it relate to our continued instructional and curricular efforts?"

Ms. Cortinas took a deep breath and said, "Today, what we'd like to do is to ask you to look at the data and discuss it among yourselves. There are various questions that we have come up with to guide our review and discussion. As you sit with your team members, I want you to consider what areas of concern come to light and what successes do the data evidence. We will begin with the campus needs during the first few minutes of our session together and then move to the campus resource documents and spend more time in our deliberations. Finally, we will examine the state assessment records. Our goal today is to help define and possibly redefine our school mission statement and revise our curriculum based on what we learn from an analysis of the data."

The deliberation phase requires that school personnel be willing to move forward with the task at hand. Because schools are complex organizations where professionals often bring divergent perspectives to the table, so to speak, curriculum leadership is about brokering through those perspectives, acknowledging them and bringing all members of the learning community onto the same curricular page. Brokering through competing desires and views, the effective principal is able to open areas of curriculum agreement by which members of the learning community are able to work through their differing imperatives.

Moreover, through the sharing of the various data and campus documents, it is possible for a principal and team to determine, in an environment of inquiry and collegiality, what must be revised relative to the school mission statement and the campus curriculum. Not every issue that surfaces because of the systematic study of the data will be necessarily encompassed. However, everyone will quickly recognize the need to commit to pursuing what at the time seems feasible and possible. The latter is accomplished in the design phase.

THERE IS AN ACTUAL METHOD TO THIS MADNESS!
The Design Phase

A few weeks before the beginning of the new school year, most personnel at Childers School met again as a team to continue implementing Walker's (1971) deliberative model. The minutes from the previous meeting had been distributed, and everyone had a chance to review the last proceedings. Three resolutions were noted: (1) to develop a working schedule for the actual task of redefining the school mission statement and, thus, revising the campus curriculum; (2) to determine how the work would be carried out; and (3) to discuss when and how other stakeholders such as parents, local business people, community groups, and even students could be brought in to participate in the revision of the campus mission statement and curriculum.

Pause and Consider

- Discuss Principal Wonkermann's implementation of the deliberative model. How did he proceed? Were his methods practical and effective? Why or why not?

- What would you do differently?

- What challenges and opportunities do you identify in the implementation of this model?

Final Thoughts

Curriculum leadership in action is nothing more than a deliberate effort to connect curriculum, instruction, assessment, and evaluation. It is also about engaging all school personnel in a critical but complex endeavor known as deliberation. Although Principal Will Wonkermann might not have been an expert when it came to curriculum design and renewal, his systematic approach to the problems of revising the school's mission statement and the overall curriculum allowed him to appreciate and subsequently implement a model that was fluid enough to bank on the ideas and insights of his staff and to further delineate the direction the school needed to take and to specify the ways in which the Childers team would accomplish the task. Walker's (1971) deliberative model of curriculum development allows flexibility, and at the same time, it provides a structure with which a principal can lead and a team can work and succeed when it comes to curriculum development, revision, and implementation.

Discussion Questions

1. Consider curriculum leadership as a verb. How is it manifested in action in your school?

2. Think of the school leaders you have encountered in your professional life. Describe attributes and actions that make these leaders educational brokers. Describe attributes and actions that make them cultural translators. What has prevented any of these leaders from being educational brokers/cultural translators? Explain in detail.

3. Consider Walker's (1971) deliberative model of curriculum development. What extension or adaptations can you make to address particular curricular issues at your school?

4. What other models are you familiar with that might provide you with a systematic approach to curriculum leadership?

CASE STUDY APPLICATION
Who Decides What and How?

In her three-year tenure as principal at Paso del Norte High School, Dr. Maria Cortez turned around the chronic cycle of low achievement. Her success was attributed to her no-nonsense approach. With support from the district, a cadre of new teachers, and a newly appointed assistant principal, Dr. Cortez brought the school to an improved level of achievement.

Though teachers and staff at Paso del Norte had been loyal to Dr. Cortez, the road to gradual but significant improvement had not been easy. Given its turbulent past and underperformance record, many at the school welcomed her strong leadership and agreed it was needed. Still, a few teachers remained skeptical about her emphasis on state

(Continued)

(*Continued*)

standards and benchmarks. However, because school personnel knew that a failing record was no longer an option, everyone conceded that a focus on improving test scores would be critical if the campus was to avoid reconstitution.

At the end of the school year—and despite the various successes—the exhaustion of personnel at Paso del Norte High School was evident. The emphasis on an outcome-based and teacher-directed curriculum had seemingly extracted the initial energy and enthusiasm with which most had set out to work to improve the school. Teacher turnover continued, and after state testing, teacher absenteeism was at an all-time high.

Untiring, Dr. Cortez announced on the last week of the school year that a different approach to the teaching of science would be implemented the following year, as the school still needed to show improvement in this curricular area. In her mind, the shift in curriculum would contribute to renew teachers' enthusiasm and provide them with new tools to become more effective in their instruction. However, to many, but especially the science teachers, the sole mention of having to take "a different approach" was burdensome. They had just began to see some encouraging results with the implemented changes in the last three years, and now, they were posed with the idea of moving on to another curricular approach.

Notwithstanding the fact that the climate at Paso del Norte High School was one of exhaustion, Dr. Cortez insisted on the new approach. "Move-It Science," the principal advanced, would promote the conceptual learning of science. It would, as she explained, nurture and develop students' scientific thinking. "Everyone," she said sensing teachers' fatigue and disinterest "should be excited." "The new science curriculum," she claimed, "would also improve students' science test scores."

Despite Dr. Cortez's confidence, a few weeks after the new science curriculum was introduced, most teachers in the science department identified issues of concern. The concerns related, for the most part, to time issues, questions of implementation, and content. In addition, most science teachers—comprised of a group of relatively new science teachers and a few veterans—saw the strong push for the new curriculum as one that would interfere with teachers' professional judgment at a time when students' test scores had shown some modest gains. During the summer, when science teachers were to report to receive training in the new curriculum, many of the teachers failed to attend; and others, as reported in an exit evaluation survey, were there just to comply.

Application Questions

1. Discuss Dr. Cortez's approach to improving student performance at Paso del Norte High School. What should be the role of the principal in determining *what* teachers should teach? What should be the role of the principal in determining *how* teachers should teach?

2. Should the goal of improved student performance be sufficient to convince teachers to follow a particular curricular approach? Why? Why not?

3. What are some of the issues that this case study identifies with regard to teachers' sense of autonomy and efficacy?

4. By what means can a principal lead a school to higher levels of academic performance and, moreover, convince all teachers of his or her course of action?

5. In Dr. Cortez's specific situation, what could she have done to persuade teachers on the use of the new science curriculum? Substantiate your response(s) with detailed argumentation.

6. What can Dr. Cortez do now to overcome teachers' skepticism with the curriculum? Substantiate your response(s) with detailed argumentation.

Other Resources

Brubaker, D. L. (2004). *Revitalizing curriculum leadership: Inspiring and empowering your school community*. Thousand Oaks, CA: Corwin.

Glatthorn, A. A., Boschee, F. A., & Whitehead, B. M. (2008). *Curriculum leadership: Strategies for development and implementation*. Thousand Oaks, CA: Sage.

Wiles, J. W., & Bondi, J. C. (2010). *Curriculum development: A guide to practice*. Upper Saddle River, NJ: Prentice-Hall.

6

Where the Action Is

Building Relationships With Teachers

Even the grandest design eventually degenerates into hard work.

—Rick DuFour (2007)

Leadership and Followership:
You Can't Have One Without the Other!

Effective principals focused on curriculum leadership readily acknowledge that a team does not exist simply because the instructional leader places a group of teachers together and calls them a team. Building strong relationships with teachers is a two-way street. Principals influence teachers; teachers influence principals. This influencing of one another, teachers and principals, builds meaningful interpersonal relationships dependent on interconnecting levels of expertise, innovative ideas, and moral integrity. DuFour (2007) was correct when he noted in the introductory quote that leading is a difficult task, especially when it relates to building relationships. Lyman Porter (1968), more than four decades ago, revealed a nugget of truth that remains relevant today: Leaders and followers who value one another, who work to establish strong professional relationships, and who have positive attitudes about the issues at hand will experience less conflict, find mutual support, and be more satisfied in their efforts.

ROBERTA'S JOURNEY, PART I

Principal Wonkermann continued to explore his curriculum leadership role. He realized he'd overlooked a most valuable resource. Childers School was blessed with a number of outstanding teacher leaders. Admittedly, some teachers still had a way to go, but he knew he could learn a lot about curriculum leadership from the Childers's team. He thought about Roberta Ayala and her teaching journey. She had grown into an outstanding educator after a bumpy start.

Roberta was absolutely without a doubt the world's worst first-year teacher. She had a teaching certificate from a premier university, a 3.75 grade point average, and a deep desire to work with students, but that didn't seem to help much. Roberta taught English/language arts. She cried most days, but never in front of the kids. If it hadn't been for the fact that Roberta's husband was in school and she was the family paycheck, she would have walked out.

Roberta was in a "pod" with two other veteran teachers. Their classes were well behaved and quiet. They didn't help Roberta, but they let her know that her classes were out of control. Roberta was too scared to ask for help, and they were too busy to intervene. The system was at fault.

Supplies and textbooks were nonexistent. Books were up for adoption the next year and the district had chosen not to obtain any extras since they would only be used once. The new teachers didn't have books. Since there were no departmental meetings, Roberta was left alone to prepare lessons and figure out what to teach. The principal never visited Roberta's classroom, although, somehow, Roberta received a good evaluation. When the year ended, Roberta's contract was extended. By then, she had developed a routine, and she had managed to be assigned a room with a door, so she didn't have to worry about bothering everyone else in the pod. Isolation had set in.

The next year, Roberta's husband graduated, and they moved. She quit teaching never intending to return to the profession.

Pause and Consider

- What conditions can the curriculum leader influence that will lead to a better beginning for teachers like Roberta?

- From a curriculum leadership perspective, what could Roberta's peers have done to help this struggling first-year teacher?

- In your opinion, what aspects of the curriculum intimidate first-year teachers and, thus, create teacher burnout? Why?

As you think back to your first teaching days, chances are you can identify with some of Roberta's experiences. Each year, thousands of teachers leave the teaching profession. Currently, about one-third of new teachers leave within five years, and since the 1990s, the annual number of exits from teaching has increasingly surpassed the number of entrants (Darling-Hammond, 2003).

Isolation

In traditional schools throughout the United States, thousands of teachers each day enter their classrooms and shut their doors. Teachers do their own thing in loosely coupled schools where their daily work is largely unsupervised and unsupported. When teachers like Roberta are isolated, their chances of survival are

> **Arrested teacher development** occurs when new or beginning teachers are left alone to determine their own way, to devise their own resources, to make decisions in isolation. Characteristics of arrested teacher development are low morale, isolationism, and burnout. Frequent side effects are negativity and low student performance.

minimal and their ability to develop the autonomous and flexible thinking demanded in a complex teaching environment is nonexistent. Roberta is a prime example of **arrested teacher development**. She never had an opportunity to grow professionally.

According to Glickman, Gordon, and Ross-Gordon (2007), faculty who experience arrested teacher development, those who are overwhelmed in the teaching and learning environment, those who fail to think in the abstract and have difficulty working independently, will simplify and flatten curricular and instructional processes.

Student achievement is the result of the dedicated efforts of teachers. Isolated teachers who receive no systemic feedback stand little chance of offering meaningful contributions to a successful school, but teachers in well-run, collaborative settings find satisfaction and renewal from their work with colleagues in addition to the rewards that come from the interaction with their students. Campus leadership either facilitates or inhibits this process. The principal as curriculum leader is responsible for the growth and well-being of each staff member on the campus. When teachers and other staff members are not performing successfully, the principal must take a long hard look at campus practices and systems. Just as teachers are responsible for student success, principals are responsible for teacher success.

10 Curriculum Leadership Building Blocks for Preventing and Treating Arrested Teacher Development

Ten building blocks focused on school organization and teacher productiveness form an essential part of curriculum leadership and provide direction for leaders of teachers such as Roberta—teachers who have the potential to mature into superior educators focused on the intellectual and emotional development of all students. Using these building blocks prevents and treats arrested teacher development.

Building Block 1: Teachers Do Make a Difference

Those in education for any length of time are familiar with a body of research known as effective schools research (Lezotte & McKee, 2006). For many educators, this research provided assurance that effective curriculum leadership could make a difference in the lives of all students.

The Coleman Report

The Civil Rights Act of 1964 required an Equality of Education Opportunity Study (EEOS) commissioned by the United States Department of Health, Education, and Welfare. This report, released in 1966, assessed the availability of equal educational opportunities to children of different race, color, religion, and national origin. Funded by the United States Office of Education, the report was written by a prominent education researcher, James Coleman (Kiviat, 2000).

Concluding that public schools didn't make a significant difference, Coleman's report credited the student's family background as the main reason for student success in school. Report findings proposed that children from poor families, lacking the prime conditions or values to support education, could not learn, regardless of what the school did. In a sense, Coleman was placing the blame for student failure on the home and conveniently giving schools a "pass" on accountability for student academic success (Kiviat, 2000). Effective schools research emerged in response to the findings of this controversial report.

Effective Schools

Ron Edmonds (1935–1983), a University of Michigan professor who later became the Director of the Center for Urban Studies at Harvard University, responded vigorously to Coleman's findings. Edmonds

(1979) and others refused to accept Coleman's report as conclusive. They acknowledged that family background does indeed make a difference, but they argued that it isn't the overriding factor. Edmonds and his colleagues set out to identify schools where kids from low-income families were highly successful, and thereby, prove that schools can and do make a difference (as cited in Lezotte & McKee, 2006).

Edmonds (1979) and other researchers looked at achievement data from schools in several major cities—schools where student populations were comprised of those from poverty backgrounds. Nationwide, they found schools where poor children were learning. Though these findings contradicted Coleman's conclusion, Edmonds and Brookover were left without an answer as to why certain schools made a difference and others did not (Brookover et al., 1982; Comer, 1989).

To answer this puzzling question, successful schools were compared with similar schools in like neighborhoods where children were not learning or learning at a low level. Characteristics describing both types of schools were observed and documented. This comparative research study found unique characteristics and processes common to schools where all children were learning, regardless of family background. These characteristics correlated with student success, thus, they were called "correlates." This body of correlated information began what is now referred to as the seven correlates of effective schools research.

The Seven Correlates of Effective Schools Research

1. Strong instructional leadership

2. Clear and focused mission

3. Safe and orderly environment

4. Climate of high expectations for student success

5. Frequent monitoring of student progress

6. Opportunity to learn and student time on task

7. Positive home-school relations

The Importance of the Coleman Report and Effective Schools Research

Leading effective schools spokesperson Larry Lezotte (1997) defines an effective school as one in which all the students learn the specified curriculum regardless of factors in their backgrounds, which ordinarily have been identified as those that prevent such learning. In other words, the effective schools premise is that a school's personnel can control enough of the variables to allow all students to be successful. Just knowing they do indeed make a difference blunts arrested teacher development.

The Coleman report slapped educators in the face when it elevated home environment and student background and alleged that teachers and schools didn't have much impact. Reacting to this affront, effective schools researchers provided solid evidence that schools had the capacity to dramatically affect the learning of students who lacked a school friendly home environment. The school factors identified as impacting student success have become ingrained into the culture of successful schools. Now, almost 50 years later, the effective schools correlates still serve as benchmarks for curriculum development and renewal and overall school improvement.

Building Block 2: Continuous Improvement

Educators are generally familiar with some aspect of a continuous improvement process. Continuous improvement is rooted in systems thinking popularized by Peter Senge. Senge's works, most notably *The Fifth Discipline* (1990) and *Schools That Learn* (Senge et al., 2000) influenced much of the current reform in business and in schools. Senge looked at schools as learning organizations with a compilation of systems that affect one another. According to Senge (1990), learning organizations employ five core disciplines: (1) systems thinking, (2) personal mastery, (3) mental models, (4) building shared vision, and (5) team learning. In learning organizations, people expand their capacity to create desired results, nurture new and expansive thinking patterns, embrace collaboration, and continually learn to see the whole together.

The continuous improvement process grew in part out of Senge's (1990) work, and today, successful school principals approach their curriculum development and renewal processes from the perspective of continuous improvement. In schools, the continuous improvement model most often follows a cycle that includes collecting data and completing a needs assessment, setting goals and objectives, choosing strategies and activities, implementing a plan, providing professional learning activities needed to carry out the plan, and conducting assessments that provide the data for the next cycle of improvement (Sorenson & Goldsmith, 2006). Think back to the section in Chapter 3 titled Expectation 3: Quality Analysis. Schools driven by continuous improvement are always looking for ways to reach higher levels of achievement for students and teachers.

The Importance of Continuous Improvement

Succinctly stated, continuous improvement means we will never arrive; we will never have it just right. The adaptive changes and complexities in schools today require the continuous improvement mindset. Continuous improvement grants beginning and growing teachers permission to admit they do not know everything when they start teaching. Principals who honor this reality and foster continuous improvement suppress arrested teacher development.

ROBERTA'S JOURNEY, PART II

Principal Will Wonkermann thought again about Roberta and all the systems she had been a part of. By the time she got to Childers School, she had taught in several schools in three different states. Principal Wonkermann also thought about the happenstance way in which Roberta had been mentored. He resolved again to initiate a system at Childers School to provide a safety net for novice teachers. Will was reminded of the rest of Roberta's story.

Roberta's husband graduated and Roberta didn't teach again for 10 years. When her youngest child was in kindergarten, Roberta had an unexpected opportunity to teach fifth grade in the school her children attended. Mary Jean, the other fifth grade teacher, was friendly, encouraging, and thought they'd make a good team. Roberta volunteered at the school all the time anyway, so she decided she might as well get paid.

Mary Jean was a master teacher, and her room was right next door. Roberta knew she could adapt what Mary Jean did, but she also felt the freedom to develop her own style. Mary Jean and Roberta planned together. They looked at student scores and teaching strategies and developed some common assessments to see how the students were progressing. Occasionally, they combined classes and divided students into different learning groups to focus on specific skills and needs. Roberta found she had more to offer than she realized. Some of those concepts that she had learned in that premier university resurfaced.

Mary Jean openly shared her ideas, remaining nonjudgmental and supportive. The absence of fear allowed Roberta to grow. Roberta later realized God put her with Mary Jean. Their learning community of two changed Roberta's life. She absolutely loved that experience and those kids.

Building Block 3: Collaboration Teams

Roberta's metamorphosis into a mature teacher able to navigate the complexities of teaching began when she became part of a collaborative team. She experienced the synergy that comes when professionals work together to solve problems and create solutions.

The Teaming Process and Shared Decision Making

Since the mid-1980s, various businesses and industries have shifted to include a variety of team-based approaches. Former University of Maine professor Tom Feinberg (n.d.) gives the following insight from a business perspective in his article, "Team Based Organizations":

> Some school systems permit only principals to lead. In such systems, the employees are not involved in decision-making and problem-solving processes. In fact, in these school systems, the principal is responsible for researching and evaluating data and information in order to make decisions and solve problems that affect the school's future. Effective site-based school systems initiate a team-oriented approach that permits principals to empower their employees and therefore promote a collaborative decision-making and problem-solving process. Site-based or team-oriented schools are successful as all parties are involved. The result is a stronger principal-teacher relationship whereby school goals are achieved. If teaming is to work, people must feel they have meaningful input that is seriously considered and appreciated.

Effective principals recognize the need for collaboration. They understand that collaboration in planning instruction thwarts arrested teacher development. Barth (2001) believes in the value of a team-based approach in school organizations. A strong proponent of teacher leadership and a collective effort, he writes, "All restructuring efforts I know are based on the assumption that serious change will come only from a collective effort—for example, a school team, a school improvement council—that stimulates, envisions, observes, plans, implements, and monitors change" (p. 178).

Building Block 4: Creating Community

Building on effective schools correlates and the cycle of continuous improvement, professional learning community concepts add important pieces to the process of teacher growth and development.

A fundamental professional learning community assumption states that the key to improved learning for students is continuous job-embedded learning for educators (DuFour, DuFour, Eaker, & Many, 2008). Six basic characteristics define the professional learning community (DuFour, DuFour, & Eaker, 2009):

1. *Shared mission, vision, values, and goals focused on student learning.* Principals and teachers in a professional learning community know why they are teaching, and they have a plan and a strategy to help students learn.

2. *A collaborative culture focused on learning.* Principals and teachers work together and are singularly focused on student learning. They have perfected the skills of teamwork and developed roles and protocols fitting their learning environment.

3. *Collective inquiry into best practice and current reality.* Principals and teachers seek new information and evaluate it against the reality of their campuses. They work together to find new strategies that can be adapted to campus needs.

4. *Action orientation: Learning by doing.* Principals and teachers in a professional learning community are not afraid to try new strategies. They are not afraid to take risks.

5. *Commitment to continuous improvement.* Principals and teachers know that they are involved in an ongoing cyclical process.

6. *Results orientation.* Principals and teachers recognize student success is the evaluation tool for all campus efforts.

In general, schools know their stated purpose—to educate students. Some, however, lack direction and follow through with timelines and targets. The ability to move faculty toward continuous academic improvement is an essential skill for campus curriculum leadership.

Working and Learning Together

The practices and structures highlighted in this chapter do not always go by the name "learning communities," but they do align with the practices of learning organizations. It doesn't matter what we call them, but it is important to know the essential elements. Professional learning community concepts have been around a long time. In many schools, meaningful collaboration takes place every day.

Numerous research studies present a compelling argument for the merits and effectiveness of this organizational structure. More than 10 years of research cites the importance of professional learning practices as a key to sustained, substantive school improvement (Darling-Hammond, 2001; Fullan, 2005; McLaughlin & Talbert, 2001; Newmann & Associates, 1996; Reeves, 2006; Saphier, 2005; Schmoker, 2006; Sparks, 2005).

Practices associated with PLCs have been endorsed by the National Staff Development Council, the National Association of Secondary School Principals, the National Association of Elementary School Principals, the National Commission on Teaching and America's Future, the National Board of Professional Teaching Standards, the National Council of Teachers of Mathematics, the National Council of Teachers of English, the National Science Teachers Association. The list goes on and on. Nearly every professional organization champions the PLC. All present compelling arguments are in favor of this concept (DuFour et al., 2008). Study after study recounts benefits for educators and students including the following:

- Reduction of isolation of teachers
- Shared responsibility for student development and success
- More satisfaction and higher morale
- Decreased dropout rates
- Lower rates of absenteeism
- Larger academic gains in math, science, history, and reading
- Smaller achievement gaps between students from different backgrounds

Developing a campus learning community requires more than mental assent. Teachers and principals have proven repeatedly that they are not afraid of difficult tasks, but such tasks are not only challenging, they are often a different kind of work. The current menu of schooling available to the American public calls for changes to address the challenges that students present today.

Building Block 5: Closing the Gap

If we want to do more than survive, if we want our children to excel and thrive, we must address what Heifetz (1994) calls the adaptive challenge: "a gap between the shared values people hold and the reality of their lives, or a conflict among people in a community over values or strategy" (p. 254). Adaptive challenges abound in schools and adaptive challenges are solved through innovation, learning, and developing a capacity for tackling an ongoing stream of hard problems. Marzano and Waters (2009) recognize these adaptive challenges referring to "first order" and "second order" change. First-order change is incremental and straightforward to what a school needs to do next. Second-order change is not incremental. It requires a substantially different approach in defining and resolving a problem. No matter which terminology is used, solving some problems requires seismic directional shifts and new ways of thinking and acting. This is not rearranging furniture; this is remodeling the whole house. It is no wonder principals and other school personnel are grappling with ways to work effectively together.

Consider the adaptive challenge posed by the following statistic from the National Center for Children in Poverty:

> Nearly 13 million American children live in families with incomes below the federal poverty level, which is $20,650 a year for a family of four. The number of children living in poverty increased by 11 percent between 2000 and 2006. There are 1.2 million more children living in poverty today than in 2000. Not only are these numbers troubling, the official poverty measure tells only part of the story. (Fass & Cauthen, 2006, para. 1)

Impoverished situations . . . language issues . . . learning differences. Clearly, schooling today is not for the faint of heart. Needs and challenges abound. As curriculum leader, what's a principal to do? Rather than just biding time, savvy curriculum leaders find ways to address adaptive challenges and create learning environments that reflect the 21st century rather than the 19th. These structures and processes do not have to cost a lot of money, but they take a heartfelt commitment and a willingness to go the distance when the implementation dip sets in. Educators have the knowledge base. Hidden beneath bureaucratic formulas and designs, in their heart of hearts, teachers and principals know what leads to better results. Teachers and principals who can answer, "Do we have the courage and perseverance to follow through?" with a resounding "Yes!" are free from arrested teacher development.

Building Block 6: A Learning Culture for All

A school culture based on shared decision making, collaboration, and trust drives this process (Sorenson & Goldsmith, 2006). Numerous texts and much worthwhile literature address these areas. Suffice it to say, the principal drives the school culture. When principals are in the trenches collaborating with teachers, the more power they give away the more power and influence they gain. This is counterintuitive. The concept of the more power given away, the more power gained is hard for many leaders to accept. A quote commonly attributed to sixth-century philosopher Lao Tzu, gets to the heart of this message. "A leader is best when people barely know he exists, when his work is done, his aim fulfilled, they will say: we did it ourselves" (ThinkExist.com Quotations, 2010). Working successfully with teachers involves developing personal skills and relationships that form a basis of trust and respect between the teachers and administrators. Indeed, positive relationships are the bedrock of any school improvement and increased student achievement (Sorenson & Goldsmith, 2009).

Recall the discussion of loosely coupled organizations in Chapter 1. Because schools are loosely coupled with teachers unsupervised approximately 99% of the time, principals and others in curriculum leadership cannot force needed changes. They must unearth knowledge, will, and skill leading the teachers to say, "We did it ourselves," as revealed in Chapter 5. Principals are challenged to build working relationships that instill commitment and effort when no one is watching. No outside source can chart this course or do this work. This work can only be done collectively by those who serve a particular set of students in a particular time and place. As was addressed through the deliberative model and process in Chapter 5, curriculum leaders lead the way, but they cannot do the learning for the teachers. Learning must be done together. By creating systems that promote growth and, most important, by participating in learning with teachers, principals model the lifelong learning necessary to address adaptive challenges. Effective leaders ask questions, guide discussions, delegate tasks, communicate with all parties, encourage innovations, and are willing risk takers.

Building Block 7: No Status Quo

DuFour and colleagues (2008) attest that educators already know how to improve schools and districts but that school leaders have "lacked the resolve to do what is necessary to convert their organizations into professional learning communities" (p. 79). Principals and prospective principals must possess the will and skill needed to lead deep cultural shifts that must occur in the school improvement process. The status quo or business as usual will continue to produce mediocre results and less-than-optimal student achievement and faculty satisfaction.

What sets the professional learning agenda apart from other programs and flavor of the month initiatives? Why should educators invest their time and energy and risk their professional reputations to transform their schools into a community of learners? Isn't this just another educational fad that is here today and gone tomorrow? Schmoker (2005) asserts that learning communities "may represent the richest, most unprecedented culmination of the best we know about authentic school improvement" (p. 136). Newmann, King, and Youngs (2000) remind us that effective schools develop the collective capacity of the full staff to improve achievement through the following:

- Developing teachers' skills
- Improving the quality of interaction among staff
- Achieving a coherent focus
- Mobilizing resources
- Developing school leadership

Schools serious about learning engage in disciplined inquiry and deliberative processes that promote continuous curricular and instructional improvement. Teaming efforts go far beyond congeniality and pleasant working relationships, although these are frequent benefits. These efforts tackle adaptive work that will raise the bar and close the achievement gap.

Building Block 8: Buy-In

How many times has the question, "Will teachers really buy-in to this?" been asked? Buy-in begins when a core number of faculty unite solidly behind a course of study, an innovation, a project—whatever it is—and are convinced that this cause will benefit the students in their classrooms. Establishing buy-in can come in several ways. Read Will Wonkermann's firsthand account of how he established buy-in for professional development at Childers School.

PROFESSIONAL DEVELOPMENT CONFESSIONS OF WILL WONKERMANN

I have some professional development battle scars. First, I must confess as a teacher I used professional development days as R&R. As a rookie principal, I used the same helter-skelter approach for professional development on my campus.

But somewhere along the way, I saw the potential of productive professional learning and my perspective on professional development changed. I realized that professional learning should be connected to the campus improvement plan, so I no longer approved any professional development unless it could be directly tied to the plan. No exceptions.

Next, I required people to attend professional development in groups. I stopped allowing just one person to attend a session. When teachers attended professional development sessions alone, I found they would come back excited but no one else shared the excitement. Eventually, the enthusiasm waned and no change occurred. Seldom would fewer than three teachers be permitted to attend a professional development session.

The third requirement got personal. I started attending professional development related to campus-wide initiatives. One summer, the local education service center was offering a 10-day training session on math manipulatives. The campus site-base planning committee reviewed the training and decided all math teachers would be encouraged to attend. I agreed to attend as well. Since this was summer, attendance could not be required, but enthusiasm for the training caused almost all of the math teachers to attend. Earlier that summer, we'd come across Walker's (1971) deliberative model of curriculum development, and the teachers and I used it to help with curriculum planning. The campus site-based planning committee agreed that those who received the training would receive the necessary manipulatives to implement the program in the following year. As a principal, I gave major authority to the campus site-based planning committee in developing the school budget. This leadership philosophy greatly increased teacher buy-in. The program was implemented and influenced instruction, assessment, and achievement.

I've got one more war story. That same summer a majority of my teachers volunteered to attend a five-day training session on cooperative learning led by Roger Johnson, a major player in cooperative learning. The local education service center funded the training for us. While the teachers received the teacher version of this training, I attended the principal version.

This professional development combined with the math training had us spending 15 days in professional development in the summer! We grew closer together as an instructional team—an unintended consequence. Yes, we did the obligatory griping about how we were working all summer, but when fall came, this professional development strongly impacted instruction on our campus; plus, as a team, we had grown more collegial and collaborative.

Professional development can work for you as the curriculum leader. It can work for your school too, but only if it is planned, meaningful, and not done in isolation.

Teachers must believe in the endeavor, and they must have time together to process how it will be implemented on the campus. What will it look like in an Algebra I class? What form will this take in language arts? How will it work in third grade? A critical number of teachers must buy-in to the validity of the effort. They must be willing to be inconvenienced and to risk themselves as teachers. Most teachers are emotionally connected and deeply invested in their work with students. Recall from Chapter 4 that stepping out to try a new innovation involves change and emotional risk. Any initiative has the potential to negatively affect student achievement. Teachers must be convinced that this endeavor merits the risk and has long-term potential. Educational fads and pendulum swings foster a cycle of nonproductivity.

The principal as curriculum leader must be aware of the current research and best practices relating to a school's needs. Through ongoing needs assessment and a cycle of continuous improvement, target areas will surface. Listen carefully to what the teachers say. What are their concerns? What problems do they note? What are their issues with discipline? What are their concerns with low math scores? As curriculum leader, you—the principal—may not have the answers. You can, however, find the answers by listening and analyzing. Consider the Sticks and Stones scenario in Chapter 7. Through your example and interest, you heighten sensitivity so that everyone is looking and investigating, searching for ways to improve the quality of teaching and learning.

The curriculum leader primes the pump with articles, research findings, stories, campus visits, and whatever means are available. In short, become an instructional resource for the teachers. Whet their appetite and wait to see what happens. Give ideas time to germinate. Many effective initiatives are cast aside because they were not given time to germinate and grow. Teachers must take ownership and run with the initiative, otherwise it will become yet another flavor of the month.

Perhaps a favorite saying of a former colleague is appropriate here: "You can lead a horse to water, but you can't make him drink. You can, however, run him hard and salt his oats." The principal's role is to salt the oats and whet the appetite. This requires investing time with the teachers and getting to know them as people. This is accomplished by working collaboratively with faculty on curricular and other instructional projects, supporting one another's efforts. This give-and-take grows trust. Principals salt oats with rich experiences aligned to the campus improvement plan and the campus needs. They salt oats when they demonstrate care and concern or when they develop positive relationships and visit classrooms. Oats are salted when faculty are perceived as hardworking people with families, financial concerns, and day-care issues. Principals know who is caring for an elderly parent or is going through a divorce. They listen and show by their actions that they value the people who work in their buildings. There are countless ways to salt oats, and fortunately, most of them don't cost a dime. Step back and allow teachers to take the lead. Continue to salt oats by finding time for meaningful collaboration, which, according to Hargreaves and Shirley (2009), is the spirit of the professional learning community. A professional learning community is, in essence, a learning/teaching environment where principals develop responsible and qualified teachers who strongly desire to work together as a curriculum team in a culture of discovery, revitalization, renewal, and continual improvement. Arrested teacher development cannot exist is such a community.

Building Block 9: Making Time, Not Doing Time

The authors have collectively spent more than a hundred years in education and have heard hundreds of times, "There isn't time." We've used it ourselves. One reason there isn't enough time is that a large portion of the general public in the United States believes that teachers who are not in the classroom directly working with students are not working. In fact, if truth be told, a number of principals and superintendents don't want teachers out of the classroom either. Neither do parents. Add to that the abysmal state of much of what is called professional development and the fact that most teachers would rather be working with their students, and you can see why collaborative teaming and time spent working with other adults at the campus level is not a priority item.

Teachers need to be primarily working with students. Students should be at the top of the hierarchy as advocated in Chapter 1. Schools purportedly exist to serve their needs. But how are students best served? How important is structured collaborative planning time for teachers? Most industrialized countries consider planning time a critical part of a teacher's schedule and allot time accordingly. The United States ranks lowest among all industrialized nations in the portion of work time reserved for class preparation. While countries like Korea, Japan, and Germany reserve up to 50% of a teacher's work hours to prepare for classes and collaborate with colleagues, U.S. teachers have fewer than 20% of their work hours dedicated to such essential tasks (Organization for Economic Cooperation and Development, 2009).

According to the National Staff Development Council's 2009 report, *Professional Learning in the Learning Profession: A Status Report on Teacher Development in the United States and Abroad* (Wei, Darling-Hammond, Andree, Richardson, & Orphanos, 2009), teachers in the United States spend about 80% of their working time teaching in the classroom versus about 60% for most other industrialized nations. Teachers in the United States average 3 to 5 hours a week in lesson planning sessions versus 15 to 20 hours a week in Europe and in Asia. Considerable research shows that students in classrooms where their teachers have ample opportunity to work with fellow teachers perform better (Von Frank, 2009; DuFour, DuFour, Eaker, & Many 2009). Likewise, the Education Trust's 2005 publication (Robinson, Stempel, & McCree, 2005), *Gaining Traction, Gaining Ground*, shares results and strategies from "high impact" high schools. Although these schools were not among the highest performing schools, they did show greater-than-expected gains with previously underperforming students. These schools had varied practices and strategies for improving achievement for at-risk students, but several commonalities emerged including teacher collaboration to ensure the consistency of course content no matter who delivered it.

How to Find Time

The need for collaboration time for teachers, time that is well spent and profitably used, is undisputed. How can curriculum leaders provide this time without compromising student time on task? Devising a schedule that allows colleagues to learn with one another is not easy, and it must be tailored to the school, district, and community. Raywid (1993) identified many schools throughout the country experimenting with creative ways to make time for planning and shared reflection. Her *Educational Leadership* article "Finding Time for Collaboration" lists successful practices unique to individual schools. They include the following:

- Common lunch periods followed by common preparation periods.
- Student engagement in community service projects while teachers plan.
- Increasing class size by just one or two students, yielding a surplus sufficient to finance teams of substitutes used to cover classes on a regular basis, permitting teacher teams to meet frequently.
- Adopting a year-round calendar, with three-week intersessions between quarters, permitting concentrated, two- or three-day meetings for teacher planning, for which participants receive compensatory time.

- Lengthening the school day by 20 minutes for four days to dismiss students at noon on the fifth day. Persuade local churches, scout troops, and other youth activities to meet on early release days. Assign a small group of faculty to supervise (on a rotating basis) the youngsters of working parents unable to make other arrangements.

This list provides examples of what others are doing or have done. There are many alternatives to the time issue if we think creatively. Don't have any good answers? Ask the teachers. Let this become a collaborative project. Here's how the teachers at Childers School found some time.

CHILDERS SCHOOL'S WACKY DAYS

The teachers at Childers School recognized the power of collaborative planning. It had grown out of Walker's (1971) deliberative model of curriculum development introduced a couple of summers ago by Principal Will Wonkermann. They also knew that resources were tight and there was no extra money. The busy schedule and the community culture would not allow for early release days. The parents in their working-class community depended on the regularity of school hours. Mothers and fathers working several jobs wouldn't take kindly to students being released early on a regular basis.

The teachers at Childers School put their heads together and devised a plan. With the help of the specials teachers (physical education, music, the librarian, and the counselor) and with the blessing of their principal, they created *Wacky Days*—an enrichment program that benefited their students and provided them with collaboration time.

Friday afternoons were designated as Wacky Days. During Wacky Days, the specials teachers combined to teach all students on a rotating basis. The students engaged in activities planned and supervised by the specials staff while the other teachers had uninterrupted planning time. During Wacky Days, students enjoyed presentations on bicycle safety, fire safety, and visits from local community celebrities. They learned about all sorts of interesting topics from pet care and weather forecasting to nutrition and gardening. The high school became involved, and the football team came to sign autographs and read with the students. Sometimes high school students who were interested in teaching careers came to work Wacky Days as an internship. Students and teachers benefited from Wacky Days because of careful planning. Everyone helped plan and schedule the Wacky Days activities. Sometimes parents shared a favorite skill and community members appreciated having an additional way to support the school. After several years, there was a long list of potential programs. Wacky Days had become an integral part of the Childers School culture.

Educators are only limited by their imaginations. When people want something badly enough, they will find ways to make it happen. The principal is either a facilitator or a roadblock. Which are you? A variation of the Wacky Days example noted in the previous scenario was incorporated by each of the authors into their schools, to some degree during their tenures as school principals. Whatever the name, Wacky Days can effectively benefit any instructional program.

A fundamental premise in team leadership requires people closest to the problem to solve the problem. The teachers on your campus have good ideas. If the teachers believe that finding time is a priority, they will find time to form a team. Gain buy-in from community members, and enlist central office support.

Building Block 10: Effective Planning

In some ways, Building Block 10 is the most important of all. The old adage, "failing to plan is planning to fail" holds true for life in general, and schools are no exception. Effective planning buys time, prepares leaders and teams to meet adaptive challenges, allows everyone to collaborate, and encourages trust. A hallmark of continuous improvement and effective schools, planning enriches a school's culture and promotes teacher buy-in. Most people, young and old alike, do better with the structure, security, and predictability of an environment that planning provides.

TEAM PLANNING AT CHILDERS SCHOOL
Roberta's Journey, Part III

The principal of Childers School, Will Wonkermann, had learned a lot since his beginning days as school leader. He was now more of a true curriculum leader, who believed in and practiced team leadership. Will knew he wasn't well versed in the entire curriculum. He admired and respected the Childers teachers and expected them to build the curriculum that would meet student needs. He had learned how to feed the teachers so they wouldn't eat the students (Connors, 2000), and he knew to let the teachers discover new concepts and learning designs so they felt they did it themselves.

When school started in the fall, the school district devoted one day to a general districtwide meeting. Usually, there was a motivational speaker, a message from the superintendent, and a chance to catch up with colleagues who taught on other campuses. Although large group in-service like this isn't deemed effective for actually learning new skills that benefit students, it is useful for building esprit de corps throughout a district.

The second in-service day, faculty and staff reported to individual campuses. The morning at Childers School consisted of a general campus meeting where Principal Wonkermann went over campus procedures, new policies and regulations, and introduced new faculty. This information was important, but most of the teachers were thinking about room preparation and getting ready for their students.

Although it was fun to see friends from other campuses and catch up with teachers in other disciplines, these activities did little to improve teaching or prepare teachers for the year to come.

By the afternoon of the second day, teachers were released to "work in rooms." This is when Roberta's official work began. As department chair, Roberta Ayala served as a liaison between administration and the department and assured good instruction was occurring in each class. Roberta did not have an official administrative role, but she assisted teachers who were having problems with academic or classroom management. Roberta was the language arts department's instructional leader. Principal Wonkermann realized he should leave Roberta and her department alone, and they would get the job done. The students consistently performed well on state academic exams and excelled in post high school settings. Although the teachers didn't win with every student, they did with the vast majority.

The department was strong. The teachers were competent and a planning process ensured everyone was prepared and pointed in the right direction. The planning process supported teachers new to the campus or new to teaching. No one was allowed to fly solo. Time was scheduled for each teaching team to meet at least once each grading period. This time was set aside to plan, develop teaching practices, and discuss student work. The carefully constructed curriculum had been developed by the teachers and administrative team collaboratively over time. Using the state learning outcomes and planning backward, the teaching teams ensured they taught the mandated objectives before test time. Benchmark formative assessments identified student instructional needs and intervention strategies provided assistance for students who needed extra reinforcement. Principal Wonkermann had led the teachers to expand the curriculum beyond test-prep and the national and state standards. New research-based practices and innovative instructional programs were initiated.

Each teaching team developed a planning calendar for the academic year. This document served as a broad outline and sequentially ordered the learning outcomes. This planning process provided a way to use limited resources efficiently. More important, it bonded the teachers together as an instructional team with an agenda and an academic road map.

The Childers School planning process is simple, but it requires organization and team effort. If students are assessed over concepts they are never taught, the faculty should not be surprised when students do not excel. As was previously noted in Chapter 5, a thoughtfully structured planning process avoids this predicament. Learning to plan together is a new skill for teachers who have operated in isolation. Team-building skills, meeting agendas, and guidelines help teachers make the most of their time together. These processes guide and structure time and indirectly teach collaborative skills. Begin in small ways to build a culture of trust and consideration on your campus. If a schedule cannot be developed where all departments/ grade levels have a common planning period, try to arrange for pairs of teachers who teach the same subject/grade level to have a common planning time. Finding common planning time is the first step.

Much of our world today emphasizes and expects teamwork. The model of schooling set up in the 1800s works against these efforts. It's not only that people are resistant to change and lapse into comfortable routines but the system of schooling itself inhibits collaboration. Many teachers have never been expected to work together, and they don't know how to do it. In a classroom with students, teachers need to set the tone and be in charge. Effective classroom skills are not always effective collaboration skills. Bringing an effective classroom management skill set into the teaming process can lead to miscommunication and diminished productivity. When teachers are brought together to collaborate, communication can quickly turn into a gripe session. Team building and trust activities lay a necessary foundation for working smarter.

Although current research and best practice indicates that a school organized into a collaborative professional learning community is more likely to provide a productive environment conducive to student achievement, the system of schooling predominant throughout the United States continues to work against this process. Sometimes the unspoken message is teachers are not working if they are not in classrooms with the students! Some teachers themselves feel this way, and most teachers prefer to be in their classrooms working with students. Our whole system has not fostered the idea of professional growth or continuous learning together as a part of the teacher's commitment to the students.

The principal, as curriculum leader, helps teachers experience a sense of satisfaction and meaning from working together to solve issues and create better learning for all. The level of skills required for students to succeed in society today demands this, and no one teacher alone has enough resources, time, or expertise to provide all that today's students need. The principal must instill in teachers the importance of their own learning. Barth (2001) reminds us that it is not whether our faculty and staff can learn but it is what conditions are required so they can learn. Students will develop only when our schools support adult development.

Collaborative problem solving is an integral part of the teacher's responsibility to students. Although many in the business world view continual learning as a necessary part of the job, many in education show by their actions that they have yet to embrace this idea. Sometimes, any attempt to create a professional learning community is met with passive, if not active, resistance.

Principals must identify what matters most professionally to their teachers and build on it. This is the first step toward becoming a professional learning community. Often the best way to find out what matters is to ask, but don't ask unless you are prepared to act in some way on what you find.

Final Thoughts

A school leader, renowned for his expertise and his ability to bring out the best in students and teachers, was asked how he managed to get so much out of students and teachers. His response was, "I find out what the teachers need, and I give it to them." By this he meant that he knew the teachers well enough to know what would motivate each one, and he used that to lead them to accomplish more than they could have ever thought possible in their difficult school situation.

Each principal must approach this in his or her way. Many teachers and many principals do not know how to collaborate because this has never been a required skill set. The need to be in charge and to be the disciplinarian in the classroom or school requires a set of skills that works against collaboration with peers. No collaboration fosters limited curriculum development and renewal.

Building a relationship of trust and understanding is difficult especially if teachers and principals are entrenched in "the way we've always done it." Veteran faculty is often skeptical of new administration or new ideas. Do everything possible to create a no-fear, risk-free environment that promotes professional collaboration and meaningful discussion. Learning is depending on it.

Discussion Questions

1. Roberta's journey was shared in three parts. How can the teachers at Roberta's school help prevent Roberta from developing a case of arrested teacher development? How can the principals at Roberta's school help prevent Roberta from developing a case of arrested teacher development?

2. The PLC characteristics were considered in Building Block 4: Creating Community. Using the planning tool provided next, rate your school on each of the six PLC characteristics. Provide an explanation for your rating.

PLC Characteristic	Evidence/ Explanation	Rating			
		Not Observed	Emerging	Developing	Advanced
1. Shared Mission					
2. Collaborative Culture					
3. Collective Inquiry					
4. Action Orientation					
5. Commitment to Continuous Improvement					
6. Results Orientation					

How does an effective campus planning process promote growth as a professional learning community?

3. Which of the 10 Building Blocks would you employ first on your campus to build relationships with teachers? Defend your choice.

4. Now that you have identified the building block you would first employ to build relationships with teachers, identify three more Building Blocks that would be the most beneficial in your situation to build relationships with teachers. Defend your choices.

5. Where you do see overlaps between effective schools research, systems thinking and continuous improvement, and professional learning community concepts?

Roaring Plains Public Schools

Zachary School is located in the city of Roaring Plains, a suburban community of 80,000. Roaring Plains was once the suburb for young upwardly mobile families. Fifty years ago, the sleepy village of Roaring Plains became almost overnight a thriving suburb of Port City. Subdivisions were aggressively developed. Most people who moved to Roaring Plains commuted to work in Port City. During its zenith, Roaring Plains Public Schools (RPPS) opened a new school nearly every year. Enrollment was climbing and so was revenue. All the new buildings were state of the art—that is for 50 years ago. In fact, RPPS was a major reason families moved to Roaring Plains. Not only did RPPS have a perceived superior academic program, it also had strong cocurricular and extra-curricular programs. The Roaring Plains Lion Stadium and its amenities were the envy of the state as was the football team's winning tradition. The district's fine arts program was superior, and the music program was unusually strong for a district of its size. The district excelled in athletic and fine arts competitions and received many state awards.

But 50 years later, things have changed in Roaring Plains. Roaring Plains has seen better days. Its population has remained somewhat constant at 80,000, but the demographics of the population have changed significantly. The upwardly mobile working professionals have, for the most part, left for newer suburbs. As they moved out, blue-collar families and the working poor have moved in. At one time, only 4% of the students in RPPS qualified for free or reduced lunch. Today 89% qualify.

The racial composition of the school system has also changed. In the 1960s, RPPS was 85% Anglo, 3% African American, 8% Hispanic, and 4% other groups. Today, RPPS is 38% Anglo, 26% African American, 30% Hispanic, and 6% Asian American.

Interestingly, most of the Asian American students are first-generation Americans. Also a significant percentage of the African American population is made of refugees from an assortment of African nations. French is the native tongue of many of these families. Of the Anglo population, about a fifth is also first generation, and many of them speak a Slavic language at home.

Walmart is the single national employer in the town. RPPS is the largest employer followed by the City of Roaring Plains. Abba Systems, a restaurant service provider, is a major employer as is Regional Hospital, Ward Correctional Center, and Salinas Food

(Continued)

(*Continued*)

Processing and Packaging. Most of the employment opportunities are with fast-food restaurants, aging motels, and small businesses such as Bubba's—a chain of convenience stores that populate the area.

The tax base for RPPS has eroded as the community continues its transformation from a premier suburb to an aging one. This process negatively impacts the local tax base and shrinks the number of dollars available to RPPS. The state funding formula for schools does not replace the lost local revenue. RPPS is forever seeking creative solutions to stretch the declining revenue. The problem is further complicated because many of the original buildings were built in the 1960s and need to be replaced or substantially remodeled.

Currently, a task force of local businesspersons, the Chamber of Commerce, county and city officials, and the Roaring Plains Economic Development Corporation (RPEDC) are collaborating with school officials and other community and parent groups to develop a recommendation for a major school bond proposal. The RPEDC, which uses a pool of local tax money to provide incentives for businesses to relocate to Roaring Plains, is days away from announcing the relocation of a firm to Roaring Plains that will guarantee 100 new well-paying jobs with a promise to add 300 additional positions over the following five years. This anticipated announcement coupled with a possible bond election is creating more excitement than the community has seen in years.

Zachary School

Zachary School was built in 1961 and named after a retired superintendent. The school's structure is the typical wing structure made popular in the 1950s and 1960s. When air-conditioning was added in 1973, the windows were covered to improve the heat and cooling factors. When the multipurpose room (gym) was constructed in 1993, the school's electric system was upgraded to handle a larger presence of technology. Although this upgrade was very helpful, the school needs additional wiring.

Zachary was built with little attention given to landscaping and little has been given to it since—with one exception. The only outside improvement is the marquee that was donated by the Devary family in memory of their daughter who was killed in a boating accident.

Nearly all of the housing around Zachary School is single-family three-bedroom homes. Some homes have been well maintained and evidence owner pride; others do not. A few aging apartment complexes with subsidized rent exist. The Roaring Plains Housing Authority constructed the Fairchild Apartments—known as the Projects in 1980.

Zachary School has had principals come and go. Many use Zachary as a way to get into administration and then leave at the first opportunity, a practice causing all aspects of Zachary to decline. Beginning teachers (fewer than 5 years experience) make up half of the faculty while the others are veterans with 15 or more years of experience. The faculty generally ignores these short-term principals.

Other facts about Zachary School:

- The PTA disbanded in 1999.

- Absenteeism for students is 50% higher than the district average.

- Personnel absenteeism is the lowest in the district.

- The secretary, Beth Larimore, has been at Zachary for 23 years. She is well liked and speaks fluent Spanish. She grew up in Venezuela, the daughter of American petroleum engineers.

- The campus planning committee meets three times a year. Customarily, the principal updates the campus plan and brings it to the committee in the spring to be adopted and then filed with the superintendent. A copy is kept in the principal's office should a teacher want to review it or discuss it with the principal. This seldom happens.

- The YMCA has expressed an interest in starting a program at the school for the last two years, but no one at the school has followed-up on this interest.

- Big State University received a $900,000 grant to develop a working relationship with a public school. The university expressed an interest in partnering with Zachary School, but the principal has been stalling. He is not sure how wise it is to have university students and faculty on the campus.

- Test scores are low.
- There are low expectations of students.

The Superintendent's Challenge

Last year, Dr. Sylvia Mendoza became RPPS's first female, minority superintendent. She has finished her first year at Roaring Plains and is gaining the support of even her staunchest critics. When the previous principal of Zachary School resigned, one of Dr. Mendoza's first tasks was to create a principal interview team, the first in Zachary's history to have input into the selection of the principal. The faculty, veteran and new alike, were surprised to get input in the hiring process and took

(*Continued*)

(*Continued*)

their assignment seriously. Congratulations! You are the new principal of Zachary. You were the first choice of Dr. Mendoza and the interview team. School starts in three weeks! Zachary is also the recipient of a $150,000 grant for the campus planning committee to use as they transform Zachary School into a professional learning community. Using strategies from the Ten Curriculum Leadership Blocks and additional resources at your disposal, develop a plan to turn Zachary School into a professional learning community. Include a rationale for the plan's implementation and how you would use each strategy.

Other Resources

Daggett, W. R. (2005, June). *Preparing students for their future*. Presented at Model Schools Conference, Washington, DC.

DuFour, R., Eaker, R., DuFour, R., & Karhanek, G. (2004). *Whatever it takes: How professional learning communities respond when kids don't learn*. Bloomington, IN: Solution Tree.

Erickson, L. H. (2007). *Concept-based curriculum and instruction for the thinking classroom*. Thousand Oaks, CA: Corwin.

Marzano, R., Pickering, D., & Pollock, J. (2001). *Classroom instruction that works: Research-based strategies for increasing student achievement*. Alexandria, VA: Association for Supervision and Curriculum Development (ASCD).

National Commission on Teaching and America's Future (2005). *Induction into learning communities*. Washington, DC: National Commission on Teaching and America's Future.

Nelson, D., & Low, G. (2003). *Emotional intelligence: Achieving academic and career excellence*. Upper Saddle River, NJ: Pearson Education.

Palmer, P. (2007). *The courage to teach: Exploring the inner landscape of a teacher's life* (10th Anniversary Edition). San Francisco: Jossey-Bass.

Schmuck, R. A. (2006). *Practical action research for change* (2nd ed.). Thousand Oaks, CA: Corwin.

7

Systematically Integrating Curriculum and Instruction

Even so, we were two tough cowpokes, out to see the countryside, and completely ignorant of the trouble that lay ahead.

—Alta Abernathy (1998, p. 27)

The Role and Vision of the Principal in Defining Curriculum and Instruction

The book *Bud & Me* presents a true story of two brothers who systematically crisscrossed the nation in the early days of the 20th century, integrating the use of horses, automobiles, and motorcycles, as they trekked from Frederick, Oklahoma, to Santa Fe, New Mexico; from Frederick, Oklahoma, on to New York City; and from New York City back to Frederick, Oklahoma. The boys accomplished such traveling feats at the ages of five and nine, without adult supervision! Much like the partnership of Bud and his brother Temple, curriculum and instruction are a unique combination, and when systematically integrated, where the two shall meet, only the visionary mind of an effective school principal can foresee.

The Curricular Role of Visionary Principals

Visionary principals are seldom ignorant of the trouble that lies ahead when it comes to integrating curriculum and instruction. Visionary principals clearly mark the curricular improvement and instructional excellence trail by avoiding the trials and tribulations that can easily throw the best of leaders off the beaten path to organizational success. Visionary principals identify and solve curricular problems that negatively affect instructional programs and student achievement. Visionary principals collaborate with members to systematically integrate curriculum and instruction. Visionary principals use direct and active leadership when integrating curriculum with instruction. Visionary principals assert a powerful presence in their schools through their choice of words and through the degree and quality of their actions. Visionary principals articulate how to develop effective school curriculum and then show how words must be put into action through the systematic integration of curriculum and instruction.

[Handwritten margin notes: ○ Identify, ○ collaborate, ○ use direct & active leadership, ○ assert powerful presence, ○ articulate]

Brown and Moffett (2002) surmise in *The Hero's Journey: How Educators Can Transform Schools and Improve Learning* that a visionary leader is one who guides, informs, and brings direction to a school. Visionary principals imbue decisions and practices with meaning, and they place powerful emphasis on reasons why curriculum must be integrated across the content areas. Visionary principals use orderly methods and purposeful approaches to get the job done. It was Lipsitz (1984) who suggested of visionary principals: Decisions can't simply be made for practical reasons; decisions must be made based on underlying principles.

In this chapter, we identify effective visionary principal practices as related to the integration of curriculum and instruction. We examine the curricular leadership principles and relevant research as related to integrating curriculum and instruction. Finally, step-by-step examples demonstrate how school principals can lead faculty in providing relevant, challenging, integrative, and exploratory curriculum and instruction.

What Is Curriculum?

In Chapter 4, curriculum was defined as *what* is taught in schools. Taking this definition a step further, let's examine the root meaning of the word "curriculum." The word curriculum, according to *The Oxford English*

> **Curriculum** is an educational process (a procedure, method, manner, or means—the "what" that is taught—a pedagogical course of action) by which the function (purpose) of schooling (teacher instruction, student learning) is set in motion.

Dictionary (Weiner & Simpson, 2009, p.114), is derived from the Latin word *currere,* loosely translated to mean "a current" or "to run as a current," much like a "current runs along the course of a waterway in a definite direction." Today, the Latin term could be interpreted to denote "to run the course of study" or "a series of study."

A review of the research literature reveals a continuously changing conception, if not definition, of the term "curriculum." To emphasize this point, Lunenburg and Irby (2006) defined curriculum as being a systematic integration of culture, programs, and instruction, all of which are connected by the needs of the community, the needs of the students, the needs of society, and the needs of the school as established in vision and mission statements. Walker and Soltis (1997) surmised that curriculum is the list of courses offered and taught as well as the purposes, content, and activities of the instructional program as created by members of the learning community. Ornstein and Hunkins (1998) state that curriculum is the central focus of a school. Curriculum integrates objectives, content, experiences, and evaluation. Finally, Miller and Seller (1990), some two decades ago, asserted that curriculum is an intentional integrative set of actions that promotes student learning and further initiates experiential activities by means of lesson content.

We believe curriculum is everything that has been previously defined, with one important caveat (whether we like it or not)—mandated accountability standards. Therefore, we define *curriculum* as an educational process by which the function of schooling is set in motion, according to local standards as well as state and national principles, dictates, and/or mandates.

What Is Instruction?

If curriculum is *what* is taught in schools, then instruction is *how* the *what* is taught in schools. Instruction is the strategies, techniques, materials, media, and place where the curriculum is taught. Allen Ornstein in his model of planning and developing the curriculum relates instruction is *how* curriculum is implemented within a school (Ornstein & Hunkins, 2009). Tomlinson and McTighe (2006) assert that instruction is multilayered. In other words, various types of instruction (see Table 7.1) must be integrated to meet the numerous "factors that students bring to school with them in almost stunning variety" (p. 1). Tomlinson and McTighe further stipulate "few teachers find their work effective or satisfying when they

> **Instruction** is *how* the *what* is taught in schools. Instruction can be defined as the strategies, techniques, materials, media, and place where the curriculum is implemented in schools.

simply 'serve up' a curriculum—even an elegant one—to their students with no regard for their varied learning needs" (p. 1). What are these "varied learning needs" that affect the instructional process?

Today, diverse students bring a variety of learning needs to the classroom. These needs can be attributed to diversity in ethnicities, cultures, languages, experiences, disabilities, motivation levels, interests, and support systems. Therefore, instructional techniques, methods, and strategies must be assorted in their approaches and differentiated in their applications. This poses another question: What is varied and differentiated instruction? The authors suggest that varied and differentiated instruction is based on instructional approaches defined as self-assessed, game centered, guideline based, question and answer centered, lecture dominated, cooperative or group based, text-only focused, graphically designed, audio formulated, kinesthetic developed, video presented, case-based interactive, podcast devised, computer generated, and self-directed studied (see Table 7.1). This list is not intended to be comprehensive.

Table 7.1   The Sorenson-Goldsmith Model of Varied and Differentiated Instruction: Designs Described and Defined

Types of Instruction	Instructional Approach Described and Defined
Self-assessed	*Self-assessed* instruction allows for a student to complete a comprehensive review of subject matter and then be self-assessed or tested relative to the knowledge acquired.
Game-centered	*Game-centered* instruction is presented in a game format. When questions are answered and choices are made, a student's score goes up or down. Students may compete against themselves or against other players or teams.
Guideline-based	*Guideline-based* instruction is centered on students describing and/or explaining a consensus statement or guideline, often generated from the textbook by the teacher or student.

Types of Instruction	Instructional Approach Described and Defined
Question-and-answer centered	*Question-and-answer centered* instruction simply provides students with a question or series of questions (frequently multiple choice) and then provides an immediate feedback answer or explanation of the correct and the incorrect choices with either brief or extended instruction about the topic consideration.
Lecture-dominated	*Lecture-dominated* instruction attempts to stimulate student interest and discussion via "the sage on stage" approach to learning. Students listen to the teacher's words, often presented in a PowerPoint format. The teacher can pause, go back, or extend forward the instruction as presented in the spoken word.
Cooperative-learned or group-based	*Cooperative-learned* instruction allows for learning from and using peers. Students work in groups, with their peers, in an effort to increase active responses and practice with immediate feedback. Peer or cooperative learning increases motivation, provides practice in social skills, increases social integration, and allows for risk taking in small groups minus the potential for large group embarrassment.
Text-only focused	*Text-only focused* instruction permits the student to read a periodical or book chapter or online print. It is a convenient, yet often overused, form of teacher instruction where students read and then answer end-of-chapter questions or teacher-generated queries.
Graphic/visually designed	*Graphic/visually designed* instruction, although similar to text-only learning, focuses on the student using charts, tables, drawings, photographs, and animated designs to better understand the subject matter presented.

(Continued)

Table 7.1   *(Continued)*

Types of Instruction	*Instructional Approach Described and Defined*
Audio-formulated	*Audio-formulated* instruction enables students to learn by hearing. Some students prefer to learn by hearing, others by seeing, and others by touching and doing.
Kinesthetic-developed	*Kinesthetic-developed* instruction increases student involvement, especially for those students who have difficulty sitting and listening. This instructional method increases student interest and motivation, provides opportunities for students to respond in nonverbal processes, and is often more project-centered than other instructional strategies.
Video-presented	*Video-presented* instruction permits learners to see or observe places and things to which they have never been exposed. For example, students can learn in reading or through lecture about the Grand Canyon and then actually observe the canyon via video presentation.
Case-based interactive	*Case-based interactive* instruction provides the learning with opportunities to apply or simulate previously received instruction. Such instruction is frequently presented through the application of case studies, as is noted within this text.
Computer-generated	*Computer-generated, online,* or *multimedia* instruction permits students to learn "anytime, anywhere" from organized knowledge banks, resources, and materials of specific training.
Podcast-devised	*Podcast-devised* instruction is provided through an audio file that can be played through a portable device like an iPod or an MP3 player. Much like computer-generated instruction, podcasts provide for very student-centered and technologically advanced methods of learning.

Types of Instruction	*Instructional Approach Described and Defined*
Self-directed studied	*Self-directed studied* instruction allows for students to read or review instruction during a specific time period. There are synchronous or asynchronous interactions between the student and the method of instructional delivery (i.e., computer, correspondence learning, and online instruction).

To exemplify varied and differentiated instruction, consider the following scenario. After reading the scenario, review and respond to the Pause and Consider questions.

FROM THE MORGUE TO THE CLASSROOM

Norma Garza sat at her desk in the newly designed science lab at Childers School. Norma loved her teaching assignment. As a biology teacher, she was finally getting an opportunity to apply certain aspects of her previous work experience to the instructional arena. Norma, until two years ago, had been a coroner's assistant in Juarez, Chihuahua. Her work in Mexico had been interesting and exciting, yet dangerous. She earned her teacher certification at Fort Rio Bravo State University while working nights for Ciudad de Juarez Despósito de Cadáveres. Her time to teach had arrived, and she was taking full advantage of the opportunity to apply her instructional love: biology and the associated medical implications. This evening, she was designing the instructional methods, techniques, and strategies to be incorporated in next week's lessons.

The subject matter centered on malignant melanoma, a cancer of potentially fatal consequences. She decided to focus her students on three types of skin cancer: (1) basal cell carcinoma, (2) squamous cell carcinoma, and (3) malignant melanoma. She wanted her students to examine the risk factors of malignant melanoma, including sun exposure, fair complexion, and family history. Additionally, she wanted her students to recognize how melanoma could be discovered in the human body via asymmetrical borders, color, and diameter.

To meet the lesson goals, Norma's lesson plans included behavioral objectives, activity descriptions, lesson rationale, needed materials, direct instructional methods, structured discovery, lesson applications, and lesson closure. Designing lesson plans was easy for Norma. The difficulty came when attempting to determine what types of

(Continued)

(Continued)

instructional delivery to incorporate. However, the challenge of the task was what Norma craved. This instructional process, in Norma's opinion, was what separated effective teachers from the ineffective ones.

Norma decided to open the lesson with a video presentation related to the three predetermined types of skin cancer. This presentation would be computer generated, streaming from an online Internet source. Following the video presentation, Norma would ask the students to get into cooperative learning groups where the students could generate a list of risk factors related to malignant melanoma.

Then, Norma would ask differing student groups to access online, via their laptop stations, various methods of detecting melanoma. The students would then develop PowerPoint or YouTube presentations showcasing how malignant melanoma could be detected. Other student groups would be asked to create a series of questions and answers centered on the subject matter. This instructional method would allow the students to self-assess their mastery of the subject.

Next, Norma would ask the students, as a method of structured discovery, to read Chapter 9: Cancer-Danger Points and Related Biological Issues. Norma would wrap up the lesson with a brief teacher lecture stressing key lesson points. The lesson would be further applied through an evening podcast that would provide the students with an audio file of key points allowing each student to be further self-assessed via a game-centered learning approach.

Norma concluded her lesson planning that evening with a personal thought: "I think these kids will really understand the lesson. This lesson effectively relates to the district science curriculum and the objectives tested on the state accountability exam!"

Pause and Consider

- Turn to Table 7.1 and place a checkmark next to the types of instruction incorporated by Norma Garza.

- Which other types of instruction could have been applied to the lesson planning process by Norma Garza? Why and for what reason(s)?

- Which of the types of instruction applied by Norma Garza would be less than effective when ensuring student mastery of the subject matter? Explain.

Integrating Curriculum and Instruction

Previously in this chapter, we defined curriculum and instruction. Now, let's consider how these two important aspects of the educational process are interrelated. How can curriculum and instruction be integrated? What purpose does the integration of curriculum and instruction serve? How can students benefit from the incorporation of curriculum and instruction?

To answer these questions, let's first return to the scenario involving Norma Garza, the biology teacher at Childers School.

CURRICULUM INTEGRATION, ARE YOU KIDDING ME?

Norma Garza arrived at school earlier than usual on the day she was to present the cancer-centered lesson she had developed for her biology students. It was a cold, damp, and dreary day—the kind of day that students loved to come into the school building, get into a warm classroom, and then doze off to the dreary drones of a boring teacher. Norma inwardly smiled and thought, "I don't think any of my students will be bored today! This lesson will keep them on their toes!"

After getting settled into her classroom, Norma began to work at the lab stations around the room. As she was setting up a particular aspect of her planned lesson, Marisa Negrete, science coordinator for the Childers School District, walked into the room and announced, "Buenos dias, Norma!" Norma looked up and said good morning in return to Marisa. Then, Marisa told Norma that she was on campus to observe several of the science teachers and wanted to begin her day with Norma. "I'm here to determine how you are integrating your lessons across the differing curriculums and content areas," noted Marisa. Inwardly, Norma panicked! She had designed a great lesson but thought nothing about the other subject areas. Nervously, she welcomed the science coordinator into her classroom but couldn't help but develop a sense of alarm, thinking, "Curriculum integration, are you kidding me? What am I suppose to do?"

As you may have surmised, the lesson went exceedingly well. The students were actively engaged. They were far from bored or desirous of a quick catnap. In fact, the students remained on task the entire class period and left the room with smiles on their faces, positively interacting with one another about their evening assignment. To say the least, Norma was pleased, as was the science coordinator.

Norma turned to Marisa: "How did I do?" Marisa noted that Norma did a great job and that the lesson was exceptional. "You should be really proud," said Marisa. "By the way, can you replicate the lesson next Thursday after school at our district gathering for secondary science teachers?" asked Marisa. "Sure," replied Norma. Then Marisa dropped a bombshell: "Norma, I want you to do some more work with your lesson before you present it next Thursday. Let's talk more in depth about curriculum integration." Norma then

(Continued)

(*Continued*)

asked, "What do I need to do about curriculum integration? I had a curriculum integration class my junior year at the university, but I vaguely recall the topic." Marisa replied, "Don't worry, Norma. We'll get started today during your conference period and after school if we need to." Norma smiled and then thought, "I can think of a lot of other things I'd rather do, but I want my lessons to improve. I surely don't want my lessons to become the same old boring stuff for my students!"

Later that morning, Norma and Marisa sat down in the lab and began a discussion relative to curriculum integration. Marisa suggested that they begin their conversation with a simple definition of the term. "Now, this is what I perceive curriculum integration to be," stated Marisa. "Curriculum integration occurs when teachers, working in collaboration with their principal, bring in content from one subject area while emphasizing skills and exploring concepts of another subject area. Thus, while teaching about melanoma cancer, you could provide examples of how physics, biology, and medical history in America correlate with one another. Curriculum specialist Allan Glatthorn (Glatthorn & Jailall, 2009) once described this process as correlative and informal curriculum integration." Norma thought aloud, "Integrated curriculum sounds like a great gift to effective teachers!" Marisa smiled and then thought to herself, "If only all teachers were as excited as Norma!"

"Now that we have defined curriculum integration," Marisa said, "let's put the definition to work!" Norma, looking somewhat bewildered, replied, "Okay, what's next?" Marisa said, "Well, let's begin with the basics—math, English, and social studies. How would you interweave or integrate biology into mathematics?" Norma quickly replied, "Oh, that's easy! I'd get in contact with James Fannin, the math department chairperson. He's easy to work with and I know we can weave my biology lesson into a trigonometry lesson related to algorithms. In cancer biology, human cancer cells can be correlated and hierarchically clustered with algorithms (Cohen, 2004). Our subject areas interact so well together!" Marisa responded enthusiastically and then asked about other subject areas.

"Well, English shouldn't be too difficult," said Norma. She continued: "Let me talk to Cullen Place. Ms. Place is the English department chairperson. I think Cullen and I could develop a writing assignment that would effectively incorporate the two curriculums! I'm thinking, off the top of my head, about a cute and witty story titled *Happy Endings*. I read it several years ago while in high school. It's a story that could connect well with biology and the topic of cancer. Various experimental treatments for cancer are tried in biological laboratories, with multiple outcomes, all in an effort to cure the dreaded disease. *Happy Endings* is also experimental by nature, and it offers five different outcomes in an effort to cure the ills of human and social intercourse [Atwood, 2001]. What I like about this short story is the way it begins. Think about it! Biology is so relatable."

Happy Endings	*Experimental Treatments*
John and Mary meet.	Cancer and biology meet.
What happens next?	What happens next?
If you want a happy ending, try A.	If you want a happy ending, try A.

The science coordinator laughed! Norma grinned and then said, "Oops, I forgot about Carl Hamlin, the social studies department chairperson. He's a bit crabby, but I think I can work with him. I've got an idea about integrating my biology lesson with one of his social studies lessons."

Norma suggested to Marisa that the biology lesson could be woven smoothly into an American History lesson. Norma thought that the teaching of blood transfusion treatments for melanoma cancer would coordinate really well with a chapter she saw one of her students reading earlier that morning before the start of class: *How Doctors Changed America*. She noted that the student was specifically reading about Charles Drew, an important black medical doctor who studied blood and how healthy blood, kept in blood banks, could rejuvenate important blood cells and, thus, improve the health and lives of people (Bernstein & Sorenson, 1990).

Norma and Marisa talked for several more minutes about curriculum integration plans. Norma was beginning to feel quite confident that she, working in collaboration with the other department chairs, could really pull off a great lesson. Norma finally said to the science coordinator, "If we can do one lesson integrating the differing curriculums, why can't we do more?" Marisa replied, "I think you're on to a great idea, Norma! Don't forget to talk to Will. He needs to be included in this process." Norma thought to herself, "True enough, Marisa's right. Principal Will Wonkermann does need to be included. I like him, he's a willing risk-taker!"

Pause and Consider

Let's return to the three questions originally posed prior to the Curriculum Integration, Are You Kidding Me? scenario.

(Continued)

(*Continued*)

- How and by what means were curriculum and instruction integrated in the previous scenario?

- What purpose did the integration process serve?

- How would students benefit from the integration of curriculum and instruction as proposed in the scenario?

Curriculum Integration: The Pros

For curriculum improvement to actually occur, many curriculum specialists believe that the integrative process serves as an effective guide (Drake, 2007; Ellis & Stuen, 1998; Erikson, 2007; Fogarty, 2002; Fogarty & Stoehr, 2007; Goldbort, 1991; Goodlad & Su, 1992; Jacobs, 1989; Kaufman, Moss, & Osborn, 2003; Lipson, Valencia, Wixson, & Peters, 1993; Vars, 1991, 2001). Best-practice evidence, consistent within the research literature, strongly recommends curriculum integration as an appropriate course of action (Northwest Regional Educational Laboratory, 2001).

One method of curriculum integration involves exploratory education. This process affords the curriculum leader the opportunity to build the needed coherence across the curriculums that unites the subject areas for meaningful and relevant learning. It was Dewey (1902), more than a century ago, and later Whitehead (1929) who noted that the integration of curriculum creates an opportunity for instruction to become more practical to students and relevant to their personal life experiences.

Vars (1991, 2001) suggests that curriculum be developed in an integrative format to meet the practical need of making the subject matter more realistic and comprehensible and for better ensuring that students understand the new knowledge being presented in teacher lessons. Tanner and Tanner (2006) assert that curriculum integration allows for positive and necessary changes within instructional programs. Curriculum integration permits schools to do the following:

- Identify methods of removing barriers between subject areas so meaningful and relevant learning can occur
- Encourage student interest and self-direction
- Facilitate student guidance in understanding the instruction taught
- Establish more effective instructional practices as teachers interact, cooperate, guide, and learn best practices together

With these pretexts in mind, principals who continue to permit teachers to rely on worksheets, rote learning, and lessons geared toward state accountability exams will never be able to expect curriculum integration to occur because these teachers and school leaders, alike, remain staunch believers that single-subject instruction is the key to student success.

When principals initiate an integrated curriculum in their schools, traditional departmental barriers dissipate and are replaced by faculty groups who focus on interdisciplinary actions and lessons, rather than focusing on traditional and separate subject areas. This approach to curricular leadership enables positive and professional attitudes to develop toward teaching and learning. Thus, a comprehensive approach to curriculum integration ensures the instructional program will provide students with important concepts, ideas, relationships, and learning applications, as opposed to overloading students with strictly factual and rote information.

Interestingly, as far back as 1975, Moody and Amos (1975) conducted a study that concluded that the involvement of principals in curriculum planning and integration had significant and positive effects on teachers' ability to help students excel at higher levels of affective and cognitive learning and achievement. More recently, a Colorado school district emphasized a radically different, more student-centered approach to teaching and learning. The district is training teachers to involve students in the lesson planning process where students articulate their goals. Students are also involved in "power-voting" where they use Post-it notes as a means of having a voice in curricular decisions, all in an attempt by the school district to give students a greater sense of independence as well as ownership in their learning (Paulson, 2009).

Regrettably, schools continue to be influenced by political forces that work to narrow national priorities to strict accountability standards rather than permitting teachers and principals opportunities to improve their schools and student learning and achievement through the fulfillment of integrated curriculums that more truly mirror campus mission and vision statements.

Curriculum leaders, at the campus level, who strictly follow a disciplinary approach to curriculum development, ignore the research literature and, thus, neglect any opportunity for curriculum integration and synthesis. Unfortunately, these leaders push their schools toward curricular fragmentation. This line of thinking generates two important questions:

Question 1: What are the implications of integrating curriculum and instruction?

Question 2: Is curriculum integration superior to disciplinary approaches to curriculum development? Why or why not?

If we agree with Tanner and Tanner (2006) that the functions of a school's curriculum are (1) to develop fundamental skills, (2) to preserve cultural heritage, and (3) to promote individual as well as social growth and development, then consider how instructional specialization and fragmentation has had concomitant effects on curriculum development in schools. When teachers are isolated by departmentalization and subject area specialties, the achievement of curriculum integration and the development of effective curricular standards is significantly diminished (Fogarty, 2002).

Curriculum Integration: The Cons

Although there is a genuine interest in curriculum integration, some aspects of the research literature suggest too much integration can have adverse effects on curriculum and instructional processes (Brophy & Alleman, 1991; Bruner, 2000; Goodlad, Wineburg, & Grossman, 2007; Roth, 2000; Vars, 2001). Opponents of curriculum integration argue students frequently gain very superficial knowledge (Roth). Others believe that subject-focused or content-area-oriented curriculum better validates knowledge gained (Bruner). Certain aspects of the research literature remain in opposition to an integrated curricular approach and caution that integrated curricular/ instructional models are typically poorly designed, loosely connected, and weak in providing for a quality education for those students most in need (Brophy & Alleman; Gardner & Boix-Mansilla, 1994).

Conversely, Glatthorn and Jailall (2009) suggested that if a curriculum leader or team expresses concerns about the integration of curriculum across the content areas, the principal, working in collaboration with the curriculum team, must determine the nature and extent to which integration is necessary. We concur with Glatthorn and Jailall's assessment but suggest that principals take the process a few steps further.

Five Steps to Successful Curriculum Integration

Before a principal and curriculum team decide that curriculum integration is the most or least effective model, a principal must initiate five important steps to ensuring curricular, instructional, and student success. These steps relate to (1) reviewing empirical research, (2) determining the degree and feasibility of integration, (3) noting the teacher experience factor, (4) piloting the integrative model, and (5) initiating a four-quadrant analysis.

Step 1: Principals are responsible for carefully leading a review of the empirical research literature relative to student learning, teaching effectiveness, and increased academic achievement in the area of curriculum integration.

Step 2: Principals are responsible for analyzing school data to determine exactly what areas of the curriculum should— if at all—be integrated, for what specified reasons, and to what degree the integration will not only be feasible but successful. Principals should never decide that curriculum integration, or any other curricular model or approach, for that matter, be initiated because other principals or school systems are incorporating a certain model or process.

Step 3: Principals are responsible for weighing the experience factor. For example, have any of the teachers previously incorporated or used curriculum integration models or approaches as a means of enhancing student learning and teacher instruction? What were the results? How did the students and teachers respond?

Step 4: Principals are responsible for involving all parties in any curriculum integration decision-making processes and must further examine how practical and pragmatic any new approach can and will be, especially as it relates to student learning. Effective principal leaders "pilot" any new approach, and carefully monitor, observe, and evaluate the overall results.

Step 5: Principals are responsible for considering each of the four quadrants in Table 7.2, Principal Responsibilities for Ensuring Effective Curriculum Integration, as adapted from Recommendations for Curriculum Integration by Glatthorn and Jailall (2009, p. 106). Three of the four quadrants are based on principal responsibilities as related to curricular and instructional integrative processes. The final fourth quadrant indicates the curriculum integration responsibilities of district-level officials/personnel.

Table 7.2   Principal Responsibilities for Ensuring Effective
Curriculum Integration

Responsibilities: Elementary School Principals	*Responsibilities: High School Principals*
• Focus on the development of higher-order thinking skills in the content areas of reading, writing, and mathematics.	• Continue to emphasize learning outcomes and other instructional concepts through an integrative process to better ensure student mastery of the content areas.
• In the prereading content area, incorporate both phonetic and whole language instruction and relate to prewriting activities.	• Emphasize reading, writing, and mathematics across all content areas.
• In the mathematics content area, apply the skills mastered to the science subject area.	• Correlate the advanced sciences with mathematic instructional areas.
• In the science content area, focus on the scientific method and apply the skills mastered to both mathematics and social studies content areas.	• Integrate English content areas (composition and literature) with social studies, science, and the arts.
• For the social studies content area, integrate reading, writing, and language arts.	• Develop instructional materials that integrate all content areas—most notably reading, writing, mathematics, technology, and the sciences.
• In all content areas, develop instructional materials that integrate the mastery of reading and writing.	

Responsibilities: Middle School Principals	*Responsibilities: District-Level Personnel*
• Emphasize learning outcomes and all instructional materials are developmentally appropriate for middle school learners.	• Ensure principals and school-site personnel read and review pertinent literature relative to the integration of curriculum and instruction.

Responsibilities: Middle School Principals	*Responsibilities: District-Level Personnel*
• Emphasize all content areas through an integrative approach, specializing in mastery of reading, writing, and mathematics. • Integrate the language arts (reading and writing) curriculum with the social studies curriculum. • Integrate instructional units across the content areas of mathematics, science, health, and technology. • Emphasize mathematical concepts and skills that prove relevant to students' daily lives. • In all content areas, develop instructional materials that integrate the mastery of reading and writing.	• Use the best lead teachers in each of the content areas to aid with the integrative process. • Hold regular meetings with principals and curriculum teams as a method of disseminating information and receiving critical feedback. • Provide the essential resources—human, material, and fiscal. • Develop, in collaboration with principals and curriculum teams, integrated units of instruction. • Provide time in meetings for reflection and risk-free comments. • Ensure that all aspects of the integrative and other curricular processes are negotiable. • Develop appropriate cross-content area assessments and evaluative tools.

The Integration of Curriculum and Instruction: How Relevance and Interest Help Students Become Better Learners

Harold Rugg (1927), more than eight decades ago, asked a most important question relative to the curriculum development process: "What use, if any, shall be made of the interests of children?" (p. 8). What a great question! It was an appropriate question in yesteryear, and it remains germane to date. Principals, as curriculum leaders, must ask the same question when integrating curriculum and instruction: Is this process relevant and of interest to our students? To better understand and answer this question, let's examine the research literature.

Cennamo and Kalk (2005) relate that the most significant element, for the principal and curriculum team, in the curriculum and instruction integrative process is the learner and recognizing what is of interest and relevance to the learner. As curriculum leader and the initiator of curriculum and instruction integration, it is imperative that principals become advocates of learner needs and interests. This is achieved through an assessment of what students perceive relevant and practical. By what other means might the curriculum leader begin to understand the interests and needs of students? First, determine what the students already know. Second, seek to understand what they need to know. Third, identify what aspects of knowledge and learning are of relevance and importance to the students.

Students possess different needs and interests. Therefore, curriculum—as integrated with instruction—must be differentiated. Effective instruction, when integrated with curriculum, provides students with differentiated tasks, materials, and time constraints (Tomlinson & McTighe, 2006; Turville, 2007). Curriculum and instruction, when properly integrated, allow for students to become partners with teachers in determining what is taught, how it is taught, why it is taught, and which goals and objectives play a role in identifying learning that is of relevance, practicality, and interest to students. To fail in the establishment of a curriculum and instructional program that focuses on student interest is to fail in helping students achieve and succeed in the classroom, in the community, and in life (Kameenui, Carnine, Dixon, Simmons, & Coyne, 2002; Marzano, 1992; National Board for Professional Teaching Standards, 1989; Tomlinson et al., 2004).

Athanasou and Petoumenos (1998) revealed that the decline of student interest in learning is well documented and is often associated with the curriculum chosen, the style of teaching used, and the relevance of the coursework. This particular study further stipulated that four instructional components must be integrated within the curriculum. These components included (1) clear objectives, (2) making the subject content interesting, (3) demonstrating the relevance of the subject content, and (4) providing opportunities for student questioning and feedback as associated with the practicality of the subject content. Relevance and interest in the content area was also shown to be correlated with how the teacher is able to effectively explain why the content is of importance to the students and their lives. Athanasou and Petoumenos also noted that curriculum must be developed and then presented (taught) in a method that aids students in understanding why the lesson and content area is practical.

Hidi (1990) along with Athanasou (1994) found a direct correlation between students' interest in the curriculum and content area, students' perceived vocational choice, and students' level of academic achievement. Schiefele, Krapp, and Winteler (1991) discovered that interest in content area is related to the learning contexts, the curriculum, the methods of instruction, and of course, the perceived practicality of the content being taught. Finally, Tobias (1994) noted that student interest in content area is at least equal to if not greater in importance than the quality of instruction. Keller and Suzuki (1998) found the issue of relevance and practicality in curriculum, as integrated with content and instructional methods, generates student interest and motivation in learning.

Finally, let's consider the research conducted by Lisa Pray of Vanderbilt University Peabody College and Rebecca Monhardt (2009) of Utah State University who readily acknowledge that integrating curriculum and instruction can seem daunting at first but have in fact developed a four-step process to help students, most notably English language learners (ELLs)—one of the fastest growing populations in our schools today, with mastery of the science curriculum. This four-step process incorporates instructional strategies into science lessons, a subject of significant difficulty for ELLs because these students often face difficult transitions from their native language to the spoken English language to the scientific academic terms and language. Listed next are the four steps as proposed by Pray and Monhardt (2009):

1. Determine the content objectives and correlate language activities, such as reading, writing, listening, and speaking, to the content objectives.

2. Use student's background, experiences, and interests and correlate to the content material.

3. Select teaching/learning activities that allow students to interact and use science vocabulary terms.

4. Evaluate whether the students have achieved the content and language objectives.

As teachers learn to experiment and incorporate this four-step process as a method of curriculum integration into their lesson plans, a positive impact on student achievement is the likely consequence, especially if the teachers, working in tandem with the curriculum team and principal, reflect on areas of improvement to continually enhance lesson delivery.

Curriculum Integration and the Kohn Perspective

Most interestingly, and frequently ignored in curriculum development and integrative processes, is the conducted research and written works of Alfie Kohn (1993, 2001, 2006, 2008a, 2008b). Kohn is a former teacher who speaks widely on human behavior, mandated curriculum, and social theory. Kohn, in his provocative text *Beyond Discipline: From Compliance to Community* (2006), proposes a curriculum alternative in which the classroom is a community of learners where students have a major role in making meaningful decisions about their schooling. This curriculum alternative is one in which principals and teachers transform instruction by asking students what they need to learn and how their learning needs and interests can be met.

Kohn (2006, 2008a) insists that principals and teams consider alternatives, such as integrated approaches to curriculum development, and, thus, create learning environments where students feel trusted, respected, and empowered. Kohn further asserts that the quality of student behavior and actions in the classroom relates extensively to the quality of curriculum and student enthusiasm and interest for the instruction and instructional program.

Kohn (2001, 2008b) emphasizes the constructivist model whereby students are active learners. Kohn notes that active learners are those who acquire essential skills, not through memorization or constant drill and practice as related to mandated curriculums and state accountability standards, but through meaningful experiences relevant to their upcoming careers and life. Kohn's (1993) model encourages teachers to permit students to engage in discussions concerning what should be expected in class, in curriculum, in instruction, and how relevant changes in curriculum and instruction can be made.

Kohn (2006) also points out that student misbehavior diminishes when students are actively involved in the curricular and instructional decision-making processes. Furthermore, Kohn asserts that students are curriculum theorists and, thus, the best critics of curricular approaches and instructional methods and techniques. He believes that schools should be student oriented, student directed, learner centered, and democratic. This approach means that students, working in collaboration with teachers and curriculum leaders, are provided time for sharing, deciding, planning, and reflecting on curricular and instructional approaches to include integrative curriculum models.

Finally, Kohn (2006) believes if school principals and teachers really desire academic excellence and achievement for *all* students, they must ensure that students are

- excited about their school—the curriculum and instruction;
- experiencing a sense of being valued and respected;
- connected to a curriculum that is relevant and practical;
- learning something of value and interest; and
- safe in openly proposing changes in curricular approaches, instructional methods, and teaching techniques and strategies.

Ultimately, Alfie Kohn (2006) proposes that principals, as curriculum leaders—working in collaboration with curriculum teams, faculty, students, parents, and district officials—criticize the status quo, and then, change it! Kohn challenges all educators to recognize that many of the misbehaviors of students are strictly related to mandated curriculums, and then he further recommends that teachers and administrators carefully examine all mandated curriculum to better ensure that our students are receiving the best possible education.

It's a Fine Line!

Principals, as integrative leaders of curriculum and instruction, must keep in mind the needs and interests of students and how each relates to curriculum and content relevance and practicality. The spirited H. Ross Perot, in his early 1980s quest for a cure-all remedy for the perceived diminished instructional skills of teachers in Texas schools, once stated before a select committee on education, "We've got to drop a bomb on them. We've got to nuke them. That's the way you change these organizations" (as quoted in Cleave, 1985; Isikoff & Von Drehle, 1992). Ross Perot was wrong. Consider what Linda McNeil (2000) calls one of the "contradictions of school reform" (p. 152): That is, the educational cost of a standardized or mandated curriculum is a curricular approach and instructional program based on test-prep. To illustrate this point, contemplate what McNeil, in her important text *Contradictions of School Reform: Educational Costs of Standardized Testing*, cited as an unsolicited correspondence:

> The town's head librarian loved to encourage the children of her small, isolated farming community to read. She frequently went to the local school to read to the children. Most recently, she had been reading to a class of "at-risk" eighth graders–students who have been held back two or more years in school. They loved her reading and her choices of books. She reported feeling very frustrated: the department chair had told her not to come any more to read to the students–they were now too busy preparing for their standardized test. (p. 229)

A second correlation to McNeil's (2000) "contradictions of school reform" is reflected by Waxman (2009) who writes of what he labels "institutionalized child abuse" (p. 5B):

> Students are held hostage by standardized tests. Districts actually write weeks of test-prep into the curricula, forcing us to teach the test. Among the ways we prepare our students for a 50 to 60 question, high-stakes exam is to make the students take 50 to 60 question state-released exams multiple times for practice.
>
> Then, the big day arrives and students are forced to sit in an atmosphere of tension and oppression, where they are treated like cheaters before the exam even begins.
>
> They must spend hour upon hour trying to pass a test that's more suited to measuring test-taking skills, as opposed to actual knowledge. As a result, rather than developing our students' creativity, critical thinking, and problem-solving ability, we're fostering test anxiety and repetitive stress disorder. Then we wonder why our students lag behind those of so many other countries.

When curriculum is mandated, most notably from the state level, it far too often becomes institutionalized; it becomes tested, and thus, the curriculum and subject or content areas become nothing more than test-prep sessions. As a result, state-mandated curriculum can—if not carefully analyzed, developed, and renewed—negatively affect the quality of instruction.

State-mandated curriculum presents a serious challenge to principals and faculty, especially as they attempt to integrate curriculum and instruction as well as initiate curriculum reform. So how do we find the time to teach what really needs to be taught when the curriculum mandates what *really needs to be taught* is test-prep? Not long ago, a lead teacher noted the following:

> It's a fine line that we have to tread here in our school. The mandated curriculum versus our campus-developed curriculum. Thank God, our principal supports what our students really need and what really needs to be taught. Because our principal has led curriculum initiatives that center on integrated approaches to instruction, our focus is less on preparing our students for the test and more on student learning. The result has actually been an increase in test scores. (Sorenson, 2007)

Lunenburg and Irby (2006) suggest principals have to recognize that the curriculum must meet students' needs, yet at the same time, it must also conform to some mandated guidelines and goals for what the states believe students should know.

Are you, the school leader, ready to walk this fine line? Are you ready to do what is right by the students you serve? Are you prepared to be the curriculum leader? Principals must know their role in curriculum integration, and as was the case with Bud and Temple in *Bud & Me: The True Adventures of the Abernathy Boys* (Abernathy, 1998), principals must never be "completely ignorant of the trouble that lay ahead" (p. 27).

The Principal's Role in Curriculum Integration

Glatthorn and Jailall (2009) noted that effective school principals must possess more than a general understanding of curriculum and, furthermore, recognize the importance of their role as curriculum leaders. We agree. Research continues to support a strong correlation between the level of a principal's leadership role in curriculum integration and the success of any integrative project (Glatthorn & Jailall, 2009; March & Peters, 2002; NREL, 2001).

The National Middle School Association (2003) reports that effective principals, as visionary leaders of curriculum integration, incorporate three frameworks essential to guiding teachers beyond departmentalization and subject area specialties, so common in schools today. These frameworks include (1) examples of other teachers' practice; (2) models of other schools' integrative curricular approaches; and (3) collaborative procedures that allow for frequent teacher interaction, discussion, reflection, and critique of the integrative processes.

Principals who act as facilitators, relative to the process of integrating curriculum across the content areas, build capacity for critical self-reflection and analysis with and among teachers—all of which enables continued curriculum reform. When principals create an atmosphere for critical self-reflection and the empowerment of faculty, the result is teachers recognize the need for and demand a more intense analysis of the curriculum integration research literature (Wasley, Hampel, & Clark, 1996).

The question remains: What is the principal's role in the curriculum integrative process? Let's begin answering the query by noting that principals must establish high expectations, develop a shared vision for organizational as well as student success, and structure and deliver high-quality instructional programs. To do so, a principal must be the leader of curriculum, the leader of instruction, and the leader of change. Not an easy task, but one that is essential to integrating curriculum and instruction. Now, let's examine a listing of leader contributions, as related to the integration of curriculum and instruction, all of which are essential to effective service in the principal role (see Table 7.3), along with a scenario exemplifying the principal's role in curriculum integration.

Table 7.3   The Principal's Role: Integrating Curriculum and Instruction

Principals who effectively integrate curriculum and instruction do the following:

_____ Engage faculty in activities that are mentally stimulating and challenging

_____ Ensure faculty enjoyment and satisfaction in the work to be accomplished

_____ Allow for active collaboration and facilitate all work sessions

_____ Establish high expectations for faculty that dictate a focus on outcomes that actively engage students and create a learning environment that is of interest and relevance to the students

_____ Set goals and develop objectives that measure committee progress, analyze curricular processes, and evaluate the effectiveness of curricular/instructional programs

_____ Provide release time for professional development focusing on current practice and anticipated change

_____ Observe teachers and students in the teaching/learning environment as a method of evaluating the extent of curricular and programmatic change and enhancement

_____ Establish a positive climate and open culture where risk taking is welcome and failure is never an option

_____ Support and empower members of the learning community by finding necessary resources to facilitate the change process

_____ Provide opportunities for shared leadership that embody the adage "all of us are smarter than any one of us"

_____ Seek and collect appropriate data, relevant research, and essential information

_____ Allow for shared responsibility in developing a curriculum that integrates instruction across the content areas

_____ Avoid any opportunity to find a simple solution to a complex problem

_____ Focus, first and foremost, on students and their achievement (Every concern, consideration, comment, concurring and opposing viewpoint must be met with this statement: "Explain to me how this is in the best interest of our students!")

STICKS AND STONES WILL BREAK MY BONES BUT WORDS WILL NEVER HURT ME!
Addressing a Bullying Dilemma at Childers School Through Curriculum Integration

Will Wonkermann, principal at Childers School, was immediately cognizant of a concern at his school, a terribly important concern. It was not only a student-centered concern it was a concern that interconnected administration, faculty, and students with the evaluation and reform of curriculum and instruction. It was also a behavioral concern.

Jaye Miller, the school's music teacher, brought the issue to Mr. Wonkermann's attention. She walked into his office and asked a rather pointed question: "Will, to what degree do you believe bullying takes place on our campus?" Will responded: "Now Jaye, come on—tell me what's really on your mind!" Jaye Miller laughed and answered her principal's question with three additional questions: "Will, have you ever been bullied? How did it feel? Have you ever bullied anyone?" Will inwardly smiled and thought to himself, "It's just like Jaye Miller to respond to my question with another set of questions!" He respected this exceptional lead teacher, and he knew the school's problem was his problem and, thus, his responsibility.

First, Principal Wonkermann decided to begin solving the bullying issue by asking himself two very important questions:

1. Am I part of the problem?

2. What types of measures do I need to take to ensure that the problem is solved?

(Continued)

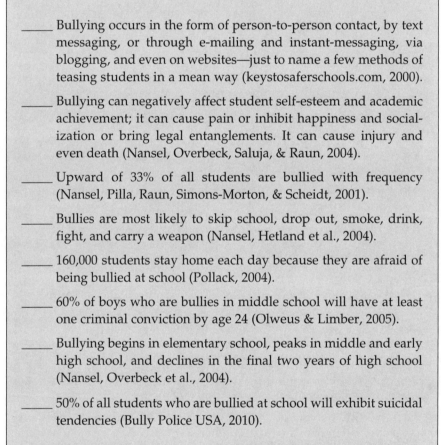

(*Continued*)

Jaye had done her homework. She had recognized the bullying problem about a week earlier, and she had subsequently searched the Internet for relevant programmatic information and empirical research to help bring the issue of bullying at school to a screeching halt. Then, she shared with Mr. Wonkermann some telling statistics about bullying in schools. Standing once again in the principal's office with notes in hand, Jaye exclaimed, "Will, let me share with you some of the data that I have collected. We must address this information in both behavioral policies and curriculum enhancements!"

_____ Bullying occurs in the form of person-to-person contact, by text messaging, or through e-mailing and instant-messaging, via blogging, and even on websites—just to name a few methods of teasing students in a mean way (keystosaferschools.com, 2000).

_____ Bullying can negatively affect student self-esteem and academic achievement; it can cause pain or inhibit happiness and socialization or bring legal entanglements. It can cause injury and even death (Nansel, Overbeck, Saluja, & Raun, 2004).

_____ Upward of 33% of all students are bullied with frequency (Nansel, Pilla, Raun, Simons-Morton, & Scheidt, 2001).

_____ Bullies are most likely to skip school, drop out, smoke, drink, fight, and carry a weapon (Nansel, Hetland et al., 2004).

_____ 160,000 students stay home each day because they are afraid of being bullied at school (Pollack, 2004).

_____ 60% of boys who are bullies in middle school will have at least one criminal conviction by age 24 (Olweus & Limber, 2005).

_____ Bullying begins in elementary school, peaks in middle and early high school, and declines in the final two years of high school (Nansel, Overbeck et al., 2004).

_____ 50% of all students who are bullied at school will exhibit suicidal tendencies (Bully Police USA, 2010).

Principal Wonkermann was impressed with the shared data, and as was his style, he immediately began addressing the problem. He too recognized that the bullying at Childers School was much more than a behavioral issue—it was also a curricular issue! Will, working in collaboration with the campus site-based decision making committee and the curriculum team, contacted the U. S. Department of Education (1998) to obtain a publication titled: *Preventing Bullying—A Manual for Schools and Communities.* Principal Wonkermann, furthermore, initiated a 10 best-practice campus curriculum strategy to include the following:

1. Taking the issue of bullying seriously

2. Focusing on changing the campus social climate and norms that elevate bullying

3. Establishing a bully prevention team to meet regularly to access, plan for, and evaluate specific bully preventive curricular and instructional activities

4. Developing a bully prevention curriculum (see Table 7.4) to be integrated across the content areas

5. Providing professional development for faculty, training for students, and curriculum development across the content areas related to bullying in school

6. Establishing and enforcing all school rules and policies

7. Increasing administrator and teacher supervision in hot-spots across campus

8. Intervening promptly and consistently when bullying occurs

9. Devoting instructional time (20 to 30 minutes each week) to bully prevention

10. Integrating anti-bullying messages and strategies throughout the curriculum

Will Wonkermann thought the 10 best-practice campus curriculum strategy was an effective beginning to initiate an integrative curriculum approach related to bullying at Childers School, but he continued to closely monitor several key websites—all of which were associated with bullying and all of which provided pathways to integrating anti-bullying curriculum into the instructional program (see Table 7.4).

Table 7.4 *Bullying in Schools: Integrating Curriculum—the Principal's Role*

Website	Name of Organization
Bullypolice.org	Bully Police USA
http://www.txssc.txstate.edu/txssc.htm	Texas Safe School Center

(Continued)

Table 7.4 (*Continued*)

Website	Name of Organization
keystosaferschools.com	Keys to Safer Schools
http://www.clemson.edu/olweus	Olweus Bullying Prevention Program
http://dpi.wi.gov/pubsales/pplsvc_2.html	Wisconsin Department of Public Instruction
http://pathwayscourses.samhsa.gov/bully/bully_intro_pg1.html	CSAP's Prevention Pathways: Online Courses—*The ABCs of Bullying. Addressing, Blocking, and Curbing School Aggression*

Pause and Consider

- Examine, as a part of adopting an anti-bullying project at your school, the following website (http://www.stopbullyingnow.com). Consider how a school leader could systematically integrate this web-based project into the curriculum and instructional program.

- Consider what you have learned from reading the chapter section Curriculum Integration and the Kohn Perspective and specifically think about the issues of quality of curriculum, instructional programming, and student interest, and how Principal Will Wonkermann must handle bullying in Childers School from a curricular as well as a behavioral perspective.

- Consider which of the Five Steps to Successful Curriculum Integration, examined earlier in this chapter, relate to the bullying dilemma facing Principal Wonkermann at Childers School.

The 7Bs of Curriculum Integration and Effective Leadership

Finally, when integrating curriculum and instruction across the content areas, it is important for a principal to instill in all members of the learning community the 7Bs of effective curriculum leadership:

1. Be a team player and expect the players to team

2. Be a curricular and instructional expert

3. Be transparent and ethical in all endeavors, sharing expertise and advice

4. Be sensitive to the needs of others, recognizing that individual differences exist in people

5. Be cognizant of the differing stages of adult learning and how levels of change adaptation will vary

6. Be organized and prepared, ready to deliver to the curriculum team essential training, goods, resources, and services

7. Be an effective leader who accepts the challenge of curricular change

From a principal's perspective, particularly when working to integrate curriculum and instruction, two of the 7Bs ring especially true: Be a team player and expect players to team and be transparent and ethical in all endeavors.

Team Leadership

School teams working to initiate change and desiring to bring an integrated approach to curriculum and instruction are led by principals who develop a shared sense of purpose, who attribute all school honors and recognitions to the learning community and not to self, and who are always willing to accept criticism and blame, if necessary. These leaders build confidence in others, are actively engaged and involved, and are willing to mentor and assist members of the team. Each of these leadership traits serve as building blocks toward effective curriculum teams and effective school teams. Remember, leaders team and teams lead!

Several years ago, the authors of this text worked with a most successful school principal. She was attempting, at times with limited success, to integrate the curriculum across the content areas. Here's the story of how she did *it*. What is the "it"? Simply, the "it" is how she built a team to lead, deliver, and manage curriculum change and content integration.

Alma Munoz of Portland, Texas, at the time principal of an intermediate school, suddenly found herself confronted with the necessity of injecting enthusiasm into a discouraged and disorganized team of teachers. Calling a faculty meeting, she urged her teachers to tell her exactly what they expected of her. As they talked, Alma wrote their ideas on a marker-board. Then she said, "I'll give you all of the qualities that you expect from me. Now, I want you to tell me what I can expect from you."

(Continued)

(Continued)

The replies started coming one after the other: "Loyalty. Honesty. Initiative. Optimism. Respect. Dedication. Enthusiasm. Willingness to change." Alma wrote, as fast as she could, each term, trait, and characteristic the team members shouted out.

The faculty meeting concluded with a new resolve—people agreed to work together, and together, they began to work! "The faculty made a bargain with me," said Alma, "and as long as I lived up to their expectations, they would team together and live up to mine. Meeting with the faculty and asking what they expected of me and what I could expect of them led to a venture in academic success for teams, students, parents, and community."

Ethical Leadership

George Shelley (*The Columbia World of Quotations*, 1996) wrote, "Beware of the individual who has no regard for his own reputation, since it is not likely he will have any regard for yours." Moses proclaimed, "Neither shall you allege the example of the many as an excuse for doing wrong" (Exodus 23:2, New International Bible). Mary Waldrop asserted, "It's important that people know what you stand for. It's equally important that they know what you won't stand for" (*Words of Wisdom*, 1995). Each of these individuals conveys a simple yet imperative message: Leaders must be ethical in their behaviors and practice. Regrettably, the "practice" of ethical "behaviors" in far too many instances and in far too many organizations is an underrated and underrepresented priority.

Ethical Leadership Defined

Northouse (2007) defines ethics, from a leadership perspective, as being related to behavior and virtue. Northouse further suggests that ethical leaders must be morally decent in their actions and interactions. Beckner (2004) defines ethics by means of a description of the ethical leader as one who promotes human welfare; is virtuous; values others; and is worthwhile, principled, righteous, and of impeccable integrity. Nash (1996) describes an ethical leader as someone who is moral in all behaviors—personal, social, and professional. Sorenson and Goldsmith (2009) define ethical leaders as those individuals who are "able to take an even closer, if not a more discerning, look at themselves—at whom they've become, and in truth, who they really want to be" (p. 47). Vince Lombardi, Jr., in his book *Twenty-Six*

Lessons From Vince Lombardi, The World's Greatest Coach (2005), wrote that ethical leaders "have to impress who and what they are . . . on the people around them. You do what is right. You do what you say. You conform to the ethics and values that you espouse. Your behavior is predictable, because you are consistent in your choices and your actions" (p. 46). Ethical leaders, as principals, are those who are honest and truthful with themselves and with others, and they are always responsible for and respectful of those in their care.

The Principal as Ethical Leader in Curriculum Integration

In the realm of curriculum integration, ethical leadership, as exhibited by the principal, serves as a means of respecting the learning community. The principal as ethical leader in curriculum integration is a willing servant who provides not only guidance and direction but also the necessary materials and human and fiscal resources to ensure that the curriculum is incorporated across the content areas as well as permeating the overall instructional program. The principal as ethical leader in curriculum integration is fair in all interactions with members of the curriculum team, where no one individual or group receives special treatment or considerations at the expense of others. The principal as ethical leader supports teamwork and is attentive to the interest of the curriculum team members, as well as the entire learning community, by being appreciative of the purposes and the work of others and by never ignoring the honorable intentions and worthwhile initiatives of any one or group of individuals.

The principal as ethical leader determines with the curriculum team what aspects of the curriculum should be integrated—where, when, why, and by what means. The principal as ethical leader works with the curriculum team to ensure that curricular changes comply with board policy. The principal as ethical leader is honest in all motivations. The principal as ethical leader in curriculum integration processes seeks to foresee potential problems and consequences (both pro and con). The principal as ethical leader ensures that all decisions are fair and further guides the curriculum team and the learning community in making and applying curriculum integration decisions that are in the students' best interests. Ultimately, the principal as ethical leader in any curriculum integration process solves problems and makes decisions according to a personal and educational philosophy by which students are always first and foremost in any and all considerations!

Shapiro and Stefkovich (2005) share that accountability, responsibility, student and teacher rights, professional standards of conduct, cultural awareness, equity, equality, and appropriate pedagogy are hallmarks (explicit signals) of the principal who serves as an ethical leader in curriculum integration processes. It was Richard Thornburgh, former U. S. attorney general, who espoused that true leaders assert specific signals to best ensure there is no confusion or uncertainty relative to what is or is not acceptable conduct (as cited in Gergen, 2000).

Ubben, Hughes, and Norris (2007) remind us that principals must be ethical leaders in the curriculum integration process. Ethical principals must be responsible in their efforts to empower faculty to lead in curricular initiatives. Ethical principals must provide structure to the curriculum—including both curricular and extracurricular. Ethical principals must allow teachers to take ownership in transforming a school, a curriculum, a program, or a classroom. Ethical principals must provide oversight by means of effective analysis and evaluation of integrative curricular models and by improving the instructional program.

Finally, ethical principals, in the curricular and integrative processes, must be principled in all of their leadership approaches, behaviors, and endeavors. Ethical principals develop, design, deliver, and evaluate integrative curriculum processes as well as all other curricular change and reform efforts. Recall, it was Mahatma Gandhi (*The Columbia World of Quotations*, 1996) who said, "Be the change you want to see in the world." Today, the principal mantra might read, "Be the ethical change you and others want to see in your school."

Final Thoughts

The National Commission on Teaching and America's Future (1996) advised, "The first priority is reaching agreement on what teachers should know and be able to do to help students succeed" (p. 18). This advice remains relevant today, especially in light of the need for systematically integrating curriculum and instruction. Principals who are able to effectively lead schools are visionary. They look beyond the current realities of existing curriculum and instructional programs. These principals are able to recognize the need for curricular change and encourage personnel to expect more from themselves, the work they presently accomplish, and ultimately, achieve higher goals to include increased student achievement (Hughes, Ginnett, & Curphy, 2009).

If curriculum is the *what* taught in schools and instruction the *how*, effective principals must serve as initiators of curricular improvement, to include the integration of curriculum and instruction. This process warrants the removal of barriers that preclude meaningful and relevant learning that ignore students' interest and self-direction. Principals who integrate curriculum and instruction dissipate traditional, single-subject instruction and focus faculty on interdisciplinary actions, teaching, and lessons. These curricular changes help students become better learners, and just as important, they allow teachers to become better instructors.

Eugene H. Peterson (2007) writes in *The Message*, "A good leader motivates, doesn't mislead, doesn't exploit" (p. 77). When initiating curricular change or reform (i.e., integrating curriculum and instruction), principals must lead through motivation, not exploitation. John C. Maxwell (2003a) believes that the best method of influencing others is through a nurturing process. To do so, principals, as curriculum leaders, must have a genuine concern for the teaching team. To exhibit concern, a leader must love the work, love the team, and love the individual members of the team.

Now, we would be somewhat remiss, if not quite idealistic, to think that we will always like everyone and be liked by everyone. That is probably not humanly possible. We can, in our hearts, learn to *love* everyone, everyday, despite their foibles, as well as our own. Love equates to respecting, nurturing, and positively influencing employees, colleagues, and friends. This line of reasoning truly epitomizes the term, *leadership*. Maxwell (2003a) further intimates that so many people are eager for a little encouragement, some basic nurturing. The encouragement and nurturing of people can positively impact their lives. As noted in this chapter, the curriculum leader—who is also a team nurturer and leader of change—can plan on having a major, and even a positive, impact on the entire school organization when integrating curriculum and instruction.

Discussion Questions

1. Sorenson and Goldsmith (2009) in their text *The Principal's Guide to Managing School Personnel* suggest that "working with school personnel can be a difficult prospect for principals who neither anticipate nor prepare for the numerous challenges, persistent individual needs, and unremitting situations that evolve when

(Continued)

(*Continued*)

confronted with the leadership role of maintaining and improving the capabilities of a campus workforce" (p. xv). How does this assessment relate to principals who initiate the integration of curriculum and instruction? How does this statement relate to ethical leadership? Be specific in your answer.

2. Examine Table 7.1, The Sorenson-Goldsmith Model of Varied and Differentiated Instruction: Designs Described and Defined, and then identify which types of instruction you incorporated into a recent lesson you conducted. Which additional types of instruction could improve your lesson? How and by what means?

3. Rethink the lesson you conceived in Question 2. What aspects of the lesson, if any, integrated other content areas? Which content areas, when integrated into your lesson, could improve student learning of the lesson objectives? After responding to this question, do you believe that the integration of curriculum and instruction is beneficial to teacher instruction and student achievement? Why or why not?

4. Examine Table 7.3, The Principal's Role: Integrating Curriculum and Instruction. Review each of the indicators listed and place a checkmark by those that you or your current principal incorporated this past week. Which of the principal role indicators would best serve you or your principal in making for a more effective instructional team and learning environment and better ensure the integration of curriculum and instruction at your school? Explain why.

5. Alfie Kohn has been described as a provocateur—a critic of curricular, instructional, and disciplinary programs in our schools today. He believes in alternative approaches, such as the integration of curriculum and instruction, essential to turning schools into learning communities where students feel valued and respected. After reading Curriculum Integration and the Kohn Perspective in this chapter, do you believe that Alfie Kohn is on target in terms of his educational philosophy and path-breaking sentimentalities regarding schooling (specifically, integrative curricular approaches) in America today? Support your answers.

6. If you were to initiate the integration of curriculum and instruction in your school today, how would you begin? Relate your answers to this and previous chapters within the text.

CASE STUDY APPLICATION
Well, It's the State-Mandated Curriculum!

Emma Murphy, a fifth-grade teacher at Harrisburg Elementary School, spent Sunday afternoon reading one research article after another for a project required in her Introduction to the Principalship course at Riverton State University. One article in particular really caught her attention because it related to her work as a teacher—specifically to the curriculum she was implementing, or not implementing. The article, titled "Beyond the Pendulum: Creating Challenging and Caring Schools," (Lewis, Schaps, & Watson, 1995) had been found in a past issue of *Phi Delta Kappan*. What compelled her to dig deeper into her thought processes was a sentence that kept ringing true, but Emma knew for a fact wasn't being implemented at Harrisburg Elementary School. The sentence read,

> How could we create a caring community in the classroom where children's own needs—to make sense of the world, to be known and liked by others, to influence the environment—were being ignored by a skill-and-drill curriculum, a curriculum that holds little intrinsic interest for children? (p. 550)

Emma thought to herself, "I've got to talk to Felipe about this article!" The more Emma pondered, the more she was convinced that she had to meet the next day with her principal, Felipe Rendon. She knew he was a first-year principal, but she also knew he cared and that he would listen.

Early Monday morning, Emma went up to Felipe who was greeting students, parents, and teachers as they came across the parking lot toward the school's entrance. "Morning, Ms. Murphy," hollered Felipe even before Emma was close enough to speak. That was just like Felipe. Always gregarious, always wanting to make everyone feel welcome. As Emma got closer, she said, "Well, Mr. Rendon, how are you this bright spring morning?" Felipe smiled and said, "I'm doing great, and I can already tell that you've got something on your mind!" Emma nodded and Felipe motioned her toward the administrative office door.

"Come on in Emma. What's on your mind, with this week just starting?" inquired Felipe. Emma sat down and began a most interesting discussion that ultimately had to be postponed until that afternoon following the dismissal of school. The later conversation unfolded.

Principal Rendon: Okay, Emma, start from the beginning if you will. I've had a thousand and one conversations since we met first thing this morning. Refresh my memory.

Emma Murphy: Felipe, as you know I am enrolled at Riverton State in their principal-prep program and Professor Ray

(Continued)

(Continued)

Cross assigned us a project that required a great deal of digging into the research literature. Well, I was reading an article out of *Phi Delta Kappan* about what a challenging yet caring school is suppose to look like. Pardon me, Felipe, but I don't think we measure up here at Harrisburg Elementary.

Principal Rendon: Okay, Emma, tell me more. Why and how are we not measuring up? You know me, I'm willing to listen, and I'm willing to try whatever is in the best interest of our students.

Emma Murphy: Felipe, I know you're about the best interest of our kiddos, and that's why I'm here. I think we've got to make some curriculum changes. I don't think we're about the needs of children. I think we're all about drill-and-kill, teaching the test. You know what I mean?

Principal Rendon: Emma, I know what you mean, but . . . well, it's the state-mandated curriculum. How can we change, Emma, when the curriculum is dictated to us by the state and the district? I'm a willing risk-taker, and I'm willing to do whatever it takes to ensure that our students learn and succeed. But how do you negotiate a nonnegotiable?

Emma Murphy: Felipe, I've been teaching 22 years, and I think I'm pretty good at what I do. I've been a teacher-of-the-year recipient three different times over those years, once at the state level. I strongly believe that more nonnegotiables are more negotiable than the district lets on. You were a very effective teacher before you became an assistant principal and now a principal. Don't you agree?

Felipe sat across the desk from Emma, internalizing her every word. Then, he let a small smile turn into a great big grin!

Principal Rendon: Okay, Emma, you've got my attention. I'm with you. Yes, every nonnegotiable must be negotiated. That's what evaluating and reforming curriculum, instruction, and every other aspect of the educational program is all about. It just gets my goat when someone from central office spouts to the masses: "This or that is a nonnegotiable!" *Eso es pura papa!* Emma, *that's pure potato*, or as we would say in English, *that's a lot of baloney!* So tell me, what's the real bee in your bonnet?

Emma Murphy: Felipe, I think we need to seriously sit down as a team and talk about how our curriculum program needs to change. We've allowed the state-mandated curriculum to take our teaching genius and creativity away. You've got an excellent team here at Harrisburg Elementary School. We all know what we're doing. We also know what we're not doing!

Principal Rendon: So what are we not doing, Emma?

Emma Murphy: Let me put it as straightforward as I can! We're not doing right by our students. We don't involve our students in curriculum design. We don't strive to teach to our students what is of interest to them and what is relevant to their current and future lives. We teach the test, we practice the test, and then we take the test. That's all we do around here! We don't realize it, but I think we are forgetting that our actions speak louder than our words. Our actions are loud and clear: We simply don't care! Now Felipe, that's wrong!

Principal Rendon: Emma, those are fighting words! Are you ready for me to stir the troops—especially those in the curriculum department over at central office? Is this a battle worth fighting?

Emma Murphy: Felipe, you know me and I know you. What do you think?

Application Questions

1. Lewis, Schaps, and Watson (1995) suggest in their article "Beyond the Pendulum: Creating Challenging and Caring Schools" that the needs of students are ignored in a drill-and-kill curriculum. This type of curricular approach is far from relevant and of interest to students. How might a curriculum that integrates instruction across the content areas help schools overcome drill-and-kill and be of relevance and interest to students? Support your answer.

2. In the scenario, Emma states that "we simply don't care" about students because, as educators, we follow state and district mandated

(Continued)

(*Continued*)

curriculums. Is there any truth to Emma's assessment? Explain and support your answer.

3. Michael Fullan, in his text *What's Worth Fighting For in the Principalship* (2008), relates that school districts expect their principals to follow dictates that are district and state determined. Fullan suggests that as a result, a campus principal readily finds himself between a rock and a hard place. How does Fullan's assessment relate to systematically integrating curriculum and instruction as detailed in this chapter? What's a principal to do?

4. Tomlinson and McTighe (2006) assert that what really matters in planning for student success is a compelling curriculum, accepting responsibility for what students learn, differentiating instruction, and being aware of what is of interest and relevance (what works) for students. How would integrating curriculum and instruction serve to meet each of these proposed considerations? Respond by relating your answer to the research regarding curriculum integration and differentiated instruction.

5. Katherine Cennamo and Debby Kalk in their text *Real World Instructional Design* (2005) believe that a critical aspect of effectively designing curriculum and instructional programs must be based on collaboration and communication. How does this belief relate to the Interstate School Leaders Licensure Consortium standards, as detailed in Chapter 2, and to the case study presented in this chapter? Additionally, determine a plan of action (from a collaboration/communication perspective) for Principal Felipe Rendon to incorporate, relative to the systematic integration of curriculum and instruction, at Harrisburg Elementary School. Be detailed in your response and provide a step-by-step course of action.

Other Resources

Hale, J. A. (2008). *A guide to curriculum mapping: Planning, implementing, and sustaining the process*. Thousand Oaks, CA: Corwin.

Sowell, E. J. (2005). *Curriculum: An integrative introduction*. Upper Saddle River, NJ: Pearson Education.

Squires, D. A. (2009). *Curriculum alignment: Research-based strategies for increasing student achievement*. Thousand Oaks, CA: Corwin.

8

Professional Learning and Curriculum Leadership

Teachers and students go hand in hand as learners—or they don't go at all!

—Roland Barth (*Learning by Heart*, 2001, p. 23)

Teaching and Learning

Recall the account from Chapter 2 detailing how Principal Will Wonkermann put on his curriculum leader glasses and ruby-red Reeboks to venture on an imaginary whirlwind tour of the six national school leader standards. At each stop, Will added depth, delineation, and structure to the sometimes chaotic role of the principal as curriculum leader. The stop at Standard 2, Teaching and Learning, provided a glimpse into the expectations of principal as curriculum leader. School missions, organizational systems, and community relationships derive their importance from the central core of the school business. That central core is teaching and learning. In fact, teaching and learning relate to Interstate School Leaders Licensure Consortium (ISLLC) Performance Expectation 2. The research literature confirms what successful principals recognize: Student learning is positively impacted when adults in the schoolhouse learn as well. Student learning and adult learning go together if curriculum development and renewal are to occur. One cannot exist without the other. If schools have effective learning environments, students and teachers will succeed.

ISLLC Performance Expectation 2: Teaching and Learning

Education leaders ensure achievement and success of all students by monitoring and continuously improving teaching and learning.

Performance Expectation 2 Dispositions

Educational leaders believe in, value, and are committed to the following:

- Learning as the fundamental purpose of school
- Diversity as an asset
- Continuous professional growth and development
- Lifelong learning
- Collaboration with all stakeholders
- High expectations for all
- Student learning

Embedded in Performance Expectation 2 is an important point all principals, as curriculum leaders, must understand: Dedication to students and their learning and achievement is priority and goal Number 1. Effective principals and teachers want to do right by their students. Effective principals and teachers also recognize that with any curricular change an aura of doubt or skepticism with some cynicism thrown into the mix begins to permeate a school. Effective principals understand why. They are not surprised because they have "been there done that!" Consider the scenario below where Principal Wonkermann recalls a professional development session at Childers School not so long ago. Actually, it was one afternoon he would rather forget.

UNPROFESSIONAL PROFESSIONAL DEVELOPMENT

The teachers began to file into the library shortly after the dismissal bell at Childers School. Each teacher was receiving a small stipend to attend three hours of professional development that afternoon. The district had provided snacks and drinks, but the fatigue and wear and tear of the day showed on the teachers' faces. After all, working with students all day tends to make one tired. This was a mandatory session—one of those *nonnegotiables*. The state had come out with some new programs, and every teacher at Childers was to receive this particular training. This was the latest elixir that would solve one of the critical issues at Childers School.

The presenter arrived. She was young and full of energy, a fact that made the teachers wonder about her credibility and what she had done all day while they strove to get across the importance of the Civil War and the mysteries of fractions. Too bad the session took place in the library where the furniture was not designed for adult bodies. The library had not been remodeled in 20 years. Small and cramped, it was virtually impossible to arrange the seating so everyone could see the PowerPoint presentation focused on the screen. Seeing the screen was important because this was state mandated "training-in-a-box" that had to be delivered as scripted. Composed of more than 300 slides, the presenter figured there'd be little time for group discussion. Since it was after school, she thought little discussion might be good anyway. Teachers tended to get testy at the end of the day, and in more than one of these sessions, the presenter had reached in her bag of tricks for some activities for working with difficult participants. She would talk very fast to see if she could squeeze these three hours into two and a half, and that way, they could possibly finish early. She recognized that teachers liked finishing early. It also helped with her presenter evaluations. This particular training had been designed specifically to address curricular issues in great need of revision and renewal. The presenter's greatest worry was that the teachers would revolt at some of the suggestions for implementation.

For the life of him, Will Wonkermann could not remember the title of that session. He knew it had something to do with curriculum but he had always let central office personnel worry about curricular issues. So after he'd introduced the presenter, he'd snuck back to his office to answer e-mails and work on the district discipline report. Now, he felt uneasy when he thought about that experience from the teachers' perspective. He doubted that any of the teachers remembered the topic either. After school, the faculty was tired; they were trying to figure out what to do with their own children at home, what to make for dinner, and how to meet family obligations, like homework, while staying at school for three extra hours.

This professional development scenario is all too common in schools today. No wonder professional development gets such a bad rap with teachers. One of the first principles of meaningful professional development relates to the old adage: The brain can absorb only what the seat can endure! Just like in a classroom, the environment sets the tone. Professional development conducted in an emotionally or physically uncomfortable setting is doomed before it even begins. Principals like Will Wonkermann should resolve right now to end the practice of conducting professional development after school, especially training that relates to curriculum development, revision, or renewal. It almost always does more harm than good.

A Subtle Semantic Shift: Moving to Professional Learning

The negative connotation associated with the term "professional development" has caused the National Staff Development Council (NSDC), now called Learning Forward, to change their terminology. In an attempt to more clearly define what needs to happen, Learning Forward has chosen to use the term "professional learning." Although this is a subtle difference, the change is important. Professional development implies something that is done to someone or something, but professional learning implies personal commitment. Learning occurs deep within. It is not done to anyone. Lois Brown Easton (2008) defines professional development as occurring when one person develops or changes another. A person cannot "learn" another person. Easton suggests that "learning is ongoing, and ultimately, in the hands of the learner" (p. 2).

PROFESSIONAL LEARNING GETS THE ATTENTION OF WILL WONKERMANN

Principal Will Wonkermann wanted to believe in the power of meaningful, job-embedded, ongoing professional development but he was beginning to think it didn't exist. He had read in one of the professional journals something about professional learning—something about in-servicing that was not an add-on to a teacher's already busy schedule but was built into the fabric of the school day. Just-in-time professional learning that addressed short-term, immediate issues as well as long-term district and campus goals. He wanted the faculty at Childers School to benefit from high-quality professional experiences, but he wasn't exactly certain how to deliver the goods. He agreed with Hirsh and Killion's (2007) assertion that teachers seldom experience quality professional development enabling them to be more effective educators, especially when it came to the development and renewal of curriculum. Will was not certain how the faculty at Childers School would get there, but he knew his role as a curriculum leader was to improve teaching and learning at the campus. In fact, he saw this as a primary responsibility with great potential for lasting impact.

Will remembered Roland Barth's (2001) words in *Learning by Heart*. Barth was no fence-sitter about the importance of professional learning. He wrote that meaningful student learning would not occur in the absence of adult learning. Barth had caught Will's attention. Will wanted to know more about professional learning.

Barth's (2001) words reminded Will of Learning Forward's purpose statement: *Every educator engages in effective professional learning every day so every student achieves* (www.learningforward.org/index.cfm). He wondered if Childers School could be transformed into a school where this was the norm. Could he and his curriculum team really establish a culture where professional learning occurred at the school several times a week? Sounded impossible! Could a culture be established at Childers where professional learning was an integral part of the normal workweek? Just how easily accessible was professional learning? Will began to think about educational beliefs that could guide the curricular transformation that needed to occur at Childers School.

If effective professional learning on a regular basis for every teacher was to become a priority, the principal and teachers would need to share the planning, development, and delivery of professional learning.

SET GOALS AND DREAM BIG!

Principal Will Wonkermann understood that common values and shared beliefs drove campus actions. He saw this played out at Childers School every day. Agenda items that mattered to the teachers were completed. What they deemed unimportant fell by the wayside. Will thought about faculty representation during curriculum development and renewal processes. The faculty ranged from veteran teachers already eligible for retirement to novice teachers who were only one or two years out of teacher preparation programs. The way novice teachers thought and viewed teaching differed from that of veteran teachers. But that was understandable, and Will recognized that all parties must be accepted and respected when it came to the development or renewal of campus curriculum. He could ill afford to overlook any generation within the Childers School faculty. Currently, Childers's faculty spanned four generational categories:

(Continued)

(*Continued*)

- Veterans born between 1922 and 1943

- Boomers born between 1944 and 1960

- Generation Xers born between 1960 and 1980

- Millennials, born between 1980 and 2000 (Zemke, Raines, & Filipczak, 2000)

Will knew it was important to view the generational differences across the campus as a strength. School personnel must be recognized, included, and appreciated.

Principal Wonkermann also knew his tendency to take control when tense situations arose at the school. Of course, there were situations where the commander-in-charge leadership style was necessary. Will was very much aware of situational leadership. He recalled the time last year when the natural gas line broke and the building had to be evacuated. There was no time for faculty collaboration. He made the immediate decision to solve the problem—Get out of the building! However, in most situations, Will realized he must avoid the autocratic style of leadership. If he was serious about shared leadership, if he believed in a collaborative team spirit, it was essential that he practice what he preached. This meant allowing teachers to carry out plans in their way, as long as they were aligned to the school's mission, vision, and goals. The faculty at Childers School was skilled and possessed a wide variety and levels of expertise. Principal Wonkermann must demonstrate not only facilitative but also ethical leadership. Some of the Childers's teachers were far better curriculum leaders than he. He needed to find ways for them to shine, to showcase their instructional and curricular expertise. Will wanted to orchestrate the life of the campus so each person took on a leadership role. This would embed professional learning into the ongoing life of the school, and it would best ensure the effective and essential development and renewal of curriculum. Will believed that when school personnel took on leadership roles, they applied the learning in a real way. It became useful and relevant learning that benefited all parties—most notably the students!

Will smiled when he thought about dreaming big. He remembered reading about BHAGS (Big Hairy Audacious Goals) in *Built to Last* by Collins and Porras (2002).These big goals represented something that the whole school could get behind and support. They were rallying points, the big dreams that unified the school and got everyone moving in the same direction. It was easy to see the importance of goal setting in all aspects of the school, including curricular and extracurricular activities. Everybody wanted to win the game or excel in the classroom; in band, choir, or speech competitions; on the basketball court; or on the football field. He knew it took a big hairy audacious goal for the Childers Eagles to win the state football championship. This had not occurred since 1956. But the football team set their goals, dreamed big, and won game after game! Will remembered visiting with big right tackle, Number 77, Noslen G. Smith. Noslen told Will, "Mr. Wonkermann, we learned something very important this championship season: There's nothing magical about setting goals. It's all about achieving goals. Team goals are most likely to be achieved if there is a commitment to them by all members of the team." The conversation both amused and impressed Will. First, Number 77 didn't mind at all interacting with his principal; second, and more impressive, Number 77 revealed a mature-thinking truth! Thus, in a way, BHAGS grabbed everyone's attention. Will thought that closing the learning gap between all special populations was a BHAG worth pursuing. Will resolved to maintain a schoolwide focus on goal setting as it related to teaching, learning, and curriculum leadership. He knew this could positively affect the curriculum development and renewal processes, important to the organizational success of Childers School.

Will was embarrassed to admit that he knew very little about how to evaluate curriculum through a professional learning approach. About all he'd ever done was to ensure that everyone was happy when the curriculum development sessions ended. He'd focused on the room set up, the physical arrangements, and the scheduling, but he had done little to assess the impact of the professional learning on curriculum and instruction. He'd noticed whether test scores went up or down, but he had never tied this directly to professional learning sessions. He knew he had a great deal to learn about curricular and instructional program evaluation. Several people who worked in central office had expertise in this area and had mentioned more than once that they would like to form an evaluation team. In fact, they had asked Will to join them in this venture. Maybe, Will thought to himself, a couple of teachers could join in as well. After all, professional learning on the campus wasn't reserved just for the lead learner. He thought *all of us are smarter than any one of us*.

If teachers were given the time and tools, they had the expertise and would come up with viable solutions to almost any problem—solutions that were tailor made to address specific campus needs. The Childers team knew what needed to happen. It was time to tap into their abilities and let them take ownership of their learning.

(Continued)

(*Continued*)

Principal Wonkermann knew that the faculty had entered teaching, in part, because they loved learning. What had happened within the system to squelch this? How had things eroded to the point where professional development was considered a waste of everyone's valuable time? Giving the teachers ownership would go a long way toward making a positive difference. His challenge would be harnessing power, productivity, and levels of expertise of the Childers's faculty and getting things moving in a unified and positive direction. Teachers tend to be independent thinkers. As the school transitioned into a professional learning community with teams of teachers working collaboratively and in charge of their learning, teaching and curriculum development would improve.

Finally, Will thought back to his days in graduate school. His university employed a cohort model. He remembered working with his peers to develop plans and programs. Invariably, one person's comment would spark the thinking of someone else, and before long, synergy had taken over. What developed was far more compelling than anything one person could have created alone. Some of those plans had actually worked well in real-world classrooms, campuses, and districts. Besides that, the process was enjoyable and promoted a sense of respect and camaraderie.

Once viewed as just directives on a page, Will now saw how the national standards had application to his daily practice and life at his school. He was convinced that professional learning must happen every day on his campus. Although there would still be times when outside presenters needed to inform their thinking or groups of teachers would need to participate in workshops, everything would be aligned to what the teachers and the students at Childers needed.

What a mind shift Will Wonkermann had undergone. He thought back to his early days as a teacher and then as a beginning principal. He remembered the days when he viewed professional development opportunities as a day off. He resolved never again to place such a low value on professional learning that was designed to enhance student achievement. His challenge now was to create structures that would lead the teachers to value professional learning as well. Barth's (2001) words haunted him, "Teachers and students go hand in hand as learners—or they don't go at all" (p. 23).

Building Teacher Capacity

What kinds of professional learning enhance teachers' abilities and lead to increased learning for students? Principals understand teaching as the school's core technology. Teaching improves when teachers' knowledge and expertise improves. But increasing knowledge isn't enough. If professional learning is to impact student learning, it must go beyond what Vaill (1996) called institutional learning. Institutional learning is learning that never becomes embedded into daily practice as opposed to learning that develops from experiences and becomes integrated life learning. Remember those academic experiences in high school and college that required memorizing the periodic table or cramming algebraic formulas into our heads? Learning like this is retained long enough to pass the test and make an acceptable grade in the course. However, much of the useful working knowledge about these topics vanished almost immediately.

Professional Learning for Permanent White-Water Conditions

White-water rafting is a challenging activity using an inflatable raft to navigate a river. White-water rafting down the Arkansas River in Colorado during the spring thaw is not for the faint of heart. Rapids are full of dangers. Churning waves, huge rocks, large drops, and other hazards are dangerous, even life-threatening. Rafters must work together in these conditions if they are to safely navigate the river and its rapids. Vaill (1996) viewed 21st-century society as being in the throes of permanent white water, white water not created by huge waves, rocks, and drops but, instead, created by surprises, unique challenges, and untidy and costly events. Much like white-water rafters on the Arkansas River, school leaders encounter conditions that take them out of their comfort zones. These events require leaders to perform feats they never anticipated. Vaill viewed society as one of permanent white water, and today's school leadership role as one of "permanent life outside one's comfort zone" (p. 14).

Schools are certainly experiencing permanent white-water conditions. Teachers require professional learning that goes beyond institutional learning. They require professional learning that motivates them to use their capacity for effective teaching and empowers them to use their expertise and energy. Professional learning must impact their thought processes and their daily decisions. Student learning benefits from empowered, motivated teachers who incorporate their professional learning into their daily practice.

Four Factors Impacting Professional Learning

Providing professional learning opportunities at school is essential if curriculum development and renewal is to occur without teacher avoidance or revolt. Unlike other sources that deal with models of learning or specific professional development planning, principals must focus on matters of the heart. Four factors drive meaningful professional learning:

1. Generational differences

2. Career/life-cycle considerations

3. Brain research and teacher learning

4. Classroom monitoring and active engagement

These factors provide direction for professional learning. Each factor focuses on the conditions necessary for professional learning to take root and grow on a campus.

Factor 1: Generational Differences

White-water conditions stress people out, and Childers's faculty is no exception. Childers School's teachers span four generations—a situation not uncommon in schools and other workplaces. In fact, Zemke, Raines, & Filipczak (2000) researched the multigenerational nature of today's workplaces, concluding that there has never been a time when we have had such generational diversity in our workforce. This generational diversity is noticeable at Childers School, especially during times of tension and anxiety.

CHILDERS SCHOOL'S FOUR-GENERATION FACULTY

The Veterans (1922–1943)

Gravett and Throckmorton (2007) called them the Radio Babies. They were young during World War II when radio was the chief means of nationwide communication. They know how to entertain themselves without any media at all. Tom Brokaw (1998) made them famous in his best seller, *The Greatest Generation*. They are known for their work ethic and ability to make do and survive. Teachers of this generation can make the 1940s and 1950s come alive to their students just through lecture.

Harold Jones and Edna Smith have been teaching at Childers for almost 40 years. Boy, they have seen many changes. When they started, the blackboard was about the only teaching tool in the school. The overhead projector was a new innovation. Technology was a foreign term. Video consisted of 16mm reel-to-reel films that were ordered from the local education agency. Teaching and learning were contained within a single classroom, and the teacher was the one with the knowledge.

(Pssst . . . Can you identify Fibber Magee and Molly, The Shadow, and Our Miss Brooks? If so, you might be a Veteran.)

The Boomers (1945–1964)

Boomers were born between 1945 and 1964. This generation is marked by a desire to have it all. Their parents instilled in them the belief that anything was possible if you worked hard enough. They came of age during the turbulent years of Vietnam and the cultural revolution. Memories of civil unrest and assassinations blended with Woodstock and the triumph of seeing men walk on the moon. Will noted that this group of teachers seemed driven by hard work.

Phyllis Spencer and Stephanie James spend more hours on the campus than anyone else. Phyllis has been at Childers 20 years, and Stephanie joined the faculty a year later. They are best friends and like working together. Both have a subtle desire to prove they are the best. They also possess a crystallized set of skills that defines good teaching. Phyllis and Stephanie along with other members of this generation are the teacher leaders at Childers School. With their years of experience, most boomers feel they already know best teaching practices and see no reason to change. While the Internet and Google searches might be valid, they question whether these methods represent real learning. Driven perfectionists, they have paid their dues and followed the rules. At the top of the game, boomers are the power brokers on the campus. Will needs their support if professional learning is to become more than lip service.

(Pssst . . . If you typed your term papers on a typewriter, saw every episode of *Leave It to Beaver*, and watched man's first trip to the moon on live TV, you might be a Boomer.)

Generation X (1960–1980)

Many teachers at Childers fall into the age bracket designated as Generation X, born between 1960 and 1980. These teachers grew up in a world of dual-income families, emerging technology, a recessed economy, and the threat of nuclear warfare. In the 1980s many of their parents lost their jobs, and family incomes plummeted. As children, they experienced the reality of company layoffs with little corporate consideration for the employee's plight and no safety net.

Martha Malone and Sydney Scott are two of Childers School's Generation Xers. Each has had several teaching positions and talks frequently about changing careers. They make a point to keep their options open. They want many choices and tend to be independent. For Martha and Sydney, there is always an alternate plan, one that would provide a safety net for them and their families.

(Pssst . . . If you played *Asteroids* on the Atari, saw the original *Star Wars* on opening day and word processed your homework on an Apple 2e, you might be a Generation Xer.)

(Continued)

(Continued)

The Millennials (1980–2000)

On the other end of the generational extreme are Tamica Yen and Raul Menendez, both in their early 20s and in their first year of teaching. For them, technology is a mainstay. They can't envision life without texting or tweeting. PINs, passwords, and call-answering systems are part of business as usual. The Internet is their coteacher. Students routinely create PowerPoints, perform web quests, and work on group papers using wikis. Teacher and students are expected to contribute to the class blog. They routinely chat with students from around the globe. Frequently, when questions arise, Tamika has one of her students Google to obtain additional information. Millennials see themselves as facilitators of information. They know where to obtain what they need. Digital-research skills are emphasized in their classes. As digital natives born after the invention of the Internet, they have never known life without it. Will marvels at their ability to switch rapidly between tasks. He admits that, more than once, he's been irritated by their seeming inattention during faculty meetings. He struggles to understand how people can do more than one thing at once.

(Pssst . . . If you can't remember life without Nintendo, PlayStation, and the Wii, you might be a Millennial.)

A Multigenerational Faculty

Is there any validity in considering faculty generational differences? Martin and Tulgan (2006) caution against stereotyping people according to age. However, helpful information can be gained by examining generational trends in attitudes and behavior. Of course, people's individual circumstances are the overriding factors shaping their frame of reference, but Martin and Tulgan reason that common events have a profound effect on a generation's collective mindset.

The generational composition of a school's faculty is a significant contributing factor affecting the outcome of professional learning. For the first time, four distinct generations working on the same campus is a possibility, if not a reality. What menu of professional learning best addresses the demands and needs of multigenerational faculty? How are generational differences affecting relationships with students, parents, and other community members? Most have witnessed misunderstandings rooted in cross-age differences. These misunderstandings have led to hurt feelings, toxic cultures, and dysfunctional relationships—all which impede student learning. Lovely and Buffum (2007) believe for a professional learning community to exist, generational biases must be removed. As multigenerational faculty work together, they must understand that teaching is not about getting their way. Teaching is about meeting learner needs.

Factor 2: Teachers' Career Life Cycle

A second factor involves the career and life stage of each teacher on the campus. Glickman, Gordon, and Ross-Gordon (2007); Huberman (1989); and Steffy, Wolfe, Pasch, and Enz (2000) wrote about the growth and development of teachers throughout their teaching careers. Although these studies varied to some degree, they agreed that teachers progress through several distinct career stages leading either to fulfillment and job satisfaction or to disengaged teachers who were retired on the job.

Gary Waddell's 2009 *Journal of Staff Development* article "Who's That Teacher?" introduced a teacher efficacy matrix that looked at the intersection of two distinct teacher skill sets: (1) mastery of content and knowledge of standards and (2) strong student focus (knowing students individually and being able to motivate and inspire them to master rigorous content). Waddell suggests that teacher strength or weakness in these two skill sets determines their optimum type of supervision and professional learning. Teachers strong in both skill sets (master teachers) need training that is different from teachers with minimum competence in both skill sets. Beginning teachers or teachers with arrested teacher development, as described in Chapter 6, are likely to exhibit fewer strengths in both these areas. Teachers function at different levels in these two skill sets. Knowing the level of teacher mastery in these areas provides valuable insight into what professional learning would be most beneficial for teachers.

Factor 3: Brain Research and Professional Learning

Sousa's (2009) discussion of recent discoveries in brain research provides valuable information for curriculum leaders about professional learning for faculty. Imaging technologies suggest ways to create professional development that would engender deep learning. Sousa, to no one's surprise, noted that teachers, irked by mandatory professional learning, resist learning. Teachers will not necessarily share these negative feelings but are likely to engage in passive aggressive behavior, such as grading papers during the training. Sousa suggests that professional learning should do the following:

- Employ challenging, exciting, and creative instructional strategies
- Address topics identified by teachers as needed
- Build on interactive strategies using learning styles techniques
- Provide for active, ongoing feedback

Brain-compatible strategies allow teachers to connect past experiences and relate new learning to job-related goals. New material should be presented over time using active learning strategies and enough depth to allow for application. Action research around the new learning would be encouraged as well as study groups to support those who questioned the new practice (Sousa, 2009). Drive-by training and after-school sessions such as the one referenced earlier in this chapter are ineffective.

Factor 4: Active Engagement

Marzano, Waters, and McNulty (2005), in a meta-analysis of research, found that "monitoring the effectiveness of school practices and their impact on student learning" (p. 43) had a high correlation to student achievement. Likewise, Hall and Simeral (2008) found daily, intentional supervision a key element in developing teacher capacity. This research confirms that effective curriculum leadership requires principals to be out of their offices and in classrooms where the teaching occurs.

Visiting classrooms daily isn't an unrealistic expectation. One to three minutes in a classroom provides a feel for what is transpiring. Initially, teachers might be anxious or suspicious, but when a collaborative relationship focused on teaching and learning develops, faculty become at ease. These daily visits can inform professional learning needs.

Curriculum leaders improve teacher effectiveness through targeted supervision. Todd Whitaker (2003) noted that effective leaders have the same workload and demands as ineffective leaders. A key difference is that effective leaders don't allow the unimportant to replace the important. Great curriculum leaders supervise, they apply pressure to high-leverage points, and then they provide enough assistance and support for teachers to succeed.

This sounds deceptively simple, but maintaining balance between pressure and support takes careful planning and forethought. Curriculum leaders are human and will never achieve a perfect balance every time. However, curriculum leaders will get it right a greater percentage of the time if they are where the action is—in classrooms listening and observing, applying support and pressure. Hall and Simeral (2008) remind us that teachers are a school's most valuable asset and that "classrooms are where they do what they do" (p. 108).

Data Collection, Feedback, and Sustained Support

Creating meaningful individualized professional learning involves data collection, feedback, and sustained support. Decisions about how much support to offer or how much pressure to apply are made continuously based on data. What is observed in the classroom provides a rich source of data that augments other forms, rounding out the picture.

Meaningful, individualized professional learning is developed as a response to campus and individual needs. Clinical supervision focuses on assisting, supporting, and collaborating with teachers to enhance their repertoire of skills to improve student performance. Glickman, Gordon, and Ross-Gordon (2007) outline a supervisory behavior continuum that pinpoints categories of teacher behaviors accompanied by appropriate supervisor behaviors. Teachers at a highly developed level of professionalism assume more responsibility for their professional growth and the supervisory relationship spans a continuum from directive to nondirective approaches. An effective curriculum leader plays the same role with teachers that effective teachers play with students. Both address the varied needs and characteristics of those they supervise.

Final Thoughts

Knowledge of these needs is gained through studying your school. The four factors highlighted in this chapter—(1) generational differences, (2) career/life-cycle stages, (3) use of brain compatible strategies, and (4) classroom monitoring and active engagement—provide a way to examine a school from a different perspective. When these factors are rooted in principles, meaningful professional learning produces positive results for students and teachers.

The goal for the curriculum leader is to guide every faculty member with the appropriate balance of support and pressure. This comes through professional learning that is developmentally appropriate, focused on needs, and combines support and pressure. Creating meaningful professional learning comes down to one question: How well do you know your faculty?

Discussion Questions

1. Give Principal Will Wonkermann three suggestions to improve the Unprofessional Professional Development conducted on his campus. What are three pieces of advice you would give to the presenter? Give reasons for your answers.

2. Interview a faculty member from each of the four generational groups. Ask about their teacher preparation, their professional development experiences, and their preferred method of professional learning. What similarities did you discover? What differences?

3. Watch three episodes each of situational comedies popular in the 1960s, 1980s, and 2000s. Chart the generational differences you observe. Compare and contrast them. What are the implications for education?

4. What factors, within your control, would improve your ability to lead a school in implementing effective professional learning?

5. Analyze your school's schedule. Identify ways to restructure the time to allow for daily teacher learning experiences and collaboration.

6. Reflect on your experience with professional development. If you are like most teachers, you have had great experiences and some that were not so great. Using points from this chapter, discuss why some of your personal professional development experiences affected student learning and others did not.

CASE STUDY APPLICATION
Professional Learning at Sandy Shores School

Sandy Shores School is located in the Live Oaks school district and has a population of about 500 students. The school is 30% Anglo, 35% Hispanic, 25% African American, 5% Asian American, and 5% other. Approximately one-third of the students qualify for free-or-reduced lunch, 25% are identified as English language learners, and the campus mobility rate is 40%. Not long ago, most students came from white, middle-class families. Now the school has a more ethnically diverse population, with many students from working-class and/or immigrant families. Since the demographics began changing, test scores across all groups have steadily decreased.

The teaching staff is comprised of a few Veterans, Boomers, Generation Xers, and Millennials. The Veterans and Boomers have been on the campus an average of 15 years. There is tension and distrust among the faculty. The Millennials and Generation Xers view the Veterans and Boomers as antiques who don't relate to the students, and the Boomers and Veterans see their younger counterparts as inexperienced and idealistic. All agree, however, that professional development is largely a waste of time.

The new principal of Sandy Shores is Will Wonkermann's friend, Sam Smith. Sam is Sandy Shores' first principal from the Millennial generation. Sam knows he needs to approach things differently if he wants to improve Sandy Shores. Sam is all about active engagement. Professional learning is a priority too.

Application Questions

1. What are three beginning steps Sam can take to develop and articulate common values and shared beliefs?

2. List three strategies for building strong working relationships among multigenerational faculty members. Why did you choose these strategies? (Hint: Lovely & Buffum, 2007, is a good resource.)

3. Explore the interconnectedness of the ISLLC standards, the Learning Forward standards, and the four factors discussed in this chapter. Focus on how these elements work together to move professional development toward professional learning in the Sandy Shores environment.

4. Share three strategies for maintaining a schoolwide focus on teaching and learning.

5. What challenges would you expect to encounter in establishing and maintaining a professional learning community in a school? Select one challenge and suggest how you might address it.

6. Barriers to the successful implementation of effective professional learning can be categorized as cultural, organizational, political, and/or psychological. For each of these categories, identify one barrier and briefly describe why it might be a challenge for successful implementation.

7. Explain why continuing professional learning is critical to improving student learning, increasing teacher capacity, and fostering continuous school improvement.

Other Resources

Burmeister, M. (2008). *From boomers to bloggers: Success strategies across generations*. Fairfax, VA: Synergy Press.

Fogarty, R., & Pete, B. (2007). *From staff room to classroom: A guide for planning and coaching professional development*. Thousand Oaks, CA: Corwin.

Jacobs, H. (Ed.). (2010). *Curriculum 21: Essential education for a changing world*. Alexandria, VA: American Association for Supervision and Curriculum Development.

Joyce, B., & Calhoun, E. (2010). *Models of professional development: A celebration of educators*. Thousand Oaks, CA: Corwin.

Killion, J. (2008). *Assessing impact: Evaluating staff development*. Thousand Oaks, CA: Corwin.

Killion, J., & Roy, R. (2009). *Becoming a learning school*. Oxford, OH: National Staff Development Council.

Sprenger, M. (2010). *Brain-based teaching in the digital age*. Alexandria, VA: American Association for Supervision and Curriculum Development.

Yendol-Hoppey, D., & Dana, N. (2010). *Powerful professional development: Building expertise within the four walls of your school*. Thousand Oaks, CA: Corwin.

9

The Principal and Legislated Learning

Working the System and the Prospects of Curriculum Renewal

Now that I was in the principal's office, I thought I was ideally suited to make a difference for teachers and kids. Was I right?

—Kim Marshall, Former Principal,
Boston's Mather School (2010, p. 279)

Curriculum Leadership and Legislated Learning

Drawing from a conception of curriculum leadership that involves the principal's active role as an educational broker and cultural translator, as was previously examined in Chapter 5, let's explore how principals can strive to meet state-legislated standards and work diligently toward a renewal of curriculum. Because curriculum renewal and the associated instructional change (recall Chapter 4) are complex endeavors in the regimented educational policy context of public schooling, principals must carefully consider the place of curriculum theory, as a set of "intellectual instrumentality" (Dewey, 1916/1990), which can guide and inform innovative curricular renewal and instructional practice. Kim Marshall's question "Was I right?" within the introductory quote readily correlates with this chapter topic and with the principal role in curriculum renewal. Regrettably, there is no room for "*Was* I right?" when it comes to working the system and the prospects of curriculum renewal. Principals *must* be right! They must have the knowledge, skills, expertise, and perseverance to lead any curriculum renewal process when working within the system of legislated learning.

Current educational policy dictates that states design and implement a standardized curriculum (Oliva, 2009). The push for the standardization of curriculum or legislated learning is sanctioned and maintained through a notion of schooling that evokes and exalts certain values embedded in American culture and its conception of democracy (Meier, 2000). Among those values are the concepts of access, excellence, and accountability. Hence, the legislating of a set of minimum curricular content that schools must deliver in classrooms is predicated and sustained based on the idea that a standardized curriculum and an assessment process are an efficient way of ensuring that all students have equal access to an excellent education that is measured through various forms of testing and accountability. This narrow, bland approach to curriculum, as described by Ornstein and Hunkins (2009), continues to expand across the nation despite the fact that an increasing diversity of students enroll in our schools every day, and to our disappointment, if not horror, they regularly fail in our schools. This shrinking approach to curriculum development and renewal has been instigated by the demands of corporate America and the mandates of federal and state legislation. Thus, Smith (2006) suggests that the explicit political curricular goal in recent years has been an emphasis on reading, mathematics, science, and social studies. Such, regrettably, is nothing more than a narrowed curriculum focus where the arts, music, physical education, and foreign languages are typically ignored (Cuban, 2004).

Despite the fact that public schools and the formal legislated curriculum appear to share many similarities, they are highly idiosyncratic spaces. Distinct student bodies, teachers, administrators, and communities shape, in unique ways, the culture of a school and its everyday instructional functions. Thus, although a legislated curriculum might provide a foundation from which school personnel can build and develop a course of study at each grade level, principals and teachers often find that they must work to adapt standards if they are to respond effectively to the local conditions of the school and the community they serve and if the school curriculum is to be enriched and extended beyond the required competencies toward the achievement of broader educational aims.

Not surprisingly, however, it is common to find that principals and teachers are conflicted between the curriculum they know is best for their students and the federal/state-legislated curriculum. This conundrum often stems from practitioners' views of the legislated curriculum as one that is overly prescriptive and subject-centered on one hand and, on the other hand, one that is assessed through state-mandated accountability measures of academic performance. Because such measures determine, to a great extent, students' academic futures and a school's viability, delivering the legislated or mandated curriculum—regardless of its relevance, merit, or worth—becomes an absolute imperative.

Pause and Consider

Think about your school's curriculum.

- What expectations, relative to academic achievement, are conveyed to teachers at your school?

- What are the means through which those expectations are reached?

- What messages about your school's commitment to students' education are implicit in the expectations set forth by your campus leadership and the legislated/mandated curriculum?

The Principal in the Process of Curriculum Renewal and Change

In the current context of legislated and standardized curriculum, principals—like teachers—often puzzle over the prospect of renewal and related change. That puzzlement is more evident when schools are performing at or above acceptable state-defined levels of student academic achievement. A principal is pressured and incentivized to spend time, energy, and associated resources (fiscal, human, and material) to best ensure that a campus meets state and federal accountability requirements. Thus, the question of curriculum renewal becomes, often understandably, a less than pressing issue. After all, why change something when the "something" is measured against the sanctioned system of accountability and, moreover, appears to work? What would be the impetus to renew curriculum that is not only legislated but is also tested via a mandated accountability process?

Sarason (1996) and Fullan (2001) contend that any change, especially as related to the renewal of curriculum, is always problematic (recall the section in Chapter 4, Why We Resist Change). This is so true of the complex bureaucracies that constitute public schools. In schools today, participants often hold divergent notions and interpretations of their school's purpose, goals, and the means through which they will be achieved. As such, the role of the principal is to work on the difficult task of leading the school community toward common purposes and goals and toward the school's collective effort and action to obtain said purposes and goals, most notably, as related to the practice of curriculum renewal.

Intriguingly, however, in the prevalent efficiency approach to schooling that informs educational mandates and standardized curriculums (McNeil, 2000), the complexity of arriving at a shared view of the purpose of schooling appears to have been resolved. The purpose of schooling, in the current context, is limited to a focus on student-achievement test scores. Thus, an unintended outcome of the current policy context is a class of educators whose sole view of the purpose of schooling and education is circumscribed to meeting standards as not only the ends but the means of public schools. Simply put, principals and teachers often seem to work in educational settings of pretest, test-prep, posttest, reteach, pretest, test-prep, posttest, and repeat as necessary! Sound absurd? Well, it is! So what's a principal to do?

IT'S ALL STATE MANDATED ANYWAY! PART I
A Principal Attends the Annual Summer State Leadership Academy

Dr. Luisa Torres is a well-respected principal at La Villita Middle School, which is located in Riverton Valley, a major metropolitan center, several hundred miles west of the state capital. She is credited with turning around the middle school that had previously failed to meet adequate yearly progress (AYP) standards. The work of bringing the school to an acceptable accountability level was strenuous. It required that teachers, parents, and the school leadership team carefully examine what needed to be accomplished to ensure student success, academic progress, and organizational improvement. It demanded a shift in focus with regard to instructional priorities. In the end, the ensuing teamwork paid off and, now in her fourth year at La Villita Middle School, Dr. Torres and the school community have finally begun to enjoy the fruits of their labor. They achieved a recognized accountability level as determined by the state education department.

As the end of the school year approached, Dr. Torres finally felt sufficiently at ease to attend to matters beyond the state-mandated assessment process and related test preparation. Now, she could take a much-needed break and feel comfortable leaving the campus to attend the annual summer state principal leadership academy. In fact, she felt good walking into the hotel conference room, where the annual leadership academy was held, with various other principals from across the state knowing that her school had made it (in terms of accountability standards).

Unlike her school, some of the campuses that were represented at the academy had not met AYP. Notwithstanding, the assembled principals chatted as they drank coffee and helped themselves to the continental breakfast offered. Conversations led unavoidably to the topic of school performance, and some principals informally shared their concerns and frustration that though progress had been made at some of their schools, not meeting AYP was all that mattered. Most principals in the room agreed that all that counted in their districts was making satisfactory academic progress as defined by AYP and the state accountability system.

Apprehensions were suspended temporarily as the academy facilitator called for the principals' attention. Quickly, the principals were signaled to take their seats at the various roundtables that seated four participants including a table facilitator. Once everyone was seated, a formal welcoming and the obligatory introductions occurred.

Given that the state had recently released student test scores and school accountability results, the academy organizers had previously agreed to provide a leadership orientation related to the topic of curriculum renewal. The organizers reasoned that with the recent dissemination of school test scores and with the school year concluded, it was both timely and essential to engage principals in a discussion about the need for and the viability of curriculum renewal. Thus, at the beginning of the academy, Dr. Tammy Greggerson, a retired school administrator and current professor at Midessa State University, introduced the topic to the academy participants.

"Good morning instructional leaders! Welcome to the state capital, and we hope you are enjoying your stay at the lovely La Bodega Garden Inn here in Midessa City! Today, we want to invite a conversation about instructional change and the curriculum renewal process." Then Dr. Greggerson added, "We want you to consider what prospects of curriculum renewal your campus could benefit from and for what reasons these changes keep being postponed." Cued by the silence in

(Continued)

(*Continued*)

the room, Dr. Greggerson clarified, "That is, we want you to identify areas in your school where curriculum renewal is long overdue."

During the 15 minutes that followed, Dr. Greggerson spent time discussing cultural conceptions of curriculum renewal, focusing her talk on what she perceived to be the paradoxical views with which American culture interprets change and the curriculum renewal process. "On the one hand," she said, "Americans have a great fascination with change and renewal. In fact, it is continuous innovation and change that define our character as Americans. On the other hand," Dr. Greggerson stated, "we as a culture also fear any form of renewal. When it comes to change, we shy away from it. We simply resist change. We are ambivalent about curriculum renewal as it challenges our sense of stability, of what is familiar to us, and what in fact makes us feel comfortable." As she concluded her introductory remarks, Dr. Greggerson asked that the principals work with their colleagues at their assigned tables.

Instructed to share their views on change and curriculum renewal, the various principals engaged in a lively conversation. At Dr. Torres's table, participants generally agreed that change and curriculum renewal were necessary. The principals also concurred that curriculum renewal needed to be encouraged and that campus personnel required a high level of nurturing and support for change to be successful. Will Wonkermann, principal of Childers School, spoke about the challenges of bringing change to his campus and cited a litany of obstacles that prevented most curriculum renewal efforts. In sum, although he agreed that curricular change was important, and even essential at his campus, he noted that it was almost impossible to embark on such a journey because his staff had become complacent about their student test scores and accountability ratings were now at the exemplary level. Mr. Wonkermann also noted that most of his teachers were veterans and, thus, were unwilling or unable to pursue new approaches. Additionally, Mr. Wonkermann explained that parents expected him and the Childers School team to continue the "great academic traditions" they had established.

Led by Will Wonkermann's comments, the conversation shifted to a focus on the factors in a school culture that hindered change and appropriate curriculum renewal. A good number of the principals offered advice as to how to overcome resistance to change and curriculum renewal efforts. Some of these principals actually shared their personal experiences relative to the plight of bringing about curriculum renewal and instructional change. Then, Dr. Torres interjected a question for Mr. Wonkermann, "But why would you want to change the curriculum or instructional approaches at your school? It's all state mandated anyway, and your campus has been rated exemplary by the state department of education!"

Dr. Torres's question again shifted the focus of the conversation and being somewhat taken aback by her question, Mr. Wonkermann inquired, "What do you mean, Luisa?" Taking a deep breath, Dr. Torres shared her heart-felt concern. "I have been sitting here listening to the issues we all confront when attempting to change our curriculum as well as our instructional approaches, but I keep wondering whether such change is really all that necessary. I say this because at your school, Will, exemplary status has been achieved for at least three consecutive years." As she spoke, the other principals at the table listened attentively. Then, Dr. Torres asked, "What in the world would you want to change and why?" To conclude the roundtable discussion she added, "I only ask because at my school we have reached recognized status, and I don't feel that we now need to do anything differently other than continue to push our students in test-prep sessions!"

Pause and Consider

- Why do principals think of AYP as being all that matters? What should matter at your school, from a curriculum perspective, beyond accountability standards and expectations?

- Does curriculum renewal at your school keep being postponed? Why?

- If the curriculum at your school is mandated, why change it? Why not?

Toward Change and a Renewed Curriculum

Fullan (2002) suggests that long-lasting change is difficult to achieve. Yet Henson (2010) relates that change is essential to people and organizations. Cortez (2010) notes that everyone and every school resists change, especially those who are in most need of change. In fact, it has been said that the definition of a neurotic school is the one that continues to do the same thing but expects a different result. The difficulty with change, particularly as related to curriculum renewal, lies in the fact that the change process must involve what Fullan (2002) calls the **reculturing** (p. 147) of school communities.

What Is Reculturing?

Reculturing is a complex process that entails a renewed perspective of shared responsibility, a focus on professional standards, and effective use of available resources, such as social relationships (personnel), instructional programs and materials, bud-

> *Reculturing* requires a renewed perspective of shared responsibility, a focus on professional standards, and effective use of available resources, including social relationships, instructional programs and related materials, and teacher knowledge and expertise.

geted funds, and teacher knowledge and expertise. It is in the recultured school that the work toward curriculum renewal and instructional change finds fertile ground. This is possible as its members have become convinced that the goal of increasing scores on standardized achievement tests—while important—should not drive the school agenda or a curricular and instructional course of action. Instead, members of the school community must work confidently in the recognition that student test scores can improve "in the short run with tightly led and monitored changes" (Fullan, 2002, p. 147), but they must realize that the fundamental work ahead of any principal and curriculum team is to build a strong learning community for purposeful schooling.

Dr. Luisa Torres's response to Principal Will Wonkermann's concern with his school's resistance to curricular renewal serves as a reflection of the current context in which public schooling is fraught. That is, in Dr. Torres's view, curriculum renewal and instructional change are not viable courses of action if standards are met. Although her comments raise important questions about the ends and means of schooling, her response is logical and understandable in the current policy context guiding educators' practice.

Let's return to the Chapter 4 section titled Why We Resist Change. A review of this particular chapter section allows us to recognize specific reasons why Principals Luisa Torres and Will Wonkermann are concerned with curriculum renewal and instructional change:

- First, principals and curriculum team are creatures of habit.
- Second, like all of us, they fear the unknown.
- Third, many principals and team members are threatened in areas of expertise.
- Finally, everyone dreads potential challenges. Principals and curriculum teams are no exception!

Now, we've heard the old saying, "Why fix what ain't broke?" Well, our curriculum and our instructional delivery approaches may not necessarily be broken, but as with all aspects of schooling, nothing is perfect, and there is always room for improvement. True?

High-Stakes Testing, Curriculum Renewal, and Educational Practice

Although high-stakes testing impacts educational practice, curriculum leadership should guide and shape it. In this way, compliance with state standards and renewal are inseparable processes. That is, principals are accountable to meet academic performance levels as established by the state; but they also have a responsibility to exceed those *minimum* requirements. Students deserve nothing less!

Although the short-term goal of successfully meeting and exceeding state standards is arduous, academic excellence demands an unyielding commitment to curriculum renewal. New ways of working and reworking a school curriculum require the development of a common and clear sense of purpose with regard to the ends of schooling. In addition, a commitment to a careful and critical assessment of the current curriculum as it is planned, enacted, and experienced is essential to determining whether and how the course of study in place is consistent with the school's purpose and goals.

How to Critically Assess Current Curriculum for Renewal Purposes

The first known and recorded effort in curriculum renewal, if not "curriculum making" occurred in Los Angeles in 1922. Later in 1925, Virginia and Connecticut followed with a districtwide renewal model. Interestingly, the curricular renewal works in these early years of the 20th century "assumed a comprehensive approach involving very large numbers of teachers in committee and task force teams" (Hencley, McCleary, & McGrath, 1970, p. 165). McNally and Passow (1960) conducted an early study related to the curriculum renewal process, and they concluded, after an analysis of a large number of curriculum programs, that renewal assessment must begin with chief responsibility being assigned to the building unit as the school appropriately "reflects recognition of the belief that continuity, unity, and balance are best achieved when the staff focus their efforts on behalf of their own pupils" (p. 43). The study concluded by noting that curriculum renewal efforts at the campus level are "most meaningful to teachers" (p. 43).

When critically assessing current curriculum, principals and team members should follow a progression of 10 essential steps.

1. *Study conditions and trends in contemporary society as well as probable conditions and requirements.* Parkay, Hass, and Anctil (2010) recommend that principals, as leaders of curriculum renewal, must recognize that "education for the future is almost useless unless it prepares learners to meet problems that are new and that neither they nor anyone else has ever encountered before" (p. 275). In other words, we must envision the future as we renew the curriculum today. Principals and curriculum teams must look beyond the present-day problems and see what instructional innovations will provide students with a love of learning, both today and tomorrow. We must prepare our students, through curricular approaches, for work that is yet to exist!

2. *Stress a need for balance.* Barrera (2002) has warned against taking any aspect of the curriculum and/or instructional program to the extreme. Principals, as curriculum renewal leaders, have to demonstrate the need for a balanced approach when changing the curriculum. A perfect example relates to phonetic versus whole-language instruction at the elementary school level. Ideological bias against skill-based instruction cannot dissuade principals and teams from a balance reading approach when, in fact, recent research evidences the importance of balancing phonics with whole-language approaches when it comes to curriculum development and renewal.

3. *Recognize teacher isolation voids any efforts to establish a school-wide purpose.* When teachers work in isolation, they seldom share effective teaching strategies nor do they partner for instructional purposes. As a result, morale worsens, teachers focus on students from a negative orientation, and very little time is spent in faculty meetings or grade-level/departmental planning on issues related to effective teaching practices and student learning. Principals, in the curriculum renewal process, must socialize teachers to team approaches and, moreover, recognize that when teachers assume a private or isolated approach to instruction, mediocrity prevails.

4. *Initiate a teamwork approach to establish an appropriate mission for a school.* Remember the adage, all of us are smarter than any one of us! The initiation of a curriculum team is a first step to improving collegiality. When developing a mission, goal, or vision statement for a school, as part of the curriculum renewal process, a principal

is well advised to begin meeting with the curriculum team at least once a week. With principal guidance, team work sessions can serve as time for sharing curriculum ideas—a time for teachers and the principal to explore the research literature and examine data to plan methods of improving outcomes. However, the most important aspect of initiating a teamwork approach to curriculum renewal is the leadership role of the principal. The principal is—and must be—the campus visionary, the keeper of campus direction, and the steward of the school mission.

5. *Claim the curricular leadership role from central administration.* Curriculum anarchy is the culminating result at the school level if a principal does not assume the renewal leadership role. Only a principal and curriculum team can develop a coherent curricular scope and sequence. When a district-level curriculum director or specialist or an outside curriculum consultant is brought into the campus folds for the delivery of change, teachers will listen politely, nod their heads in respectful agreement, and then return to their classrooms and do what they've always done. When the principal leads curriculum renewal, in concert with team, buy-in is more likely as the teachers will recognize that when all is said and done, "We did this work; we brought these changes, ourselves!" Additionally, when the principal serves as the curriculum leader and doesn't abdicate the role to a central office employee, campus teachers recognize the principal's level of expertise, respect the principal's initiative, and are more susceptible and willing to following through in the classrooms with the intended curricular changes.

6. *Understand minimal expectations equate to minimal teaching and learning.* Recall from Chapter 3 that low expectations are a barrier to instructional improvement, teacher development, student achievement, and, moreover, effectively hamstring curriculum renewal efforts. Low expectations breed teacher pessimism and negativity. Low expectations inhibit student learning. Low expectations defeat any curriculum renewal efforts. Low expectations fail to enhance any instruction-oriented procedures. Low expectations bring a quick end to a principal's career that was once thought to be most promising.

7. *Clarify the difference between standards alignment and innovative curricular approaches.* Shooting from the hip didn't work for the gunslinger in the Wild West, and it most certainly will not work in the 21st-century school! History tells us that the best shooters were those who realized that the first shot—even a fairly well-placed or

intended shot—generally did not hit the bull's-eye. Second, hitting the bull's-eye is demanding. Third, hitting the bull's-eye takes practice—lots of practice! Effective principals, as leaders of curriculum renewal, must carefully take aim at the legislated standards (the target) but shoot for innovative approaches (the bull's-eye). This process will involve a number of near misses. This process demands principals and curriculum teams review the research literature for best practice approaches to curricular and instructional improvement. This process involves principals leading teachers in the practice of a regular curriculum audit—an examination of what's working and, just as important, what's not working. The bottom line is that effective principals understand that state and national standards, the high-stakes testing, and the accountability process are vital parts of ensuring that teachers are on target. In other words, they are on the same curricular/instructional page. However, the alignment of standards with the curriculum and instructional program is just one single aspect of any curricular renewal process. Innovative curricular approaches are the icing on the cake, the gravy on the potatoes. Teaching the test is not an acceptable practice but it is one that regularly occurs in our schools. Principals must lead teachers, through interaction, example, and modeling, to an understanding that a thoughtful curriculum is measured by much more than any state or district test. A thoughtful curriculum is student centered, and it encompasses research-based and best-practice initiatives and programs.

8. *Establish a schoolwide action or improvement plan before initiating any curriculum reform.* Exemplary schools are led by exemplary principals who guide an exemplary team with an exemplary action or improvement plan. Whole-school curricular reform will never occur without a plan in place. This action or improvement plan must include the following:

- Goals (both district and campus)
- Measureable objectives
- Strategies
- Persons responsible
- Resources (human, fiscal, and material)
- An evaluation timeline
- A formative evaluation
- A summative evaluation

Without a plan, curriculum reform and schoolwide improvement are doomed from the get-go! Remember, those who fail to plan, plan to fail.

9. *Incorporate consensus-building strategies.* Consider the plethora of questions facing education, and schools in general, when it comes to curriculum renewal. Such questions include but are not limited to the following: What within the curriculum must be renewed? Why must it be renewed? Is teaching the standards enough? Is teaching the state mandated test ethical? Do our students need a standards-based curriculum? Should the curriculum be core-knowledge oriented? Is a curriculum best when based on constructivist ideals? What is more important, career or vocational education or college-centered education or both? Must we expand phonetic instruction and deemphasize whole-language instruction or vice versa? Shall we back-burner the arts and physical education, focusing primarily on reading, mathematics, science, and social studies? Is an integrated curriculum better than a content-based curriculum? Oliva (2009) asserts that a critical assessment of current curriculum (answers to questions much like those previously posed) must begin with a principal who possesses interpersonal and technical skills essential to bringing about consensus among members of the learning community. Principals must do more than stipulating that "the research reveals" when invoking innovation, as such may not necessarily be the case. Teachers are not fools and can readily wade through a principal's spin. Any instructional innovation, any attempt to renew curriculum, must be proven better that the one being replaced. Principals must encourage teachers to come to agreement and consent to try new innovations. At the same time, principals cannot make teachers feel that all that they have done in the past, from an instructional or curricular perspective, is less than appropriate.

10. *Do the essential review of the research literature.* Just because a review of the research literature is listed as Number 10 in this listing does not necessarily mean it should be consider the last in the progression of the 10 steps. A review of the research literature is mandatory when considering any changes to a school's curriculum or instructional program, which means, do a research review early and often!

The curriculum renewal process is fraught with uncertainty. This uncertainty arises as principals and school personnel search for innovative methods of reaching the educational goals they have committed to achieve. Innovation, however, is always risky and involves moving from the familiar terrains of practice to new and uncharted territory. As such, the process can be unsettling.

Thus, because efficacious principals are expected to manage smooth educational organizations and operations, the instructional commitment to a continuous process of renewal and change is a tall order. Recall from earlier in the chapter that this commitment involves the reculturing of schools. Reculturing is a long-term process. It is also challenging as schools, like other complex bureaucracies, are inhabited by participants who often hold divergent notions and interpretations of their schools' purpose, goals, and the means through which each will be achieved. As such, reculturing requires that the entire school community work toward nurturing and sustaining an environment where differing views are welcomed, discussed, and negotiated. This approach to curriculum renewal readily relates to Enacting the Deliberative Model of Curriculum Development in Chapter 5 and the subsections titled Platform, Deliberation, and Design.

Pause and Consider

- As a prospective principal, take time over the next few days/ weeks to observe the curricula and curricular development and renewal approaches at your school. Do you note principal-led, student-centered approaches? If yes, which of the 10 steps has your principal incorporated? If no, which of the 10 steps could serve as the beginning of curriculum renewal initiatives?

- As a principal or prospective principal, team with a curriculum coordinator or a strong curriculum leader (principal or teacher) and learn from this coordinator's curricular efforts. Ask this coordinator or leader how legislative learning has influenced curriculum and renewal and reform?

- As a principal or prospective principal, ask yourself the following question: Is legislated learning (high-stakes testing and accountability standards) fair? Why or why not?

Curriculum Theory and the Renewal Process

Historically, Kliebard (2002) contends, curriculum change and renewal has occurred as a series of cyclical "pendulum-swings" (p. 76). His characterization results from what he describes as the back-and-forth movement between one "curriculum fad" (p. 76) and another, yet with very little of the substance of schooling actually being changed. Change for the sake of changes is dangerous, and as Kliebard warns, it can be just as regressive as progressive.

An effective approach to curriculum renewal must draw from the "intellectual instrumentalities" (Dewey, 1916/1990) that curriculum theory affords. Curriculum theory, in this sense, offers educational leaders a new or different set of lenses with which to observe and interpret the problems of schooling. Furthermore, because theory affords a different way of viewing what is right under our noses, it allows principals to reflect on their personal perspectives and, thus, respond appropriately and efficaciously in practice. Therefore, as theory deepens a principal's level of understanding of the complexity inherent in curriculum renewal, principals are able to help educators anticipate and identify possible instructional issues, problems, or consequences that were not previously considered or that were ignored in practice.

Moreover, as theory affords a broader perspective of schooling and curriculum matters, through that new set of lenses, principals and curriculum teams will find their problem-solving skills expanded and their decision-making abilities less circumscribed by the tyranny of tradition and customary approaches, to include legislated learning, high-stakes testing, and accountability processes. Instead, principals, as curriculum leaders, whose work is guided by the principles that theory affords, find that their assessment of curricular situations and instructional issues is enriched. As a result, an ample range of alternative approaches and solutions are more readily identified and accessible.

Final Thoughts

Legislative learning and other mandates, as reflected in standardized curriculum, high-stakes testing, and accountability measures, can render curriculum renewal an absolute impossibility. Understandably, the pressure imposed by a rigid accountability system that emphasizes student performance scores often dissuades principals and curriculum teams from engaging in innovative practices. Notwithstanding the challenges that the current educational policy environment poses for curriculum renewal, principals and curriculum teams do not have to relinquish their commitment to instructional innovation and academic excellence. Curriculum theory affords principals, as curriculum leaders and visionaries, the intellectual instruments with which to guide renewal as they seek to improve public schooling and the education of all students!

Discussion Questions

1. Discuss the various conceptions of instructional change and curriculum renewal that you might hold. How do your views of change and renewal correlate with those advanced by Dr. Tammy Greggerson, in the chapter box titled It's All State Mandated Anyway? How do your views about change and renewal differ, most notably as compared to those of Dr. Greggerson, Mr. Wonkermann, and Dr. Torres?

2. Alfie Kohn (1999) has decried a standardized, legislated, or mandated (you decide the term) curriculum. Kohn writes that such an approach to curriculum renewal "usually consists of imposing specific requirements and trying to coerce improvement by specifying exactly what must be taught and learned—that is, by mandating a particular kind of education" (p. 22). Does Kohn's description equate to the curricular approach in your school? If yes, what's a principal or prospective principal to do—exactly? Be specific in your answer.

3. The mandated curriculum is said to specify the minimum academic content that educators should strive to deliver. Do you personally agree with such a statement? Why? Why not?

4. Discuss how your school community views the legislated curriculum and the current system of accountability. What challenges and opportunities can you identify relative to the legislated curriculum? What challenges and opportunities can you identify in the current system of accountability?

5. Principals are expected to lead their schools into state-defined, acceptable-plus levels of student academic performance. As curriculum leaders, they are also expected to nurture curriculum renewal. Do you believe those two equally valued goals are compatible? Why? Why not?

6. Curriculum theory affords educational leaders a powerful set of tools with which to understand the problems of schooling and practice. Do you agree with the previous statement? Why? Why not?

7. Reflect on a recent curriculum reform or initiative you have witnessed or have heard about. To what extent was it successful or not successful? What made it successful or not successful? To what extent was the curriculum reform or initiative guided by theory? To what extent was the curriculum reform or initiative guided by tradition and convention? Justify your response.

CASE STUDY APPLICATION
It's All State Mandated Anyway! Part II: A Principal Returns From the Annual Summer State Leadership Academy

After attending the summer leadership academy organized by the state principal association, Dr. Luisa Torres was challenged to rethink how she would lead her campus. Initially resistant to discussions of curriculum renewal and instructional change, Dr. Torres left the academy convinced that the current levels of student academic performance at her school—though remarkable—would not be maintained through complacency. Though ready to revisit her plans for the upcoming school year, she was certain that much of the work would involve challenging and supporting the teachers at her campus to think of new ways in which higher scores and higher levels of academic excellence could be achieved. The questions for Dr. Torres and for the committed teachers at her school were *what* and *how* to change in a way that the campus curriculum and instructional program could be transformed from good to excellent?

Application Questions

1. What probable resistance will Dr. Torres face from her teaching staff because of her reluctance to be complacent relative to the school's current academic achievement scores?

2. How could Dr. Torres overcome teacher resistance?

3. If you were in Dr. Torres's situation, what arguments would you make to convince teachers that being a recognized campus is not good enough and that curricular, academic, and organizational excellence is what everyone at the campus should be striving for?

4. How would Dr. Torres's stance on moving from a good to an excellent curriculum and instructional program be explained to parents?

(Continued)

(*Continued*)

5. What support can be asked of parents, and can parents be expected to provide such support as their child's school strives for excellence in curricular and instructional approaches?

Other Resources

Makas, E. (2009). *From mandate to achievement: 5 steps to a curriculum system that works*. Thousand Oaks, CA: Corwin.

Perna, D. M., & Davis, J. R. (2007). *Aligning standards and curriculum for classroom success*. Thousand Oaks, CA: Corwin.

Robertson, W. H. (2008). *Developing problem-based curriculum: Unlocking student success utilizing critical thinking and inquiry*. Des Moines, IA: Kendall Hunt.

10

Trailblazing Digital Curriculum Leadership 101

New ideas always encounter stiff headwinds.

—Scott Kirsner (2008, p. 2)

Trailblazing

Charles Goodnight, a famous cattleman from the Old West, worked at almost every job there was on the American western frontier. Besides being a cowboy, he served as a Texas Ranger, a scout, and a trailblazer. He opened new trails for settlers, his most notable trail being the Goodnight-Loving Trail. Charles Goodnight was a forward-thinking man. Those who work in digital curriculum leadership are much like Charles Goodnight—forward-thinking digital trailblazers developing pathways for the digital-settling educators exploring the digital-curriculum trail.

Cowboys and cattle trails appear distant in our emerging digital age. Yet today's cowboys are adapting to the digital age by incorporating technology in herd management. Likewise, principals are adapting their schools' curriculum and instruction. The challenge for cowboys and principals is accomplishing this adaptation in a way best for their clientele.

Digital curriculum leadership requires a view beyond that of our local learning communities, as we explore new technologies, analyze trends, and confront critical challenges. It is imperative that campus leaders implement and sustain systemic reform. Accomplishing this requires us to be at ease working collaboratively with colleagues not only at our campuses but from around the world (Knezek, 2009).

To provide a greater understanding of implementing digital learning at our campuses, we examine a group of administrators' effort to positively impact digital learning in their state. We introduce the International Society for Technology in Education's (ISTE) national educational technology standards and how they assist school leaders in creating digital-age schools. We interview a chief technology officer and visit a digital academy. We tie it all together, closing the chapter with a case study.

A New Vision Project

In 2006, 35 innovative Texas superintendents formed a learning community to create a new vision for the 4.7 million students in their state's public schools. They knew it was time for a new and different kind of dialogue. The Texas Public Visioning Institute was birthed. This grassroots effort produced the *Creating a New Vision for Public Education in Texas Report* (Texas Association of School Administrators, 2008). This report, a self-proclaimed "work in progress," initiated disciplined dialogue, stimulated questions, identified problems, and framed issues (Texas Association of School Administrators). At the report's onset, the authors noted the importance of engaging the digital generation, the change in the way students learn, as well as "embracing the potential of new technologies and making optimum use of the digital devices and connections that are prevalent today to make learning vibrant and stimulating for all" (p. 2). It was acknowledged that transforming the system to meet student needs required a digital environment and new learning standards (Texas Association of School Administrators). These curriculum leaders proclaimed the digital environment the most significant impact on the transmission of knowledge since Johannes Gutenberg's invention of the printing press in 1450 (Texas Association of School Administrators). This emphasis was cemented in the first article of the report's six articles, "The New Digital Learning Environment."

Article I: The New Digital Learning Environment

Digitization and miniaturization of information processing power are expanding exponentially and are changing the world, our lives, and our communities at an overwhelming speed. To be viable, schools must adapt to this new environment. We must embrace and seize technology's potential to capture the hearts and minds of this, the first digital generation, so that the work designed for them is more engaging and respects their superior talents with digital devices and connections.

Source: Texas Association of School Administrators (2008), p. 13.

Texas curriculum leaders are not unique in grappling with the digital generation and digital learning. Curriculum leaders in all 50 states are examining digital issues impacting curriculum, instruction, and assessment.

Creating a Digital Learning Environment

Creating a digital learning environment is a formidable task. A couple of Charles-Goodnight-trailblazer-type teachers can create pockets of change in a school, but not all students benefit from this random approach. When these trailblazing teachers leave, the school typically returns to the status quo as noted in Chapter 4. To create significant and sustainable change in a school's instructional system, all stakeholders must be involved. This requires strong curriculum leadership.

Oddly enough, the answer on affecting significant and sustainable change is found in a surprising place—the budget process! The Sorenson-Goldsmith Integrated Budget Model found in Figure 10.1 was introduced in *The Principal's Guide to School Budgeting* (Sorenson & Goldsmith, 2006). This budget model, constructed around a process integrating vision, collaborative planning, and resource allocation strongly supports the National Educational Technology Standards for Administrators (NETS•A).

NETS•A Standard 1, visionary leadership (see Table 10.2 on page 238), calls for personnel to participate in the development of the school's vision (Profile 1a), engage stakeholders in developing and implementing

Figure 10.1   Sorenson-Goldsmith Integrated Budget Model FIX 5

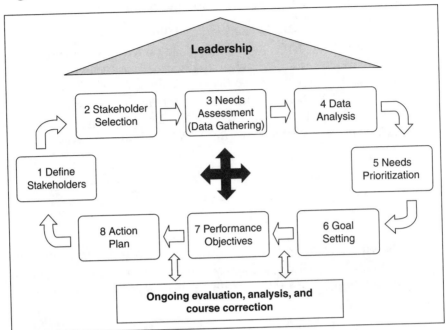

Source: Sorenson & Goldsmith, 2006, p. 65.

technology in the school, and fund opportunities that support effective technology integration (Profile 1c).

The triangle at the top of Figure 10.1 depicts collaborative leadership. The upward pointing of the triangle represents a clear, shared vision guiding all stakeholders. It is in collaborative leadership, as previously noted in Chapter 1, that others become empowered.

In Component 1, Define Stakeholders, stakeholder roles are defined, partnerships are engaged, and collaboration develops not only with the school's stakeholders but with the school's broader community. Stakeholder Selection, Component 2, is where stakeholders are elected to serve on the site planning team. In Component 3, Data Gathering, the planning team conducts needs assessment, in this case, needs associated with growing the digital learning environment. As described in Chapter 3, needs assessment is a continuous process. Gathered data are analyzed in Component 4, Data Analysis. It is here that continuous assessment and evaluation reside, where standards serve as goals. In Component 5,

Needs Prioritization, data are reviewed and consensus is obtained on actions that will move the school further toward fulfilling its mission.

In Component 6, Goal Setting, goals are assimilated into the school's culture to motivate stakeholders to achieve them. In fact, goals can become so assimilated in a school's culture that they became institutionalized and will even survive changes of administration (Razik & Swanson, 2010).

Component 7, Performance Objectives, provides added definition to the course of action. Performance objectives identify specific, measurable, and expected student outcomes. This encourages student-centered learning as detailed in Chapter 7.

Component 8, the Action or Implementation Plan, provides an easy-to-read document for implementing and monitoring school improvement. The action plan is a living, breathing document. Notice the three terms as the base of the model in Figure 10.1: (1) ongoing evaluation, (2) analysis, and (3) course correction. No matter how well we plan, unexpected events occur. We must continuously evaluate and analyze and make the appropriate course corrections. Imagine the quad-arrow in the center of the budget model rotating while continuously moving left to right. This represents the constant monitoring and changing that goes into a living document. As the principal and campus planning team conduct ongoing evaluation and analysis of the campus plan, course corrections will be needed.

> If a campus action plan isn't dog-eared, marked up, and tattered as the school year unfolds, then the plan's creation was a meaningless ritual. The plan was dead on arrival. Give it a proper burial or, if you prefer, cremate it in the school's dumpster.

Were you surprised that the budget process is such an important player in digital-age leadership? A sound campus budget process like the Sorenson-Goldsmith Budget Model using a shared vision, extensive stakeholder involvement, stakeholder empowerment, assessment, evaluation, funding, and implementation of a campus plan supports the implementation of the NETS•A. Combine these factors with a well-trained faculty and staff, meaningful policies, and ongoing professional development; the opportunity is even greater for growing a digital learning environment.

TRANSFORMING A LEARNING ENVIRONMENT

Principal Will Wonkermann and his wife Maria decided to remodel their kitchen. New in 1988, the kitchen was showing its age as well as wear. Will and Maria visited a local home improvement store searching for remodeling ideas and contractor leads. They watched several remodeling shows. Immediately, Will and Maria became keenly aware of how time and decor had passed their kitchen's design.

If you have ever remodeled a kitchen, you understand the work required to transform a dated kitchen into a modern efficient kitchen. First, remodeling always takes longer than expected. Second, it usually ends up over budget. Third, the remodel never goes exactly as planned. Fourth, the plan must be monitored and adjusted. Face it; kitchen remodeling is a messy process. Not only is the kitchen in disarray, remodeling impacts the entire home. Items must be removed and stored in other places. Construction dust seems to coat everything in the house.

Why go to the expense and inconvenience to remodel a kitchen? Generally speaking, it is done to take advantage of new technology and design. Cabinets have features not available a decade ago. Appliances have "become smarter." Faucet design has been revolutionized. Countertop options have expanded.

After a weekend of kitchen remodeling talk, Will was more than ready to return to his school. His first item of business was reviewing the *National Educational Technology Standards for Administrators* (ISTE, 2009) in preparation for a campus-planning meeting. A table (Table 10.1) about transforming learning environments caught his eye.

Will realized this table could serve as a structure for an extended discussion on the Childers School learning environment. He debated

Table 10.1 *Leading the Transformation of Learning Environments*

Traditional Environments	Emerging Learning Landscapes
Teacher-directed, memory-focused learning	→ Student-centered, performance-focused learning
Lockstep, prescribed-path progression	→ Flexible progression with multipath options
Limited-media, single-sense stimulation	→ Media-rich, multisensory stimulation
Knowledge from limited, authoritative sources	→ Learner-constructed knowledge from multiple information sources and experiences

Traditional Environments	Emerging Learning Landscapes
Isolated work on invented exercises	→ Collaborative work on authentic, real-world projects
Mastery of fixed content and specified processes	→ Student engagement in definition, design, and management of projects
Factual, literal thinking for competence	→ Creative thinking for innovation and original solutions
In-school expertise, content, and activities	→ Global expertise, information, and learning experiences
Stand-alone communication and information tools	→ Converging information and communication systems
Traditional literacy and communication skills	→ Digital literacies and communication skills
Primary focus on school and local community	→ Expanded focus including digital global citizenship
Isolated assessment of learning	→ Integrated assessment for learning

Source: National Educational Technology Standards for Administrators (2009). Used with permission from the International Society for Technology in Education, www.iste.org. All rights reserved.

with himself on how to best use this table in a collaborative process with the school's 13-member campus planning team. As he pondered this, his mind returned to his kitchen-remodeling project.

Will recognized similarities between his and Maria's kitchen remodeling project and his desire to collaboratively lead Childers School into the digital age. His kitchen had been state-of-the art in 1988, but time and technological advances had made it obsolete. His school was also constructed in 1988, what a coincidence. Its design too was dated—not just the building but the design and delivery of the curriculum. Could he use this table as a catalyst for transforming learning and curriculum the way he and Maria used their visits to the home improvement store and the shows on HGTV in remodeling their kitchen?

The more Will examined this table the more receptive he became to the idea of becoming a digital trailblazer. "Trailblazer," he said to himself. Will remembered a song his father sang to him as a little boy, "Happy Trails to You" (Rogers, 1952) and smiled at the serendipity of this childhood connection.

(Continued)

(Continued)

Will provided a copy of the Leading the Transformation of Learning Environments table to the campus planning team. He asked the team to reflect on Childers School as they studied the table. Twenty minutes later, he provided a copy of a continuum to each team member. He asked the members to place an "x" on the continuum where they felt Childers School was in the transformation process. Sanjay Patel, an assistant principal, collected the papers and compiled the results on a continuum on the conference room smart board.

```
    x x x
    Traditional–xx————xx——xx————————x——————Emerging
    x xx
```

The campus team noted that most of them placed their "x" toward the traditional end of the continuum. This observation sparked an invigorating discussion. It also began the team's galvanization into forward-thinking digital trailblazers willing to explore a digital trail for their school. They were willing to change from a traditional learning environment to an emerging learning environment. The campus team also understood it would be no easy task to go from teacher-directed learning to student-centered learning, from factual thinking for competence to creative thinking for innovation and original solutions, from traditional literacy and communication skills to digital literacies and communication skills. The digital trail while challenging was also exciting.

Let's Talk Technology Standards

Agreed, a discussion on standards quickly dulls the senses, closes the eyes, and makes time stand still. Many have had negative experiences with standards. State and federal bureaucrats have enforced punitive measures on schools based on data spewed from computers in the bowels of some agency. These data rather than being used constructively as formative assessment are at times used punitively as summative assessment to reprimand and even assign schools to "time out" with little or no opportunity to discuss or remedy the situation. When standards are involved, educators often find themselves in a situation of coercion, fear, and punishment.

In the digital age, time and distance have been compressed. We can be a 1,000 miles apart and yet be next door. We exist in different time zones, but in reality, multiple time zones can be passed through with the click of a mouse. In fact, we can be halfway around the world and still be a click away. Common ground is needed to move our schools forward. Standards, when used appropriately, provide us this much-needed common ground.

ISTE, formed in 1989, currently has more than 85,000 members (ISTE, 2005). Working as a nonprofit organization, it is a trusted source for digital learning information. ISTE exists "to provide leadership and service to improve teaching and learning by advancing the effective use of technology in education" (ISTE, 1997–2010).

ISTE led the development of national educational technology standards. NETS•S (National Educational Technology Standards for Students), NETS•T (National Educational Technology Standards for Teachers), and NETS•A (National Educational Technology Standards for Administrators) address the educational technology needs for each particular constituency while providing a system-wide approach to the national standards. The NETS•A were revised in 2009. Since this book targets principals and other site leaders, our examination will focus on the NETS•A.

ISTE took the NETS•A and added specific requirements for three different administrative roles: (1) superintendent and executive cabinet, (2) district-level leaders for content-specific or other district programs, and (3) campus-level leaders, including principals and assistant principals. Again, since this book is designed for principals and other site leaders, our examination will focus on the third category—NETS•A Profile for Principals.

NETS•A Profile for Principals

- Standard 1: Visionary Leadership

- Standard 2: Digital-Age Learning Culture

- Standard 3: Excellence in Professional Practice

- Standard 4: Systemic Improvement

- Standard 5: Digital Citizenship

Let's use NETS•A Standard 1: Visionary Leadership to better understand how the NETS•A are organized. Table 10.2 contains NETS•A Standard 1. Each standard contains performance indicators that guide us toward fulfilling the standard. Below the standard in the left-hand column are the performance indicators. In this case, there are three performance indicators. To the right of each performance indicator is a corresponding profile activity providing one way in which this performance indicator can be fulfilled. Although the performance indicator is assigned to a specific activity in the corresponding Profile area, it is only *one* suggestion. A school can add or substitute other appropriate activities in the Profile box to demonstrate proficiency of a performance indicator.

CHILDERS SCHOOL DIGITAL JOURNEY CONTINUES

Will knew he must lead Childers School forward on digital learning. He could think of no better place to start than the NETS•A. Hanging on to the status quo was not morally acceptable if he were to help Childers's students be successful in the 21st century.

NETS•A Standard 1: Visionary Leadership

As Will read the first NETS•A and saw its "Visionary Leadership" moniker, he remembered the day he cleaned the dust off his school's mission statement banner. This was a vivid memory for Will for it was his awaking to visionary leadership. Will saw evidence of his visionary leadership in that the district and campus visions were now inculcated in Childers's culture. This inculcation reinforced Childers's commitment to continuous improvement. As he read this standard (Table 10.2), Will knew he was not an expert on technology and most likely would never be one. Did he have to be an expert on technology to provide visionary leadership? He didn't think so, but he needed to be current in the field.

Table 10.2   *NETS•A Standard 1*

NETS•A Standard 1: Visionary Leadership

Education administrators inspire and lead development and implementation of a shared vision for comprehensive integration of technology to promote excellence and support transformation throughout the organization. Education administrators do the following:

Performance Indicator	*Principal Profile*
a. Inspire and facilitate among all stakeholders a shared vision of purposeful change that maximizes use of digital-age resources to meet and exceed learning goals, support effective instructional practice, and maximize performance of district and school leaders	**1a.** Participate in the development of the district vision and ensure that it is communicated, understood, and supported by school personnel

Performance Indicator	Principal Profile
b. Engage in an ongoing process to develop, implement, and communicate technology-infused strategic plans aligned with a shared vision	**1b.** Engage stakeholders in the development and implementation of a technology-infused school improvement plan aligned with district vision and strategic goals
c. Advocate on local, state, and national levels for policies, programs, and funding to support implementation of a technology-infused vision and strategic plan	**1c.** Use school-based examples and action-research results to advocate on local, state, and national levels for policies, programs, and funding opportunities that support effective technology integration

Source: National Educational Technology Standards for Administrators (2009). Used with permission from the International Society for Technology in Education, www.iste.org. All rights reserved.

NETS•A Standard 2: Digital-Age Learning Culture

Will read the second NETS•A (Table 10.3) recalling the activity he and the Childers's campus planning team completed earlier using the Leading the Transformation of Learning Environments table (Table 10.1). It wasn't that his school didn't have technology; it just wasn't being planned efficiently. Will purchased a few classroom sets of audience response systems sometimes referred to as responders or audience clickers. He gave them to the librarian and informed the teachers the clickers were available for check out. The vendor offered training, but the offer was ignored. No teacher ever checked the clickers out except Carlos Garza, a 22-year-old first-year teacher. Will thought of other technology not being used or being underutilized at Childers School. Will regretted not involving the faculty and staff in creating a digital-age learning culture. Looking at his iPhone, he thought how principals had resisted the district's effort to put applications on it to help principals with their leadership responsibilities. Will was an early adopter of this technology. If he was going to digitally lead, he would lead by example.

Table 10.3 *NETS•A Standard 2*

NETS•A Standard 2: Digital-Age Learning Culture

Education administrators create, promote, and sustain a dynamic, digital-age learning culture that provides a rigorous, relevant, and engaging education for all students. Education administrators do the following:

(Continued)

Table 10.3   *(Continued)*

Performance Indicator	*Principal Profile*
a. Ensure instructional innovation focused on continuous improvement of digital-age learning	**2a.** Work with staff to organize learning teams focused on employing a cycle of continuous improvement to advance their professional practice and student achievement through the use of digital-age tools
b. Model and promote the frequent and effective use of technology for learning	**2b.** Establish expectations for and acknowledge the effective use of technology resources at the school level to improve student learning
c. Provide learner-centered environments equipped with technology and learning resources to meet the individual, diverse needs of all learners	**2c.** Acquire, manage, and equitably provide technology teaching and learning resources to meet the identified needs of all students
d. Ensure effective practice in the study of technology and its infusion across the curriculum	**2d.** Establish and promote contribution to a school repository of effective technology integration practices
e. Promote and participate in local, national, and global learning communities that stimulate innovation, creativity, and digital-age collaboration	**2e.** Work with teachers to identify collaborative partners from other schools or communities to implement innovative school or classroom projects

Source: National Educational Technology Standards for Administrators (2009). Used with permission from the International Society for Technology in Education, www.iste.org. All rights reserved.

NETS•A Standard 3: Excellence in Professional Practice

Will cringed as he read NETS•A Standard 3 (Table 10.4). Professional learning at Childers School received lip service; it had never been a priority. Professional learning was one of those items that everyone went through the motions and checked it off the state mandates to-do list. Little to no buy-in existed. The district's professional learning program was underfunded, underutilized, and misunderstood.

Will knew he and the faculty might not be able to right everything wrong about professional learning, but they could rethink and reinvent it with a little creative resourcefulness. This would require prioritizing and allocating the necessary resources, human and financial, for ongoing professional development in digital learning. Professional learning must begin with the campus budgeting and planning process.

Childers School would not meet with success by bringing in speakers to lecture and provide handouts and binders. Although well intentioned, the binders would gather dust as teachers returned to the demands of the classroom leaving the necessary practice required for incorporating the training into their teaching repertoire for a later date, a date that was permanently later. Will recognized this standard's clarion call for active learning. Instead of providing training where a presenter models how to use a piece of software or hardware, teachers needed to *use* the software or hardware in the training process.

Will had recently read *Revisiting Professional Learning Communities at Work: New Insights for Improving Schools* by Richard DuFour, Rebecca DuFour, and Robert Eaker (2008). He understood that learning communities were a collaborative and ongoing process. Will examined the six characteristics of a professional learning community (PLC) (DuFour, DuFour, & Eaker, 2008, pp. 15–17):

1. Shared mission, vision, values, and goals—all focused on student learning

2. A collaborative culture with a focus on learning

3. Collective inquiry into best practice and current reality

4. Action orientation: Learning by doing

5. A commitment to continuous improvement

6. Results orientation

Will immediately saw three connections between the characteristics of a PLC and the NETS•A. Both emphasized vision and goals, both were about collaboration among stakeholders, and both were committed to continuous improvement. Will knew there were other connections. He was confident that a PLC would be an awesome tool for fostering the NETS•A at Childers School. He also believed that a PLC could be successfully implemented given the tight budget constraints Childers School faced.

(Continued)

(*Continued*)

Table 10.4   *NETS•A Standard 3*

NETS•A Standard 3: Excellence in Professional Practice

Education administrators promote an environment of professional learning and innovation that empowers educators to enhance student learning through the infusion of contemporary technologies and digital resources. Education administrators do the following:

Performance Indicator	*Principal Profile*
a. Allocate time, resources, and access to ensure ongoing professional growth in technology fluency and integration	**3a.** Provide opportunities for continuous professional learning in the use of new tools and resources including onsite and online support for teachers in the use and integration of technology into classroom
b. Facilitate and participate in learning communities that stimulate, nurture, and support administrators, faculty, and staff in the study and use of technology	**3b.** Contribute ideas and provide opportunities and resources to support learning communities for lifelong learning, leadership, and productivity
c. Promote and model effective communication and collaboration among stakeholders using digital-age tools	**3c.** Use online communication tools to exchange information with colleagues, staff, parents, teachers, and the community, including school news, important dates, and digital resources to support continuous learning
d. Stay abreast of educational research and emerging trends regarding effective use of technology and encourage evaluation of new technologies for their potential to improve student learning	**3d.** Stay current in emerging educational trends and research and share information with school staff to support their selection of resources for effective technology integration

Source: National Educational Technology Standards for Administrators (2009). Used with permission from the International Society for Technology in Education, www.iste.org. All rights reserved.

NETS•A Standard 4: Systemic Improvement

Will pondered Standard 4 (Table 10.5) and readily understood that systemic improvement was not a once- or twice-a-year event. It was an ongoing process. In fact, he made the important connection between the NETS•A, the Interstate School Leaders Licensure Consortium (ISLLC) standards and the Sorenson-Goldsmith Budget Model. The NETS•A and ISLLC standards support each other. The Sorenson-Goldsmith Budget Model provides the vehicle to integrate resource allocation, data gathering and analysis, ongoing evaluation, and collaborative planning of systemic improvement to bring life to the NETS•A and ISLLC standards. Systemic improvement was not another obligation he needed to add to his already crowded schedule. If he demonstrated leadership, he would bring about systemic improvement through the effective use of the campus planning team.

Will also recognized the need for Childers School to take advantage of action research as a tool for effective technology integration. Action research would allow the Childers School's faculty and staff to study its situation, try new practices, evaluate, and adjust. Action research could lead to continuous improvement of teaching and learning; it was a practical tool for Childers School. Who better to collect and analyze data or design interventions than the Childers's stakeholders?

Table 10.5 *NETS•A Standard 4*

NETS•A Standard 4: Systemic Improvement

Education administrators provide digital-age leadership and management to continuously improve the organization through the effective use of information and technology resources. Education administrators do the following:

Performance Indicator	*Principal Profile*
a. Inspire and facilitate among all stakeholders a shared vision of purposeful change that maximizes use of digital-age resources to meet and exceed learning goals, support effective instructional practice, and maximize performance of district and school leaders	**4a.** Participate in the development of the district vision and ensure that it is communicated, understood, and supported by school personnel
b. Engage in an ongoing process to develop, implement, and communicate technology-infused strategic plans aligned with a shared vision	**4b.** Engage stakeholders in the development and implementation of a technology-infused school improvement plan aligned with district vision and strategic goals

(Continued)

Table 10.5   (*Continued*)

Performance Indicator	Principal Profile
c. Advocate on local, state, and national levels for policies, programs, and funding to support implementation of a technology-infused vision and strategic plan	**4c.** Use school-based examples and action research results to advocate on local, state, and national levels for policies, programs, and funding opportunities that support effective technology integration
d. Establish and leverage strategic partnerships to support improvement	**4d.** Promote and support the involvement of local, national, and global partners to contribute to the improvement of student learning through the use of collaborative technologies
e. Establish and maintain a robust infrastructure for technology including integrated, interoperable technology systems to support management, operations, teaching, and learning	**4e.** Allocate funding and assign support personnel as needed to make effective use of technology resources to improve teaching and learning

Source: National Educational Technology Standards for Administrators (2009). Used with permission from the International Society for Technology in Education, www.iste.org. All rights reserved.

Richard Schmuck's (2006) *Practical Action Research for Change,* 2nd edition, is an excellent tool for facilitating faculty in completing meaningful research. Schmuck's straightforward explanation of the proactive, responsive, and cooperative action research models effectively eases concerns of some faculty when hearing the word "research." Schmuck relates the hardest part of action research is getting started. Campus planning teams often need to "prime the action research pump."

NETS•A STANDARD 5: DIGITAL CITIZENSHIP

The fifth NETS•A (Table 10.6) reminded Will of the fifth ISLLC standard, "A school administrator is an educational leader who promotes the success of all students by acting with integrity, fairness, and in an ethical manner" (NPBEA, 2002, p. 2). By the time Will read this final NETS•A, he realized both the NETS•A and ISLLC standards complemented each other. As he led Childers School's faculty in implementing standards, he would do so in an integrated manner involving the NETS•A in tandem with the seven ISLLC standards.

Will recognized social, ethical, and legal issues and responsibilities of digital citizenship. Two contentious digital-age issues at Childers School came immediately to his mind; the first being the school's cell phone policy. He thought of the many hours he had spent dealing with cell phone issues! Some school districts ban cell phones altogether; others place strict access limits on students. On the other hand, some schools have begun to relax their cell phone policies to accommodate mobile technology into instruction. Will thought, "What's the best policy for the students at Childers School?"

The second issue was Internet access. If the Childers School firewall was so restrictive that student Internet access was confined within the school district, would this prepare students for the real world? On the other hand, the students were minors and material existed on the Internet that was inappropriate for minors. Will thought again, "Did Childers School err on the side of access or err on the side of protection?" Will knew he was not alone; other school districts faced the same dilemma (Johnson et al., 2009). Will thought to himself, "This NETS•A standard might be the most challenging and explosive of the NETS•A to implement."

Table 10.6   *NETS•A Standard 5*

NETS•A Standard 5: Digital Citizenship

Education administrators model and facilitate understanding of social, ethical, and legal issues and responsibilities related to an evolving digital culture. Education administrators do the following:

Performance Indicator	*Principal Profile*
a. Inspire and facilitate among all stakeholders a shared vision of purposeful change that maximizes use of digital-age resources to meet and exceed learning goals, support effective instructional practice, and maximize performance of district and school leaders	5a. Participate in the development of the district vision and ensure that it is communicated, understood, and supported by school personnel

---

(Continued)

Table 10.6   *(Continued)*

Performance Indicator	*Principal Profile*
b. Engage in an ongoing process to develop, implement, and communicate technology-infused strategic plans aligned with a shared vision	**5b.** Engage stakeholders in the development and implementation of a technology-infused school improvement plan aligned with district vision and strategic goals
c. Advocate on local, state, and national levels for policies, programs, and funding to support implementation of a technology-infused vision and strategic plan	**5c.** Use school-based examples and action research results to advocate on local, state, and national levels for policies, programs, and funding opportunities that support effective technology integration
d. Model and facilitate the development of a shared cultural understanding and involvement in global issues by using contemporary communication and collaboration tools	**5d.** Promote use of digital-age tools and resources to establish collaborative learning projects among students within and outside the school setting

Source: National Educational Technology Standards for Administrators (2009). Used with permission from the International Society for Technology in Education, www.iste.org. All rights reserved.

A Voice From the Field

Dr. Chad Stevens is the Chief Technology Officer of Clear Creek Independent School District (Clear Creek ISD) near Houston, Texas. Clear Creek ISD has approximately 37,000 students with 21% of the students on free-or-reduced lunch. Most would recognize one of the district's largest employers, Johnson Space Center of the "Okay, Houston, we've had a problem here" (aerospaceguide.net, 2010) fame.

Chad was interviewed because he has served successfully as a teacher, principal, and most recently, as a chief technology officer. The NETS•A were employed as a basis for the interview in an attempt to connect practice to these standards. Chad and the interviewer, Lloyd Goldsmith, both recognized the difficulty of divorcing the five standards from one another because of their interdependence. The interview is roughly organized around the standards, but the reader should readily note comments that could be placed under multiple standards.

Lloyd: Chad, you have had the unique experience of serving as a principal and as a chief technology officer for a school district. This provides you both a campus and district perspective. I thought we might connect your career experiences with the NETS•A to provide the readers with a practitioner's perspective.

Chad: That's fine, Lloyd, but I must tell you I see these standards as highly interconnected, so my observations will likely touch on more than one standard at a time.

Lloyd: Fair enough. The first NETS•A is about visionary leadership. What challenges do principals face in providing visionary digital curriculum leadership?

Chad: Principals must help provide a vision for using digital-age resources in meeting learning goals. One of the greatest challenges in technology is having *purposeful* change. Quite often, we just throw technology at issues and do not necessarily make sound pedagogical decisions. Change isn't about adopting new technology; it's about adopting new behaviors for teachers. The technology being adopted, whether it's Web 2.0 tools or hardware, if it isn't driving systemic change and impacting the curriculum, it's not really accomplishing anything. If you put all the technology in the world in a classroom and still have a teacher teach the same way she did when she only had a chalkboard, change has not occurred.

For example, if technology is used only to put up flat information, nothing has changed. However, if the teacher and students are putting up interactive information and the teacher is engaging students, then you have created systemic change in pedagogy. Let me illustrate it this way. If a teacher tells students to "read pages three through ten," or if the teacher tells a student to "go to www.dot.com and read pages three through ten," does it make any difference in instruction? I don't think so. The student is still just reading pages three through ten. He's either reading from a book or a monitor. What's the difference? None! Our vision as curriculum leaders must be about impacting teaching. I guess you can tell I'm already hitting on the systemic improvement standard as we discuss visionary leadership.

Lloyd: So you're saying the impact of technology on teaching is an essential part of visionary leadership?

Chad: Yes. Often, principals throw a piece of technology at a curriculum issue when it's not really about the technology; it's

(Continued)

(Continued)

about how we are going to change teaching. It's about the evolution of the teacher. When I first started teaching, there was a computer lab teacher. Kids came to the computer lab to learn about technology. Our district realized that we needed to get the technology out of the lab and into the classroom, so we moved away from the lab concept and put more technology into the classroom. We redefined the technology lab teacher position to the technology integration specialist whose job it was to teach teachers how to integrate technology into their lessons. At Clear Creek ISD, I believe we're ready to make the next shift. The technology integration specialists need to become technology coaches or almost technology consultants. They can sit on the side and suggest to the teacher, "That's a great lesson, but if you did it this way, you could make it more real world, more collaborative, and more engaging for the student." As technology becomes easier, it will increase our opportunities to use it interactively in the classroom.

Lloyd: What challenges do principals face in digital curriculum leadership?

Chad: One digital curriculum leadership challenge that principals face is realizing they will *not* be experts on technology. Engineers don't know everything about technology. They possess areas of expertise. This is a paradigm shift for principals. They must break away from the old school "I've been a teacher and I . . ." to "I'm not going to be an expert, I'm a learner." Principals must also model technology and put themselves in vulnerable spots. For example, they can explore Twitter. There could be a risk in tweeting. Principals must model collaboration and let others on their campuses know it's okay to take risks. It's okay to fail and try again.

Lloyd: You appear to be emphasizing risk taking and collaboration in visionary leadership.

Chad: If a principal is not a technology user, it's hard to lead the incorporation of technology in campus planning. Leaders who do not understand certain new technologies, especially social networking, tend to dismiss that technology as something for kids. Likewise, if principals don't understand the power of collaboration, it's hard for them to use it in strategic planning. One more point, it can be intimidating to start a particular strategy as part of the school's vision, and before it can be finalized, something better has been created. That's

Lloyd: the technology challenge. Principals must remain focused and not be lured away by the next greatest widget.

Lloyd: Let's move on to Standard 2, Digital-Age Learning Culture. What insights do you have on this standard?

Chad: I can't say enough about modeling. Principals must model technology. I guess I'm referring back to the first standard, but I see them connected. Principals can do little things. For example, we fought hard to change our cell phone policy. We put Blackberry smartphones in the hands of our principals. We worked hard to put all the tools a principal needs on that device. They can complete teacher evaluations on it; they have templates by subject area to evaluate lessons. If principals use different online tools, it only makes them stronger leaders in incorporating technology in instruction. You might say they're modeling digital curriculum leadership.

Lloyd: I see the connection you are making between these two standards.

Chad: Let me share a story. We used the schoolwide enrichment model with the Renzulli Learning Software [http://renzulli-learning.com/default.aspx] in our PK–5 school. We surveyed all students to find their interest and passions. Certain times during the semester, we would group students by their interests, not by age, and placed them in a room with a teacher or volunteer with the same passion. No formal lesson plan existed; students drove the lesson. Everyone was engaged. Students could log on and do searches on the many free websites that pushed students toward their passions [See Chapter 7]. For example, if a student was interested in baseball, when he searched mathematics he would find problems using baseball to solve math problems. We discovered our students were logging on during Christmas break, spring break, and in the middle of the night. Instead of being on gaming sites, they were on educational sites. The point of my story is that with technology and Web 2.0, it's relatively easy to harness what is available to develop an individual learning network.

   You see, before the Internet, if a child was passionate about an author, there were not many opportunities to learn about the author. Now, with online access, students can follow their favorite author on Facebook, discover other people's blogs who share their passion about the author. I've personally done this. I tweeted back and forth with Michael Horn

(Continued)

(Continued)

coauthor with Clayton Christensen, in *Disrupting Class*. When would I have ever received a message from Don Tapscott the author of *Growing Up Digital* on digital learning without Web 2.0 tools in my learning network? This has taught me that if I don't start developing my network of people who can help me solve problems, then I won't be as successful. If I network with people who help me solve problems, I can experience greater success. If people can help me solve problems and obtain answers in a quick manner, it is to my advantage. I share this because students can do this too. Many principals and teachers have not tapped into this power yet because the other side of the Internet is pretty open and lots of bad things can happen.

The whole idea of meeting the needs of diverse learners and how we can leverage Web 2.0 tools to meet their needs and help them develop their own network for use after they leave school is powerful. Principals must understand this is how people work in the real world today. They don't work solo in a cubicle. They collaborate.

Lloyd: Do you have any other comments?

Chad: Collaboration with other partners, schools, or communities is easy to do if you are not scared. The fear is open access to the Internet in a K–12 environment. We are working with minors and cannot open them up to just anything. Some of us err on the side of caution; others err on the side of taking a little risk. Risk can cause trouble at times. We must have strategic access. If we put a big firewall around our schools, we do the students a disservice. If they can collaborate only within the campus or district, that is not real world.

Lloyd: The third NETS•A is about excellence in professional practice. How is professional growth accomplished in technology?

Chad: Let me share an example associated with the rolling out of Blackboard [an online course management system]. First of all, we recognized Blackboard as a tool for professional development. We trained our teachers on Blackboard as we trained them how to use Blackboard. We were basically modeling the entire time. I have learned that if you follow up training with a discussion board or another collaborative tool, you can continue the learning process well beyond the face-to-face professional development and help teachers form their learning network.

Lloyd: I've had a similar experience in training online teachers on how to use Moodle [open-source course management system] as an online tool.

Chad: We've had similar experiences. The quickest way to get teachers to learn technology is for them to use it in the training process. One more observation, I've noticed that we're on the downside of resistance to technology training. Five years ago, there was much more resistance from faculty. Today, more teachers have had experience with computers growing up and do not resist professional development in technology. In fact, the new college graduates are hard to keep up with!

Principals also need to consider making training mobile. Let teachers do their training on their iPods as they travel. Make training available in multiple formats so it is easy for teachers to access. Whether it's a webinar that can be accessed from home or a podcast, make access easy. Abandon the idea that good professional development must be face-to-face. Likewise, principals must value technology professional development enough to make it important. As a principal, I created a six-station training center on my campus where teachers could drop in and grab 45 minutes of technology training. Principals must remove professional development roadblocks.

Lloyd: What about learning communities?

Chad: Having faculty participate in learning communities is a lot like having your students participate in learning communities. Much is available for teachers in the global community. It all comes back to curriculum leadership. If principals don't strategically plan how the faculty collaborates and learns, they might get burned a little bit. If they align themselves with ASCD [Association of Supervision and Curriculum Development] or ISTE [International Society for Technology in Education], those folks have great networks.

Lloyd: Can you provide a specific example of the power of networking?

Chad: I've got a great example. Say you have an exemplary science teacher who develops wonderful lesson plans [See Chapter 7, the section titled Curriculum Integration: Are You Kidding Me?]. How hard has it been for principals to get those great lesson plans to other science teachers in the school or district? By taking advantage of content

(Continued)

(Continued)

management systems, these lessons can be made readily available to all science teachers instead of remaining isolated in a filing cabinet in a classroom. This allows the school to capture this curriculum intellectual capital. No longer does it evaporate when a master teacher moves or retires. Having the curriculum online created a better way to share it. The curriculum is available 24/7 at school, home, or anywhere. Now *this* is a professional learning community.

Lloyd: Is there something principals should avoid in providing professional learning?

Chad: Principals should not roll out any technology that doesn't have training. Period. No exceptions. It's much better to roll out only three pieces of technology in a year and do it well and connect the technology with the curriculum than to roll out lots of technology without thorough planning and have it end up collecting dust. If an interactive whiteboard is delivered to a school and no one knows what to do with it, it is likely to collect dust. A principal should not be measured by how much technology is on to the campus but by how effectively the campus technology is used. Principals must take advantage of training available from vendors.

Lloyd: We've already touched on systemic improvement several times. Do you have a bottom line on systemic improvement?

Chad: Communicating the "why" is important. Principals must make the why relevant to the faculty and staff if systemic change is to be accomplished. This is what shared vision is—communicating the why. Bring students in and listen to them for an hour or so about the vision, and you will learn a lot. Systemic improvement requires a valid why. Systemic improvement is so linked to creating the digital-age learning culture. When making systemic improvement, be sure to pay close attention to the bottom line. Finance and funding cannot be ignored. One easy mistake that is often made when infusing new technology is ignoring the total cost of ownership, such as maintenance costs. This can bite you in the budgeting process. Principals must plan and budget to sustain technology.

Lloyd: The last NETS•A is about digital citizenship. What are your thoughts?

Chad: Digital citizenship is about all school stakeholders understanding their social, ethical, and legal responsibilities in the digital world. This includes administrators, teachers, students, and parents. I want to talk specifically about our responsibility as leaders toward our students. We must make the conscious effort to teach our students the ethics involved with the digital age.

It is an unbelievable gift students have. The amount of information available is incredible. They must be held responsible with this information and the powerful collaboration abilities that technology offers them if they are to be successful in the future.

In my opinion, we, the adults in the school system and the parents, sometimes rely too much on the technology to "protect" students from making a mistake. I would make the argument that for every physical violation in the student handbook there is a corresponding cyber violation. For example, if a student breaks into a school building and vandalizes it, we would punish that student and seek restitution for any damages incurred. To me, hacking into a school's network is parallel to breaking and entering a school building. A cyber break-in must be pursued with the same due diligence as a physical break-in.

If a student makes a bad judgment and accesses websites and/or files that have been protected or filtered, we adults tend to blame the hardware or the software *and not the student*. We wouldn't do that if the student picked a lock and entered a restricted area of our school. Both are the same issue—gaining unauthorized access.

What I'm getting at is that if we want our students to be responsible digital citizens, then we must treat cyber violations the same way we treat physical violations. Bottom line—we must teach the ethics behind these powerful tools that students have access to.

Chad possesses visionary digital leadership. He is committed to engaging stakeholders in the development and implementation of technology. This was evident in his use of "we" rather than "I" throughout the interview. When it comes to digital-age learning culture, Chad draws on Quintilian who in 94 AD recognized the power of *imitatio*, or modeling, as the strongest form of teaching (Fantham, 1995). Chad uses *imatatio* to train faculty efficiently and effectively in digital learning. He uses technology to improve the delivery of curriculum and instruction. Chad is assisting Clear Creek ISD in the use of digital-age tools supporting collaborative learning as access to Web 2.0 tools and others are made available to students and faculty. Like most in digital curriculum leadership, Chad recognizes that he and the teachers will never arrive at full implementation of the NETS. They are trailblazing.

The Quaker Digital Academy Story

Let's leave suburban Houston and travel to rural New Philadelphia, Ohio. There is a dramatic difference between the geography and culture of these two locations. However, beneath the surface they have much in common. New Philadelphia Public Schools and Clear Creek ISD both are pioneering in technology albeit on two very distinct trails. Unlike our story in Clear Creek ISD with its 37,000 students implementing digital learning within the traditional public school setting, New Philadelphia Public Schools created a virtual campus initially targeting nontraditional students.

We spent three days interviewing and visiting at the Quaker Digital Academy. Dr. Richard Varrati is committed to creating a virtual school to meet the needs of all learners in the state of Ohio. He is quite an entrepreneur. He is a digital-age, learning-culture risk taker, as you will discover reading the Quaker Digital Academy story.

> "If we're not failing ten times more than we're succeeding, it means that we're not taking enough risks."
>
> —Mary Murphy-Hoyle, Intel's Director of IT strategy and technology (Kirsner, 2008)

Tucked away in a mall in the small burg of New Philadelphia, Ohio, is the Quaker Digital Academy (QDA) directed by Dr. Richard Varrati. QDA's unique story contains many lessons for those of us exploring digital curriculum leadership. It is a story of entrepreneurship, homeschooling, high-risk students, calculated risk taking, partnerships, resourcefulness, visioning, pioneering, and dare we use the scholarly term "elbow grease." Dr. Varrati gathered a team of educators committed to transforming industrial-age instruction to digital-age learning. This team has learned and is still learning in their trailblazing of digital curriculum leadership.

New Philadelphia, Ohio, a town of approximately 17,000 is located 71 miles south of Cleveland. The New Philadelphia City Schools (NPCS) provide a free public education for its 3,200 students. Dr. Richard Varrati became its superintendent in 2002.

Shortly after arriving at NPCS, Dr. Varrati discovered approximately 80 families were homeschooling their children. He sought to discover why this was occurring. A questionnaire was developed and sent to homeschool families. Five reasons were identified on why parents were homeschooling their children: (1) religious reasons, (2) didn't want their children in a brick-and-mortar school, (3) children had been bullied at school, (4) a bad experience with a teacher, and (5) a sincere desire to homeschool their children.

With this information in hand, Dr. Varrati, who had prior experience with distance learning in Pennsylvania and Colorado, sent a second letter to the homeschool families asking if NPCS created a charter school providing a strong online curriculum and teachers, would they be interested in having their children attend such a school. The parents expressed a strong interest in the school.

Dr. Varrati approached the NPCS Board of Trustees and requested permission to develop an online charter school targeting the homeschoolers as its first enrollees. To help the NPCS Board of Trustees better understand online instruction, Dr. Varrati arranged for the board to join him in visiting PA Cyber Charter School in Midland, Pennsylvania, directed by Dr. Nick Trombetta. When the NPCS board members witnessed an online lesson in real time, they were impressed. He informed the board members if 80 NPCS homeschoolers would enroll in the proposed online school, additional Ohio school revenue would be generated for NPCS. Shortly after the board returned from its Pennsylvania trip, a for-profit online school was attempting to enroll NPCS homeschoolers. This further convinced the NPCS board to take the charter school seriously.

The NPCS board approved the charter school as long as it was revenue neutral. In Ohio, revenue follows the student, so Dr. Varrati was counting on receiving state revenue as the homeschoolers joined the online charter school. After forming a separate board of trustees for the charter school, as required by Ohio law, planning began in earnest. Dr. Varrati served as the charter school's superintendent while continuing to simultaneously serve as superintendent of NPCS.

Dr. Varrati secured a $50,000 start-up grant to help research and develop the online school's conceptual plan. He also received two federal grants of $150,000 each to help get the school off the ground. The school was named Quaker Digital Academy after NPCS's mascot, the Quaker. An unintended consequence of naming the school Quaker Digital Academy was the public's confusion on whether the school was a private religious school or a public school. The school's name was shortened to QDA to avoid this confusion.

Dr. Varrati and others working with him enrolled 50 students and ended the first year with an enrollment of 25 students. He readily admits the QDA team started out "flying by the seat of our pants." Dr. Varrati was joined by Steve Eckert, a teacher committed to the project, who was willing to do anything to get the project off the ground. Both delivered computers to students out of the back of their cars and helped students deal with home Internet service issues. Their customer service efforts doubled student enrollment to 50 at the end of the school's second year.

By the end of its second year, QDA was receiving inquiries from parents outside of NPCS wanting to enroll their children in the academy. Unfortunately, QDA's charter prohibited accepting students outside of NPCS. Working with the NPCS board, QDA's state charter was amended to allow any student in the state of Ohio to enroll in QDA. The National Network of Digital Schools provided guidance and support. This greatly expanded the potential student pool, causing enrollment to climb over 300 students in its sixth year and climbing toward 400 at the printing of this book. QDA is projecting even stronger enrollment growth in the coming years. Growing enrollment is helping the school financially succeed since education funding in Ohio follows the student. Although QDA received inquiries from parents and students in neighboring states interested in enrollment, Ohio law prohibits enrolling out-of-state students. The QDA student population is gradually spreading across Ohio.

The majority of students enrolling at this time are considered academically high-risk students, many of whom did not function well in brick-and-mortar schools. However, the school's student profile is changing as more students are enrolling with solid academic credentials. The QDA team believes this is occurring because QDA advertises it is open 24/7 and tailors curriculum to meet individual student's instructional needs.

The process has been challenging for the school's stakeholders. One of the greatest challenges during the start-up time was convincing teachers an online academy was a valid educational option for students. Dr. Varrati spent a significant amount of time meeting with small groups of teachers in an effort to inform them that the academy was not a threat to them or their jobs, but instead, it was an opportunity to widen their scope of teaching.

At the beginning of the 2009–2010 school year, Dr. Varrati resigned as superintendent of NPCS to devote his efforts full time to QDA. Currently, the school has 20 part-time teachers, including three who are past union presidents. Most QDA teachers teach full time in public schools and adjunct at QDA. Ohio teachers benefit multiple ways financially. Not only are they paid to teach at QDA, their extra pay is calculated into their teacher retirement package. This financial arrangement makes it much easier for QDA to attract quality, motivated faculty. With a strong enrollment growth rate, as well as a continued strong projected growth rate, Dr. Varrati anticipates creating full-time teaching positions shortly.

QDA teachers need to be inclined to work with high-risk students. They must not hesitate to get on the phone, e-mail, text, or tweet students and their parents in an effort to keep open communication letting students know they are there to help them.

QDA is still small enough and in close enough geographic area that ample face-to-face communication exists. The faculty also communicates by phone, e-mail, and texting. However, the QDA team realizes this will change, as it should, as the faculty becomes more geographically dispersed. This will require incorporating technology such as web conferencing in conducting faculty meetings, planning, and training. Currently, all faculty activities are conducted at QDA's physical site.

New student orientation has been modified to improve communication. Students and parents are provided with information on what must happen for students to meet with success in QDA's online environment. Students are reminded that they are in charge of their education and share in setting its pace. Likewise, students are reminded this responsibility makes success dependent on how much effort they invest in their education.

To no one's surprise, students coming from strong families tend to do well because parents are monitoring their performance. QDA faculty is more likely to be involved in a surrogate parent role with secondary students who do not have strong parental involvement. QDA has employees whose sole job is contacting at-risk students and their parents or guardians. Software allows faculty to monitor student online activity or lack thereof. Students learn quickly that faculty can tell if the student is logged on and doing nothing or logged on and working. Students learn that they can't hide in the back of an online classroom.

Close student monitoring is paying dividends. QDA experienced a high completion rate last year and graduated its largest class. As further encouragement to QDA students, NPCS allows QDA students to participate in its graduation ceremony along with the district's traditional students. The cooperation between QDA and NPCS does not end with the combined graduation ceremony. QDA and NPCS have a reciprocity agreement on academic services. QDA students are allowed to participate in NPCS sports and fine art classes. They must meet the same eligibility requirements as their NPCS counterparts. In turn, QDA offers Mandarin Chinese to NPCS's traditional students.

QDA has operated summer school for the past five years for NPCS. This arrangement has been cost beneficial for both schools. Recovery and accelerated classes are offered during the summer. The summer program is delivered in a hybrid model requiring students to work online and to come three times a week to a NPCS lab for additional academic services. This academic arrangement has had a strong positive impact on course completion rates, a rate currently in excess of 90%. More students in the New Philadelphia area are attending the NPCS-QDA summer school program.

QDA has begun working with a couple of other school districts to provide particular courses. Students in those districts go to their school's lab during a scheduled period and work online taking courses such as British Literature.

QDA continues its organizational growth process. Initially, QDA's policy and procedures were folded in with NPCS documents. However, QDA soon began operating independent of NPCS. It has created its own visioning, planning, and operating documents.

The QDA team was not large enough nor did it have adequate resources to develop the wide array of courses required to launch a K–12 program. Currently, QDA contracts with five different providers for its course offerings. Using multiple providers allows QDA to be deliberate in curriculum design and delivery. For example, the course selected for Spanish is designed using a gaming environment. The QDA team selected this particular Spanish course because they believed the gaming design would appeal to the at-risk population that was initially being attracted to the academy. In this course, students selected an avatar and were dropped as secret agents onto a Spanish-speaking island. Fortunately for the students, the course's software customized their language experience to the student's Spanish-speaking level. To develop a course of this quality would have been beyond the current resources of QDA. Finally, QDA has a procedure in place where their teachers can provide feedback to the course provider on items needing to be changed or suggestions for improving the course design.

The QDA team is planning on incorporating more synchronous instruction, a plan that will require full-time staff. They are starting to test synchronous instruction with help from an arrangement with a national network using AT&T Connect. The initial offerings will be a course preparing high school students for the Ohio Graduation Test. A second course will be offered on preparing for the ACT exam. The course software provides the teacher with an analysis of student performance on the appropriate exam allowing for targeted reteaching inside the course. The QDA team will use these two synchronous courses to familiarize themselves with the benefits, challenges, and skills necessary to deliver such courses.

There is no doubt that QDA's stakeholders are trailblazers. They left the comfort of traditional brick-and-mortar schools to create a digital school on a shoestring budget. Their commitment allowed them to do whatever it takes to make QDA a success story.

Looking Forward

New Media Consortium (NMC) produces an annual report on emerging technologies and how these technologies impact the curriculum, instruction, and learning in K–12 education. The most current report, *2009 Horizon Report K–12 Edition,* identified technologies to be adopted within the next year, within two or three years, and within four or five years (Johnson et al., 2009). Collaborative environments and online communication tools were reported as the technologies most likely to be adopted within the next year. Barriers exist in implementing these technologies as mentioned by Chad Stevens from Clear Creek ISD, the most noted barrier being restricted Internet access. Johnson et al. (2009) observed that this barrier is beginning to dissipate.

Mobiles and cloud computing were identified as technologies likely to become adopted in two to three years after the report's issue (Johnson et al., 2009). This delay in technologies implementation is attributed to the fact that K–12 students are less likely to carry mobile devices with Internet capabilities as well as district policy barriers to Internet access. The final group of technology, three to five years away from adoption, is smart objects and personal web (Johnson et al.).

Johnson et al. (2009) identified five trends impacting teaching, learning, and creative expression in K–12 schools. These trends, in rank of impact on K–12 education in the next five years are the following:

1. Technology continues to profoundly affect the way we work, collaborate, communicate, and succeed.

2. Technology is increasingly a means for empowering students, a method for communication and socializing, and a ubiquitous transparent part of their lives.

3. The web is an increasingly personal experience.

4. The way we think of learning environments is changing.

5. The perceived value of innovation and creativity is increasing.

Johnson et al. (2009) also noted five critical challenges schools will confront in integrating new technologies into curriculum, instruction, and assessment. These challenges are the following:

1. There is a growing need for formal instruction in key new skills, including information literacy.

2. Students are different, but educational practice and the material that supports it are changing only slowly.

3. Learning that incorporates real-life experiences is not occurring enough and is undervalued when it does take place.

4. There is a growing recognition that new technologies must be adopted and used as an everyday part of classroom activities, but effecting this change is difficult.

5. A key challenge is the fundamental structure of the K–12 education establishment.

The challenge for principals in curriculum leadership is gauging the impact of these trends and challenges on their schools. Principals must work with the campus planning team, coordinate resources, transform the learning environment, and utilize the NETS for students, teachers, and administrators. Chad Stevens from Clear Creek ISD and Richard Varrati from QDA provided us with clues on digital curriculum leadership. Chad provided great advice when he encouraged campus curriculum leaders to realize they do not have to be technology experts. Instead, they must facilitate everyone in the process of digital curriculum leadership. Richard provided digital curriculum leaders courage to be calculated digital risk takers.

Final Thoughts

At times, trailblazing is a lonely business. You question yourself. Am I going down the right trail? Self-doubt, questioning, and second-guessing are part of trailblazing. Kirsner (2008) in his book *Inventing the Movies: Hollywood's Epic Battle Between Innovation and the Status Quo From Thomas Edison to Steve Jobs* chronicles trailblazers in the film industry. We find reassurance in our trailblazing by considering resistance issues encountered by motion picture trailblazers. Consider the following from Kirsner's text:

• Kodak's founder George Eastman said, "I wouldn't give a dime for all the possibilities of [motion pictures with sound]. . . . The public will never accept it" (p. 15).

- Daniel Comstock one of Technicolor's founders said, "Throughout the industry, the 'it can't be done' [color film] atmosphere was general" (p. 26).
- "They didn't understand how fast it [computer animation] was progressing and so they dismissed it as a science fair project" (p. 69).
- "A number of old film editors swore they would never use electronic editing" (p. 82).

Recall from Chapter 4, resistance to change is not new. For example, film editors, distributors, artists, theatre owners, studio owners, and other stakeholders in the motion picture industry opposed technological advances. They are no different from those of us in education. We grapple with mobile learning, cloud computing, smart objects, and the personal web. In fact, we have much in common with the motion picture industry. We resist change, are intimidated by it, and long for the security of current practice.

Digital curriculum leaders can't be bulldozers plowing people down. We must be patient and work with the stakeholders; for in the end Kirsner (2008) reminds us, "The preservationists and sideline-sitters are often forced to acknowledge that those annoying persistent innovators haven't destroyed the art form or damaged the business, but rather taken it someplace new" (p. 5).

One More Thing

Three trails exist in curriculum leadership. Every curriculum leader must choose one of these trails. The first trail, and possibly the most tempting one, returns us to the past. This trail takes us back to places where we have already been. Its allure is nostalgia. This trail is often referred to as "a return to the basics." The second trail, if indeed it can be legitimately called a trail, is one of permanent camping. No need exists for traveling on this trail. We just stay permanently camped. This trail encourages us to be defenders of the status quo. On this so-called trail, we "keep on keeping on." It is the lazy choice; it requires no action on our part. It is also a safe, enticing choice in that it requires no personal risk. Our third trail choice is to bring about the needed change for students to meet with success in society. This is by far the most difficult of the three curriculum leadership trails. It requires the most energy, the most time, and the most effort. This trail has many wonderful views, but it also presents many dangers and challenges that must be overcome.

Back in the Old West, Charles Goodnight had the same three trail choices we have today. Charles Goodnight chose the third trail. Had he chosen the first or second trail, history would be quite different. If we choose to travel down the third trail, we can travel together and help one another overcome trailblazing obstacles and challenges. Maybe we'll be able to hear amongst the howling of the coyotes, the growling of the bears, and the rattling of the snakes a distant voice singing encouragement and wishing us a happy trail. Goodnight wherever you are.

Discussion Questions

1. Should your school's planning team adopt Article 1 of the *Creating a New Vision for Public Education in Texas Report* (Texas Association of School Administrators, 2008, p. 3), what changes might you expect to see in your students? In the environment in which teachers and students work? What new capacities would be needed, and how would they be developed?

2. The school budget was mentioned as a vehicle to support significant and sustainable change for digital learning. How have you seen budgeting impact digital learning both positively and negatively? How could the Sorenson-Goldsmith Integrated Budget Model be used to support digital curriculum leadership?

3. Choose three of the transformations from traditional environment to emerging learning landscapes found in Table 10.1 that would be the easiest to implement on your campus. Why did you select these three transformations?

4. Choose three of the transformations from traditional environment to emerging learning landscapes found in Table 10.1 that would be the most challenging to implement on your campus. Why did you select these three transformations?

5. Select a NETS•A of your choice using Tables 10.2, 10.3, 10.4, 10.5, and 10.6. Create another possible profile activity for each of the performance indicators for the selected NETS•A.

6. In his interview, Chad Stevens commented on curriculum leaders' fears about open access to the Internet in the K–12 environment. He observed that some leaders err on the side of caution while others err on the side of risk. Would you err on the side of caution or on the side of risk? Defend your choice.

7. Dr. Varrati and the QDA team are partnering their digital school with brick-and-mortar schools. New Philadelphia Public Schools allows the QDA students to graduate at their traditional commencement ceremonies. QDA operates summer school for the New Philadelphia Public Schools in a blended online-onsite format. QDA also provides online courses to other traditional school districts. What do you perceive as the challenges, drawbacks, and benefits of such arrangements?

CASE STUDY APPLICATION
My School and the NETS•A

This case study is like none other in this book in that you and your school are the subject of the case study. Instead of looking "under the hood" of another school, you will look under the hood of your school. We reviewed the NETS•A Principal Profile, interviewed Chad Stevens the chief technology officer of Clear Creek ISD, and visited the QDA. Now, it's time to apply the NETS•A Principal Profile to your school.

An informal self-assessment instrument has been developed to assist you in this process. This instrument is located on pages 264–266.

Begin with NETS•A Standard 1—Visionary Leadership. Refer to Table 10.2 on page 238. Read Performance Indicator *a*. Reflect on this indicator and your perception of its implementation on your campus. Place a checkmark in the "below average," "average," or "above average" box to the right of Performance Indicator *a* on the Informal NETS•A Principal Profile Campus Evaluation Instrument. Repeat this process through the remainder of the evaluation instrument.

Remember the principal profile activity by each performance indicator is one illustration on how this performance indicator might manifest itself. Performance indicators manifest themselves in multiple ways (Figure 10.3).

Now that you have completed the informal self-assessment instrument, consider the following questions.

Application Questions

1. List three findings about your school and the NETS•A. What was your reaction to your findings?

2. Are you more advanced, about the same, or behind your school in understanding and using the technology standards for administrators? Why do you think this?

(Continued)

(*Continued*)

3. What are your barriers in utilizing the technology standards for administrators?

4. What would help improve your ability to lead a school in implementing technology standards for administrators?

5. If you were the infamous technology fairy and could grant your school three technology wishes to help your school better use the NETS•A, what would your three wishes be? What influenced your selection of these three wishes?

6. Look at the average scores for each of the NETS•A. If there is a score that is particularly higher or lower than the others, or if the scores are all relatively close, why did the scores fall into this particular pattern?

INFORMAL NETS•A PRINCIPAL PROFILE CAMPUS EVALUATION INSTRUMENT

Refer to Tables 10.2, 10.3, 10.4, 10.5, and 10.6 to assist you in completing this instrument. You will use a three-point scale to rate each item: 1 = below average, 2 = average, and 3 = above average. You must rate all items.

NETS•A	Below Average 1	Average 2	Above Average 3
Standard 1—Visionary Leadership			
• Performance Indicator a			
• Performance Indicator b			
• Performance Indicator c			
Standard 2—Digital-Age Learning Culture			
• Performance Indicator a			
• Performance Indicator b			
• Performance Indicator c			
• Performance Indicator d			
• Performance Indicator e			

NETS•A	Below Average 1	Average 2	Above Average 3
Standard 3—Excellence in Professional Practice			
• Performance Indicator a			
• Performance Indicator b			
• Performance Indicator c			
• Performance Indicator d			
Standard 4—Systemic Improvement			
• Performance Indicator a			
• Performance Indicator b			
• Performance Indicator c			
• Performance Indicator d			
• Performance Indicator e			
Standard 5—Digital Citizenship			
• Performance Indicator a			
• Performance Indicator b			
• Performance Indicator c			
• Performance Indicator d			

Scoring the instrument. Add the points given to all performance indicators for a NETS•A. Divide the total points given by the number of performance criteria for that NETS•A. Round to the nearest tenth (i.e., 3.4). Use the following tool to assist you.

NETS•A Standard 1—total points given: _____ / 4 = _____

NETS•A Standard 2—total points given: _____ / 6 = _____

NETS•A Standard 3—total points given: _____ / 5 = _____

NETS•A Standard 4—total points given: _____ / 6 = _____

NETS•A Standard 5—total points given: _____ / 5 = _____

Plot your averages on the NETS•A Campus Assessment Profile by creating a bar graph. See the example listed next. This campus scored 1.5 on Standard 1—Visionary Leadership.

(Continued)

(*Continued*)

NETS•A Standard	Score		
	1	2	3
1—Visionary Leadership			

NETS•A Campus Standards Assessment Profile

NETS•A Standard	Score		
	1	2	3
1—Visionary Leadership			
2—Digital-Age Learning Culture			
3—Excellence in Professional Practice			
4—Systemic Improvement			
5—Digital Citizenship			

Other Resources

Bonk, C. J. (2009). *The world is open: How web technology is revolutionizing the world.* San Francisco: Jossey-Bass.

Christenson, C. (2008). *Disrupting class: How disruptive innovation will change the way the world learns.* New York: McGraw-Hill.

Collins, A., & Halverson, R. (2009). *Rethinking education in the age of technology: The digital revolution and schooling in America.* New York: Teachers College Press.

Williamson, J., & Reddish, T. (2009). *ISTE's technology facilitation and leadership standards: What every K–12 leader should know and be able to do.* Washington, DC: International Society for Technology in Education.

Epilogue

It's been five years since Will Wonkermann arrived at Childers School. It seems like it was only the other day that he was wiping the dust off the mission statement's vinyl letters. A lot has changed since Will's late afternoon experience. First, Will acted on this experience and explored curriculum leadership. Second, he embraced a definition of curriculum leadership and pursued discovering ways to exhibit it. Third, Will quickly adopted an understanding that this would be a student-centered process.

Fortunately, Will realized developing curriculum leadership cannot be haphazard. His decision to take a curriculum-leadership-focused Interstate School Leaders Licensure Consortium (ISLLC) standards journey sparked a greater understanding of curriculum leadership's big picture. This journey ignited Will's passion to explore curriculum leadership to a greater degree.

Principals functioning as curriculum leaders must have high expectations when it comes to curriculum planning, assessment, evaluation, and renewal. Will understood the importance of high expectations and used this knowledge to increase faculty performance and student achievement. The stakeholders of Childers School were no longer satisfied with the status quo; they invested in continuous improvement.

Continuous improvement requires curricular change. This change is the basis for instructional growth, teacher development, and student achievement. Will used Childers School's vision statement to drive the necessary changes to enhance and improve student learning. Curricular change didn't just happen at Childers School. Will's leadership led the school to identify the demand for change, evaluate change, deliberately implement change, and understand the ramifications of change. Meaningful and purposeful curricular change didn't just happen at Childers School. It required curriculum leadership.

Will was deliberate in connecting curriculum, instruction, and assessment at Childers School. However, he did not accomplish this alone—he engaged all school personnel. Will knew he was not an expert in curriculum design and renewal. However, leading the school stakeholders through the revision of the school's vision and mission statements allowed him to appreciate and, subsequently, implement a curriculum model fluid enough to incorporate the ideas and insights of Childers's faculty and staff. Incorporating Walker's (1971) deliberative model of curriculum development provided the structure necessary to lead the faculty and staff to succeed in its quest to succeed in curriculum development, revision, and implementation.

Will understood that curriculum leadership required building relationships with teachers and other stakeholders. Will was purposeful in his efforts to get to know the Childers's team well enough to know what motivated each one. He used this knowledge to lead the team to accomplish more than they could have ever thought possible, given Childers School's difficult situation. Principal Wonkermann led the effort to make Childers School a place where team members could express opinions and ideas freely—a risk-free environment that encouraged professional curricular collaboration and meaningful discussion.

Will became a visionary leader. He became capable of looking beyond the current realities of Childers's existing curriculum and instructional programs. He recognized the need for curricular change and encouraged Childers's personnel to expect more from themselves and their students. Will led the effort to integrate the curriculum from single-subject instruction to interdisciplinary actions, teaching, and lessons. Principal and personnel embraced this shift in perception that made students better learners and teachers better instructors.

Will's curriculum leadership journey led him to embrace and value professional learning. For so long, he had mistakenly viewed professional learning as something he had to check off to keep the state and his superintendent happy. Will now appreciated the generational differences in the faculty and staff, understood the impact of career/life-cycle stages of Childers's personnel, and comprehended the importance of brain-compatible strategies. Will also developed a capacity to see Childers School through teacher eyes—something that opened his principal eyes. Finally, he fully comprehended that curriculum leadership could not exist without daily, intentional classroom visits to inform his leadership.

Like other curriculum leaders, Will coped with standardized curriculum, high-stakes testing, and accountability standards meted out by politicians in the state and federal capitols. Will did not allow these factors to dissuade him from exhibiting curriculum leadership. He and Childers's personnel did not relinquish their commitment to instructional innovation and academic excellence. Will practiced curriculum leadership that allowed him and Childers's personnel the intellectual instruments with which to guide curriculum renewal as they sought to improve the education of all Childers's students.

Will led Childers's personnel in growing their understanding of digital curriculum leadership by examining the International Society for Technology in Education (ISTE) standards. He knew he couldn't just bulldoze the school's personnel. He needed patience as he dealt with generational differences in accepting technological advances. Will's patience and perseverance paid off as the faculty grew in their acceptance of technology in curriculum matters. Will skillfully used students to help transition Childers School in integrating technology with curriculum matters.

Will's curriculum leadership skills brought Childers's faculty to the realization that curriculum leadership could not yearn for the way things were nor could it remain static. Collectively, Will and Childers's personnel recognized that curriculum leadership involved all stakeholders embracing the school's mission and vision and moving forward with the understanding that curriculum leadership involved continuous improvement of teaching and learning.

Childers School was forever changed for the better. Curricular change had not been easy, but staying the same would have been harder for the school's students. Will recalled a Lao Tzu quote, "A journey of a thousand miles must begin with a single step." His single step was dusting off vinyl letters on a vinyl banner. Will didn't make his journey alone. He brought his entire school with him. Can you? Will you?

Recently, Will was invited to share Childers School's curriculum leadership story with other schools seeking to embark on a curriculum leadership journey. Will would accept the invitation only if he could bring some Childers School personnel along to share the story. Will understood curriculum leadership is something that can't be accomplished alone. Would you agree?

References

Abernathy, A. (1998). *Bud & me: The true adventures of the Abernathy boys.* Irving, TX: Dove Creek Press.

aerospaceguide.net. (2010). *Apollo 13.* Retrieved February 4, 2010, from http://www.aerospaceguide.net/apollo/apollo13.html.

Anderson, R. E., & Dexter, S. (2005). School technology leadership: An empirical investigation of prevalence and effect. *Educational Administration Quarterly, 41*(1), 49–82.

Athanasou, J. A. (1994). Some effects of career interests, subject preferences and quality of teaching on the educational achievement of Australian technical and further education students. *Journal of Vocational Education Research, 19,* 23–38.

Athanasou, J. A., & Petoumenos, K. (1998). Which components of instruction influence student interest? *Australian Journal of Teacher Education, 23*(1), 62–71.

Atwood, M. (2001). *Good bones and simple murders.* New York: Nan A. Talese.

Bacharach, S. B. (1981). *Organizational behavior in schools and school districts.* Santa Barbara, CA: Praeger.

Barrera, X. (2002). *I would remind you that extremism in defense of curriculum renewal is a vice!* Unpublished interview, Department of Educational Leadership and Foundations, The University of Texas at El Paso, El Paso, TX.

Barth, R. S. (2001). *Learning by heart.* San Francisco: Jossey-Bass.

Bass, B. M. (1985). *Leadership and performance beyond expectations.* New York: Free Press.

Beckner, W. (2004). *Ethics for educational leaders.* Upper Saddle River, NJ: Pearson Education.

Bennis, W., & Nanus, B. (1985). *Leaders: The strategies for taking charge.* New York: Harper & Row.

Berlew, D. E. (1992, April 12). *Leadership and empowerment.* Workshop presented as the Seventh Annual Society for Industrial and Organizational Psychologists Convention, Montreal, Canada.

Bernhardt, V. L. (1998, March). *Invited Monograph No. 4.* Larchmont, NY: California Association for Supervision and Curriculum Development.

Bernhardt, V. L. (2000). Intersections: New routes open when one type of data crosses another. *Journal of Staff Development, 21*(1), 33–36.

Bernstein, V., & Sorenson, R. D. (1990). *America's story: Book two–since 1865.* Austin, TX: Steck-Vaughn Company.

Brokaw, T. (1998). *The greatest generation.* New York: Random House.

Brookover et al. (1982). *Creating effective schools: An in-service program for enhancing school learning climate and achievement*. Holmes Beach, FL: Learning Publications.

Brooks-Young, S. (2006). *Critical technology issues for school leaders*. Thousand Oaks, CA: Corwin.

Brophy, J., & Alleman, J. (1991). A caveat: Curriculum integration isn't always a good idea. *Educational Leadership, 49*(2), 66.

Brown, J. L., & Moffett, C. A. (2002). *The hero's journey: How educators can transform schools and improve learning*. Alexandria, VA: Association for Supervision and Curriculum Development (ASCD).

Bruner, J. S. (1960). *The process of education*. Cambridge, MA: Harvard University Press.

Bruner, J. (2000). *The process of education*. New York: Random House.

Bruster, J. (2001). *Candid remarks about the principal role*. Unpublished interview, Educational Leadership and Foundations Department, The University of Texas at El Paso, El Paso, TX.

Bryk, A., & Schneider, B. (2003, March). Trust in schools: A core resource for school reform. *Educational Leadership, 60*(6), 40–45.

Buffum, A., Mattos, M., & Weber, C. (2009). *Pyramid response to intervention: RTI, professional learning communities, and how to respond when kids don't learn*. Bloomington, IN: Solution Tree Press.

Bully Police USA. (2010). *The bully police USA report*. Retrieved August 25, 2009, from http://www.bullypolice.org

Cachet Records. (1979). *Johnny Cash: A believer sings the truth*. Los Angeles: Author.

Cannon, M. D., & Griffith, B. A. (2007). *Effective groups: Concepts and skills to meet leadership challenges*. Upper Saddle River, NJ: Pearson Education.

Carrell, M. R., Kuzmits, F. E., & Elbert, N. F. (1992). *Personnel/human resource management*. New York: Macmillan.

Cennamo, K., & Kalk, D. (2005). *Real world instructional design*. Belmont, CA: Thomson Wadsworth.

Charles A. Dana Research Center. (2003). *Building a new structure for school leadership*. Retrieved February 10, 2009, from http://www.utdanacenter.org/downloads/research/tsse_fall03.pdf

Chin, R., & Benne, K. (1969). General strategies for effecting changes in human systems. In Warren Bennis et al. (Eds.), *The planning of change*. New York: Holt, Rinehart and Winston.

Cleave, S. (1985). NFER evidence to the select committee on education, science, and arts for its inquiry into achievement in primary schools. *Education Research, 27*(2), 117–126.

Cohen, J. E. (2004). Mathematics is biology's next microscope, only better; biology is mathematics' next physics, only better. *PLoS Biol, 2*(12). Retrieved on March 2, 2009, from http://www.biology.plosjournals.org/perlserv/?request=get-document&doi=10.1371/journal.pbio

Collins, J., & Porras, J. (2002). *Built to last: Successful habits of visionary companies*. New York: HarperCollins.

The Columbia world of quotations. New York: Columbia University Press, 1996. Retrieved January 18, 2010, from http://www.bartleby.com/66

Comer, J. P. (1989). *A conversation between James Comer and Ronald Edmonds: Fundamentals of effective school improvement*. Dubuque, IA: Kendall Hunt.

Conger, J. A. (1989). *The charismatic leader*. San Francisco: Jossey-Bass.

Connors, N. A. (2000). *If you don't feed the teachers they eat the students: A guide to success for administrators and teachers*. Nashville, TN: Incentive.

Cortez, M. T. (2010, June 14). *The administrative leadership role and the change process in schools*. Paper presented at An Evening With Outstanding Administrative Leaders, The University of Texas at El Paso, El Paso, Texas.

Council of Chief State School Officers. (2008a). *Educational leadership policy standards: ISLLC 2008*. Retrieved October 13, 2009, from www.ccsso.org/content/pdfs/elps_isllc2008.pdf

Council of Chief State School Officers. (2008b). *Performance expectations and indicators for education leaders: An ISLLC-based guide to implementing leaders' standards and a comparison guide to the educational leadership policy standards: ISLLC 2008*. Retrieved October 15, 2009, from www.ccsso.org/content/pdfs/elps_isllc2008.pdf

Country Music Television Inc. (2008). Deep in the heart of Texas (1967). [Review of the album *The Best of Bob Willis, Vol. 1*]. Retrieved December 15, 2008, from http://www.cmt.com/lyrics/bob-wills/deep-in-the-heart-of-texas/964367/lyrics.jhtml

Covey, S. R. (1989). *The seven habits of highly effective people*. New York: Simon & Shuster.

Cuban, L. (2004). *The blackboard and the bottom line*. Cambridge, MA: Harvard University Press.

Cunningham, W. G., & Corderio, P. A. (2006). *Educational leadership: A problem-based approach*. Upper Saddle River, NJ: Pearson Education.

Darling-Hammond, L. (2001). *The right to learn: A blueprint for creating schools that work*. San Francisco: Jossey Bass.

Darling-Hammond, L. (2003). Keeping good teachers: Why it matters, what leaders can do. *Educational Leadership, 60*(8), 6–13.

De Saint-Exupery, A. (2003). *The wisdom of the sands*. Mattituck, NY: Amereon.

Descamps, J. (2009). *The curriculum leader in an era of change*. Unpublished interview, Department of Educational Leadership and Foundations, The University of Texas at El Paso, El Paso, TX.

Dewey, J. (1902). *The school and society and the child and the curriculum*. Chicago: University of Chicago Press.

Dewey, J. (1916/1990). *The school and society/The child and the curriculum* (Rev. ed.). Chicago: The University of Chicago Press.

Drake, S. M. (2007). *Creating standards-based integrated curriculum: Aligning curriculum, content, assessment, and instruction*. Thousand Oaks, CA: Corwin.

DuFour, R. (2007). Professional learning communities: A bandwagon, an idea worth considering, or our best hope for high levels of learning? *Middle School Journal, 39*(1), 4–8.

DuFour, R., DuFour, R., & Eaker, R. (2008). *Revisiting professional learning communities at work: New insights for improving schools*. Bloomington, IN: Solution Tree.

DuFour, R., DuFour, R., Eaker, R., & Many, T. (2009). *Learning by doing: A handbook for professional learning communities at work.* Bloomington, IN: Solution Tree.

Dylan, B. (1964). *The times they are a-changin' lyrics.* Retrieved from http://lyricsfreak.com/b/bob+dylan/the+times+they+are+a+changin_20021240.html

Easton, L. B. (Ed.). (2008). *Powerful designs for professional learning* (2nd ed.). Oxford, OH: National Staff Development Council.

Echols, A. (2000). *Scars of sweet paradise: The life and times of Janice Joplin.* New York: Henry Holt and Company, LLC.

Edmonds, R. (1979). Effective schools for the urban poor. *Educational Leadership, 37*(1), 23.

The Elephant and the blind men. (n.d.). Retrieved January 28, 2010, from http://www.cs.princeton.edu/~rywang/berkeley/258/parable.html

Ellis, A. K., & Stuen, C. J. (1998). *The interdisciplinary curriculum.* Larchmont, NY: Eye on Education.

Erikson, H. L. (2007). *Stirring the head, heart, and soul.* Thousand Oaks, CA: Corwin.

Fantham, E. (1995). The concept of nature and human nature in Quintilian's psychology and theory of instruction. *Rhetorica, 13*(2), 125–139.

Fass, S., & Cauthen, N. (2006). Who are America's poor children? The official story. *National Center for Children in Poverty.* Retrieved October 7, 2010, from http://nccp.org/publications/pub_684.html

Feinberg, T. (n.d.). *Self-managing teams.* Retrieved October 18, 2010, from http://www.isnare.com/?aid=351069&ca=Business+Management

Ferrandino, V. L., & Tirozzi, G. N. (2004). Principal's perspective. *Education Week, 23*, 31.

Fisch, K., McLeod, S., & Bronman, J. (2009). *Did you know? 3.0.* YouTube.com. Retrieved from http://www.youtube.com/watch?v=PHmwZ96_Gos

Fletcher, M. A., & Anderson, N. (2010). *Obama angers union officials with remarks in support of RI teacher firings.* Retrieved March 13, 2010, from http://www.washingtonpost.com/wp-dyn/article/2010/03/01/AR010030103560_pf.html

Fogarty, R. J. (2002). *How to integrate the curricula.* Thousand Oaks, CA: Corwin.

Fogarty, R. J., & Stoehr, J. (2007). *Integrating curricula with multiple intelligences: Teams, themes, and threads.* Thousand Oaks, CA: Corwin.

Frase, L., & English, F. (2000). When doing more means doing nothing well. *Thrust for Educational Leadership, 29*(4), 19.

Friedman, T. (2006). *The world is flat.* New York: Farrar, Straus and Giroux.

Fullan, M. G. (1999). *Change forces: The sequel.* London: Taylor and Francis/Falmer.

Fullan, M. G. (2001). *Leading in a culture of change.* San Francisco: Jossey-Bass.

Fullan, M.G. (2002). The change leader. *Educational Leadership, 59*(8), 16–21.

Fullan, M. G. (2005). Professional learning communities at-large. In R. DuFour, R. Eaker, & R. DuFour (Eds.), *On common ground: The power of professional learning communities* (pp. 209–223). Bloomington, IN: Solution Tree.

Fullan, M. G. (2008). *What's worth fighting for in the principalship.* New York: Teachers College Press.

Fullan, M. G., & Hargreaves, A. (1991). *What's worth fighting for: Working together for your school*. Andover, MA: The Regional Laboratory for Educational Improvement of the Northeast and Islands in association with Ontario Public School Teachers' Federation.

Gardner, H., & Boix-Mansilla, V. (1994). Teaching for understanding in the disciplines—and beyond. *Teachers College Record, 96*, 198–218.

Gergen, D. (2000). *Eyewitness to power: The essence of leadership—Nixon to Clinton*. New York: Simon & Schuster, Inc.

Gerhards, S. (2008). *Leadership for a change: Education, politics, and motherhood*. Unpublished interview, Department of Educational Leadership and Foundations, The University of Texas at El Paso, El Paso, TX.

Giuliani, R. W. (2002). *Leadership*. New York: Miramax Books.

Glanz, J. (2006). *What every principal should know about school-community leadership*. Thousand Oaks, CA: Corwin.

Glatthorn, A. A., & Jailall, J. M. (2009). *The principal as curriculum leader: Shaping what is taught and tested*. Thousand Oaks, CA: Corwin.

Glickman, C., Gordon, S., & Ross-Gordon, J. (2007). *SuperVision and instructional leadership: A developmental approach*. Upper Saddle River, NJ: Pearson Education.

Glickman, C., Gordon, S., & Ross-Gordon, J. (2009). *The basic guide to supervision and instructional leadership*. Upper Saddle River, NJ: Pearson Education.

Goldbort, R. (1991). Science in literature: Materials for an integrated teaching approach. *English Journal, 80*(3), 69–73.

Goodlad, J. L., & Su, Z. (1992). Organization of the curriculum. In P. W. Jackson (Ed.), *Handbook of research on curriculum* (pp. 327–344). New York: Macmillan.

Goodlad, J., Wineburg, S. S., & Grossman, P. L. (2007). *Interdisciplinary curriculum: Challenges to implementation*. New York: Teachers College Press.

Gordon, S. P. (2004). *Professional development for school improvement: Empowering learning communities*. Upper Saddle River, NJ: Pearson Education

Gravett, L., & Throckmorton, R. (2007). *Bridging the generation gap: How to get radio babies, boomers, gen xers, and gen yers to work together and achieve more*. Franklin Lakes, NJ: Career Press.

Grigsby, B., Schumacher, G., Decman, J., & Simieou III, F. (2010). A principal's dilemma: Instructional leader or manager. *Academic Leadership: The Online Journal, 8*(3). Retrieved July 9, 2010, from http://www.academicleadership.org/empirical_research/A_Principal_s_Dilemma_Instruction

Groundwater-Smith, S. (1996). The practicum as workplace learning: A multi-mode approach in teacher education. *Australian Journal of Teacher Education, 21*(2), 29–41.

Hall, P., & Simeral, A. (2008). *Building teachers' capacity for success: A collaborative approach for coaches and school leaders*. Alexandria, VA: Association for Supervision and Curriculum Development.

Hargreaves, A., & Shirley, D. (2009). *The fourth way: The inspiring future for educational change*. Thousand Oaks, CA: Corwin.

Hatch, T. (2009). The outside-inside connection. *Educational Leadership, 67*(2), 16–21.

Heifetz, R. (1994). *Leadership without easy answers*. Cambridge, MA: Harvard.

Heller, R. (1998). *Managing change*. New York: DK.

Heller, R. (1999). *Effective leadership: Learning to lead*. New York: DK.

Hencley, S. P., McCleary, L. E., & McGrath, J. H. (1970). *The elementary school principalship*. New York: Dodd, Mead and Company.

Hendrick Hospice Care. (2010). *About camp courage*. Retrieved February 3, 2010, from http://www.hendrickhospice.org/campcourage

Henson, K. T. (2010). *Supervision: A collaborative approach to instructional improvement*. Long Grove, IL: Waveland Press.

Hidi, S. (1990). Interest and its contribution as a mental resource for learning. *Review of Educational Research, 60*, 549–557.

Hilber, C. A., & Mayer, C. J. (2004). *Why do households without children support local public schools?* Retrieved January 5, 2010, from http://personal.lse.ac.uk/hilber/hilber_wp/Hilber_Mayer_2008_WP.pdf

Hirsh, S., & Killion, J. (2007). *The learning educator: A new era for professional learning*. Oxford, OH: NSDC.

Holt-Reynolds, D. (2000). What does the teacher do? Constructivist pedagogies and prospective teachers' beliefs about the role of a teacher. *Teaching and Teacher Education, 16*(1), 21–32.

Hoy, A., & Hoy, W. (2006). *Instructional leadership: A research-based guide to learning in schools* (2nd ed.). Upper Saddle River, NJ: Pearson Education.

Huberman, M. (1989). The professional cycle of teachers. *Teachers College Record, 91*(1), 37.

Hughes, R. L., Ginnett, R. C., & Curphy, G. J. (2009). *Leadership: Enhancing the lessons of experience*. Columbus, OH: McGraw-Hill Higher Education.

International Society for Technology in Education (ISTE). (1997–2010). *Mission-driven initiatives*. Retrieved October 15, 2009, from http://www.iste.org/AM/Template.cfm?Section=About_ISTE

International Society for Technology in Education (ISTE). (2005). *ISTE fact sheet*. Retrieved October 15, 2009, from center.uoregon.edu/ISTE/NECC2005/media/ISTEFactSheet.pdf

International Society for Technology in Education (ISTE). (2009). *National educational technology standards for administrators*. Retrieved October 19, 2009, from http://www.iste.org/standards/nets-for-administrators.aspx

Isikoff, M., & Von Drehle, D. (1992, June 28). Perot-schools shootout: How billionaire outdrew Texas establishment. *The Washington Post*. Retrieved February 20, 2009, from http://pqasb.pqarchiver.com/washingtonpost/search.html

Jacobs, H. H. (1989). *Interdisciplinary curriculum: Design and implementation*. Alexandria, VA: Association for Supervision and Curriculum Development (ASCD).

Jacobs, H. H. (2004). *Getting results with curriculum mapping*. Alexandria, VA: Association for Supervision and Curriculum Development (ASCD).

Johnson, D. W., & Johnson, R. T. (1999). The three Cs of school and classroom management. In H. J. Freiberg (Ed.), *Beyond behaviorism: Changing the classroom management paradigm* (pp. 119–144). Boston: Allyn & Bacon.

Johnson, L., Levine, A., Smith, R., and Smythe, T. (2009). *The 2009 horizon report: K-12 edition*. Austin: TX: The New Media Consortium.

Junior Achievement. (2010). *Educating children worldwide.* Retrieved January 5, 2010, from http://www.ja.org

Kameenui, E. J., Carnine, D. W., Dixon, R. C., Simmons, D. C., & Coyne, M. D. (2002). *Effective teaching strategies that accommodate diverse learners.* Upper Saddle River, NJ: Merrill/Prentice-Hall.

Kaufman, D., Moss, D. M., & Osborn, T. A. (Eds.). (2003). *Beyond the boundaries: A transdisciplinary approach to learning and teaching.* Westport, CT: Praeger.

Kaye, R. (2010). *All teachers fired at Rhode Island school.* Retrieved March 13, 2010, from http://www.cnn.com/2010/US/02/24/rhode.island.teachers/index.html

Keller, D. (1999). Deciphering teacher lounge talk. *Phi Delta Kappan, 81*(4), 328–329.

Keller, J. M., & Suzuki, K. (1998). Use of the ARCS motivation model in courseware design. In D. H. Jonassen (Ed.), *Instructional designs for microcomputer courseware.* Hillsdale, NJ: Lawrence Erlbaum.

Keys, R. (2006). *The quote verifier.* New York: St. Martins Press.

keystosaferschools.com. (2000). Bullying in schools. *Safer Schools News (18).* Retrieved September 6, 2009, from www.keystosaferschools.com/Newsletter_vol.18htm

Kirsner, S. (2008). *Inventing the movies: Hollywood's epic battle between innovation and the status quo, from Thomas Edison to Steve Jobs.* Los Angeles, CA: CinemaTech Books.

Kiviat, B. J. (2000). The social side of schooling. *Johns Hopkins Magazine, 51*(2), 114.

Kiwanis International. (2010). *What is a Kiwanian?* Retrieved January 8, 2010, from http://www.kiwanis.org/WhoWeAre/WhatisaKiwanian/tabid/297/Default.aspx

Kliebard, H. M. (2002). *Changing course. American curriculum reform in the 20th century.* New York: Teachers College Press.

Knezek, D. (2009). Speaking personally—with Don Knezek. *American Journal of Distance Education, 23*(2), 104–115.

Kohm, B., & Nance, B. (2009). Creating collaborative cultures. *Educational Leadership, 67*(2), 67–72.

Kohn, A. (September, 1993). Choices for children: Why and how to let students decide. *Phi Delta Kappan.* Retrieved February 10, 2009, from http://www.alfiekohn.org/teaching/cfc.htm

Kohn, A. (1999). *The schools our children deserve: Moving beyond traditional classrooms and "tougher standards."* Boston: Houghton Mifflin.

Kohn, A. (2001, January). Fighting the tests: A practical guide to rescuing our schools. *Phi Delta Kappan.* Retrieved February 10, 2009, from http://alfiekohn.org/teaching/cfc.htm

Kohn, A. (2006). *Beyond discipline: From compliance to community.* Alexandria, VA: Association for Supervision and Curriculum Development (ASCD).

Kohn, A. (2008a, September 10). It's not what we teach: It's what they learn. *Education Week.* Retrieved February 10, 2009, from http://alfiekohn.org/teaching/edweek/inwwt.htm

Kohn, A. (2008b, Spring). Progressive education: Why it's hard to beat, but also hard to find. *Independent School.* Retrieved February 10, 2009, from http://www.alfiekohn.org/teaching/progressive.htm

Lazear, J. (1992). *Meditations for men who do too much*. New York: Simon & Schuster.

Lee, V. E., & Smith, J. B. (1996). Collective responsibility for learning and its effect on gains in achievement and engagement for early secondary school students. *American Journal of Education, 104*(2), 103–147.

Leithwood, K., Louis, K. S., Anderson, S., Wahlstrom, K. (2004). *How leadership influences student learning*. New York: The Wallace Foundation.

LeRoy, M. (Producer), Fleming, V. (Director). (1939). *The Wizard of Oz*. [Motion picture]. Metro-Goldwyn-Mayer.

Lewis, C. C., Schaps, E., & Watson, M. (1995, March). Beyond the pendulum: Creating challenging and caring schools. *Phi Delta Kappan, 76*(7), 547–554.

Lezotte, L. W. (1997). *Learning for all*. Okemos, MI: Effective School Products.

Lezotte, L. W., & McKee, K. M. (2006). *Stepping up: Leading the charge to improve our schools*. Okemos, MI: Effective Schools.

Lifsey, R. (2008). *What is teaching? An outsider's interpretive perspective*. Unpublished interview, Educational Leadership and Foundations Department, The University of Texas at El Paso, El Paso, TX.

Lipsitz, J. (1984). *Successful schools for young adolescents*. New Brunswick, NJ: Transaction Books.

Lipson, M., Valencia, S., Wixson, K., & Peters, C. (1993). Integration and thematic teaching: Integration to improve teaching and learning. *Language Arts, 70*(4), 252–264.

Lombardi, V., Jr. (2005). *Twenty-six lessons from Vince Lombardi, the world's greatest coach*. New York: McGraw-Hill.

Lovely, S., & Buffum, A. (2007). *Generations at school: Building an age-friendly learning community*. Thousand Oaks, CA: Corwin.

Lunenburg, F. C., & Irby, B. J. (2006). *The principalship: Vision to action*. Belmont, CA: Wadsworth, Cengage Learning.

Lunenburg, F. C., & Ornstein, A. C. (2008). *Educational administration: Concepts & practices* (5th ed.). Belmont, CA: Thomson Wadsworth.

Mackenzie, G. N. (1949). Curriculum leadership. *Educational Leadership, 6*(5), 264–271.

Maltin, L. (2007). *Leonard Maltin's 2007 movie guide*. New York: Penguin Group.

March, J. K., & Peters, K. H. (2002). Effective schools: Curriculum development and instructional design in the effective schools process. *Phi Delta Kappan, 83*(5), 378–379. Retrieved January 5, 2009, from http://www.questia.com.

Marsh, C. J., & Willis, G. (2007). *Curriculum: Alternative approaches, ongoing issues*. Upper Saddle River, NJ: Pearson Education.

Marshall, K. (2010). Approaches to curriculum development. In Parkay, F. W., Hass, G., & Anctil, E. J. (Eds.), *Curriculum leadership: Readings for developing quality educational programs* (pp. 278–287). Upper Saddle River, NJ: Pearson Education.

Martin, C. A., & Tulgan, B. (2006). *Managing the generation mix: From urgency to opportunity* (2nd ed.). Amherst, MA: HRD Press.

Marzano, R. J. (1992). *A different kind of classroom: Teaching with dimensions of learning*. Alexandria, VA: Association for Supervision and Curriculum Development (ASCD).

Marzano, R. J., & Kendall, J. S. (1998). *Awash in a sea of standards*. Aurora, CO: Mid-continent Research for Educational Learning.

Marzano, R. J., & Waters, T. (2009). *District leadership that works*. Bloomington, IN: Solution Tree.

Marzano, R. J., Waters, T., & McNulty, B. A. (2005). *School leadership that works: From research to results*. Alexandria, VA: Association for Supervision and Curriculum Development (ASCD).

Maslow, A. (1999). *Toward a psychology of being* (2nd ed.). New York: John Wiley & Sons.

Maxwell, J. C. (2003a). *Ethics 101*. New York: Center Street.

Maxwell, J. C. (2003b). *Leadership: Promises for every day—A daily devotional*. Nashville, TN: Thomas Nelson.

McLaughlin, M. W., & Talbert, J. E. (2001). *Professional communities and the work of high school teaching*. Chicago: University of Chicago Press.

McLuhan, M., & Fiore, Q. (2005). *The medium is the massage: An inventory of effects*. Berkeley, CA: Gingko Press.

McNally, H. J., & Passow, A. H. (1960). *Improving the quality of public school programs*. New York: Bureau of Publications, Teachers College, Columbia University.

McNeil, L. (2000). *Contradictions of school reform: Educational costs of standardized testing*. New York: RoutledgeFalmer.

Meier, D. (2000). *Will standards save public education?* Boston: Beacon Press.

Méndez, Z. Y., & Sorenson, R. D. (2010). Rethinking the role of the principal leader in curriculum change and renewal. *Texas Study of Secondary Education*.

Miller, J. P., & Seller, W. (1990). *Curriculum perspective and practice*. Toronto, Ontario: Pears Education Center.

Montopoli, B. (2010). *Rhode Island teacher firings*. Retrieved March 13, 2010, from http://www.cbsnews.com/8301–503544_162–6239681–503544.html

Moody, L., & Amos, N. (1975). The impact of principal involvement in instructional planning with teacher teams on academic achievement of elementary school pupils. *Bureau of Educational Research: Mississippi State University*. Retrieved on February 18, 2009, from http://www.eric.ed.gov/ERICDocs/data/ericdocs2sql/content_storage_01/00000 19b/80/3/1/76/74.pdf

Murphy, J., & Shipman, J. (1998, April). *The interstate school leaders' licensure consortium: A standards-based approach to strengthening educational leadership*. Paper presented at the annual conference of the American Educational Research Association, San Diego, CA.

Nansel, T. R., Hetland, J., Craig, W., Carvalhosa, S., Overbeck, M., & Scheidt, P. C. (2004). Cross-national consistency in the relationship between bullying behaviors and psychosocial adjustment. *Archives of Pediatrics and Adolescent Medicine, 158*(1), 731–736.

Nansel, T. R., Overbeck, M. D., Saluja, G., & Raun, W. J. (2004). Health behavior in school-age children. Bullying analyses working group. *Archives of Pediatrics and Adolescent Medicine, 158*(8), 831–832.

Nansel, T. R., Pilla, R. S., Raun, W. M., Simons-Morton, B., & Scheidt, P. C. (2001). *School violence: Methods, issues, and contexts*. Hauppauge, NY: NovaScience.

Nash, R. J. (1996). *"Real world" ethics: Frameworks for educators and human service professionals*. New York: Teachers College Press.

National Board for Professional Teaching Standards. (1989). *What teachers should know and be able to do*. Retrieved March 27, 2009, from http://www.nbpts.org/about/coreprops.cfm#introfcp

National Commission on Teaching and America's Future. (1996). *What matters most: Teaching for America's future*. New York: Author.

National Council of Teachers of Mathematics. (1989). *Curriculum and evaluation standards for school mathematics*. Reston, VA: Author.

National Middle School Association. (2003). *This we believe: Successful schools for young adolescents: A position paper of the National Middle School Association*. Westerville, OH: Author.

National Policy Board for Educational Administration. (NPBEA). (2002). *Instructions to implement standards for advanced programs in educational leadership for principals, superintendents, curriculum directors, and supervisors*. Arlington, VA: Author.

Newmann, F., & Associates. (1996). *Authentic achievement: Restructuring schools for intellectual quality*. San Francisco: Jossey-Bass.

Newmann, F. M., King, M. B., & Youngs, P. (2000). Professional development that addresses school capacity: Lessons from urban elementary schools. *American Journal of Education, 108(4), 259–299.*

Northouse, P. G. (2007). *Leadership: Theory and practice*. Thousand Oaks, CA: Sage.

Northwest Regional Educational Laboratory (NREL). (2001). Integrated curriculum. *School Improvement Research Series (SIRS).* Retrieved February 10, 2009, from http://www.nwrel.org/scpd/sirs/8/c016.html

Northwest Regional Educational Laboratory. (2005). *Principal leadership for accountability*. Portland, OR: Author.

Oliva, P. F. (2009). *Developing the curriculum*. Upper Saddle River, NJ: Pearson Education.

Olweus, D., & Limber, S. (2005). *Bullying prevention program: Blueprints for violence prevention*. Boulder, CO: Center for the Study and Prevention of Violence, Institute of Behavior Science.

Organization for Economic Cooperation and Development (OECD). (2009). *Highlights from education at a glance*. Paris, France: Author.

Ornstein, A. C., & Hunkins, F. P. (1998). *Curriculum: Foundations, principles, and issues*. Needham Heights, MA: Allyn & Bacon.

Ornstein, A. C., & Hunkins, F. P. (2004). *Curriculum: Foundations, principles, and issues*. Upper Saddle River, NJ: Pearson Education.

Ornstein, A. C., & Hunkins, F. P. (2009). *Curriculum: Foundations, principles, and issues*. Upper Saddle River, NJ: Pearson Education.

Overton, J. (2005). *Farragut's "damn the torpedoes!"* Retrieved February 25, 2010, from http://findrticles.com/p/articles/mi_1_35/ai_n15674076

Palmer, P. (2007). *The courage to teach: Exploring the inner landscape of a teacher's life*. San Francisco: Jossey-Bass.

Parkay, F. W., Hass, G., & Anctil, E. J. (2010). *Curriculum leadership: Readings for developing quality educational programs*. Upper Saddle River, NJ: Pearson Education.

Paulson, A. (2009). A Colorado school district does away with grade levels. *The Christian Science Monitor*. Retrieved on February 17, 2009, from http://news.yahoo.com/s/csm/20090210/ts_csm/agradeless/print

Peterson, E. H. (2007). *The message: The Bible in contemporary language*. Colorado Springs, CO: NavPress.

Pollack, W. S. (2004). *Real boys: Rescuing our sons from the myths of boyhood*. New York: Henry Holt and Company.

Porter, L. W. (1968). *Managerial attitudes and performance*. Homewood, IL: R. D. Irwin.

Pray, L., & Monhardt, R. (2009). Sheltered instruction techniques for ELLs. *Science and Children, 46*(7), 34–38.

Pufahl, I., Rhodes, N. C., & Christian, N. (2001). *What we can learn from foreign language teaching in other countries*. Washington, DC: Center for Applied Linguistics.

Qualls, B. (1981). *Principal expectations*. Unpublished course lecture, Texas A&M University-Corpus Christi, Corpus Christi, TX.

The Quote Garden. (2010). Quotations about change. Retrieved February 10, 2010, from http://www.quotegarden.com/change.html

Rainer, J., Guyton, E., & Bowen, C. (2000). *Constructivist pedagogy in primary classrooms*. Retrieved January 5, 2009, from http://eric.ed.gov/ERICWebPortal/custom/portlets/recordDetails/detailmini.jsp?_nfpb=tru

Random Quotes. (2010). Alfred Edward Perlman. Retrieved February 14, 2010, from http://randomquotes.org/quote/16343-after-youve-done-a-thing-the-same-way-for-two-yea.html

Raywid, M. A. (1993). Finding time for collaboration. *Educational Leadership, 51*(1), 30–34.

Razik, T. A., & Swanson, A. D. (2010). *Fundamental concepts of educational leadership and management*. Upper Saddle River, NJ: Pearson Education.

Reeves, D. B. (2006). *The learning leader: How to focus school improvement for better results*. Alexandria, VA: Association for Supervision and Curriculum Development (ASCD).

Robbins, S. P. (2006). *Organizational behavior: Concepts, controversies, and applications* (8th ed.). Englewood Cliffs, NJ: Prentice-Hall.

Robbins, S. P., & Hunsaker, P. L. (2005). *Training in interpersonal skills: TIPS for managing people at work* (4th ed.). Englewood Cliffs, NJ: Prentice-Hall.

Robbins, S. P., & Judge, T. A. (2008). *Organizational behavior* (13th ed.). Englewood Cliffs, NJ: Prentice-Hall.

Robinson, S., Stempel, A., & McCree, I. (2005). *Gaining traction, gaining ground: How some high schools accelerate learning for struggling students*. Washington, DC: Education Trust.

Rogers, D. E. (1952). Happy trails to you. On *Route 66* [Drive Time] [Audio Download]. New York City: SONY Music Entertainment Downloads LLC.

Rosaparksfacts.com. (2010). *Rosa Parks quotes*. Retrieved March 20, 2010, from http://www.rosaparksfacts.com/rosa-parks-quotes.php

Ross, G., & Burton, T. (2005). *Charlie and the Chocolate Factory* [Motion picture]. Warner Bros.

Roth, K. J. (2000). Photosynthesis of Columbus: Exploring interdisciplinary curriculum from the students' perspectives. In J. Goodlad, S. Wineburg,

& P. Grossman (Eds.), *Interdisciplinary curriculum: Challenges to implementation* (pp. 153–179). New York: Teachers College Press.

Rugg, H. (1927). List of fundamental questions on curriculum making. In G. M. Whipple (Ed.), *The foundations of curriculum making*. Twenty-sixth Yearbook, National Society for the Study of Education, Part II. Bloomington, IN: Public School Publishing.

St. George, D. (2009). 6,473 texts a month, but at what cost? *The Washington Post.* Retrieved April 19, 2010, from http://www.washingtonpost.com/wp-dyn/content/article/2009/02/21/AR2009022101863.html

Saphier, J. (2005). Masters of motivation. In R. DuFour, R. Eaker, & R. DuFour (Eds.), *On common ground: The power of professional learning communities* (pp. 85–113). Bloomington, IN: Solution Tree.

Sarason, S. B. (1994). *The case for a change.* San Francisco: Jossey-Bass.

Sarason, S. (1996). *Revisiting "The culture of the school and the problem of change."* New York: Teachers College Press.

Sawyer, K. (2007). *Group genius: The creative power of collaboration.* New York: Basic Books.

Schiefele, U., Krapp, A., & Winteler, A. (1991). Interest as a predictor of academic achievement: A meta-analysis of research. In Renninger, K. A., Hidi, S., & Krapp, A. (Eds.), *The role of interest in learning and development.* Hillsdale, NJ: Lawrence Erlbaum.

Schmoker, M. (1999). *Results: The key to continuous school improvement* (2nd ed.). Alexandria, VA: Association for Supervision and Curriculum Development (ASCD).

Schmoker, M. (2005). No turning back: The iron-clad case for professional learning communities. In R. DuFour, R. Eaker, & R. DuFour (Eds.), *On common ground: The power of professional learning communities* (pp. 135–153). Bloomington, IN: Solution Tree.

Schmoker, M. (2006). *Results now: How we can achieve unprecedented improvements in teaching and learning.* Alexandria, VA: Association for Supervision and Curriculum Development (ASCD).

Schmuck, R. (2006). *Practical action research for change* (2nd ed.). Thousand Oaks, CA: Corwin.

Search Institute. (2003). *Insights and evidence: Boosting student achievement—New research on the power of curriculum development.* Minneapolis, MN: Author.

Seidel, K., & Short, E. (2005). Connecting students, standards, and success: Using standards-based curriculum connections to improve learning. *Alliance for Curriculum Reform.* Retrieved January 3, 2009, from http://www.acr.uc.edu/journal.html

Senge, P. (1990). *The fifth discipline: The art and practice of the learning organization.* New York: Doubleday.

Senge, P., Cambron-McCabe, N., Lucas, T., Smith, B., Dutton, J., & Kleiner, A. (2000). *Schools that learn: A fifth discipline field book for educators, parents, and everyone who cares about education.* New York: Doubleday.

Sergiovanni, T. J., Kelleher, P., McCarthy, M. M., & Fowler, F. C. (2009). *Educational governance and administration.* Upper Saddle River, NJ: Pearson Education.

Shapiro, J. P., & Stefkovich, J. A. (2005). *Ethical leadership and decision making in education: Applying theoretical perspectives to complex dilemmas.* Mahwah, NJ: Lawrence Erlbaum.

Shipman, N. J., Topps, B. W., & Murphy, J. (1998, April). *Linking the ISLLC standards to professional development and relicensure.* Paper presented at the annual conference of the American Educational Research Association, San Diego, CA.

Smith, M. S. (2006, November). Chat wrap-up. In G. Cawelti, The side effects of NCLB. *Educational Leadership, 64*(3), 64–68.

Smith, S. C., & Piele, P. K. (Eds.). (2006). *School leadership* (4th ed.). Thousand Oaks, CA: Corwin.

Sorenson, R. D. (2004). Principal leadership and the art of influencing others. *Texas Study of Secondary Education, 13*(2), 15–18.

Sorenson, R. D. (2005). The complexity of change: The school leader as a change initiator. *Texas Study of Secondary Education, 15*(1), 13–15.

Sorenson, R. D. (2006). *Information analysis: An examination of problematic causal factors at the campus level.* Unpublished course material, The University of Texas at El Paso.

Sorenson, R. D. (2007). *They talk: Voices from the field of school administration-Part II.* Unpublished interviews of school principals and lead teachers, The University of Texas at El Paso. The Department of Educational Leadership and Foundations.

Sorenson, R. D., Cortez, T. M., & Negrete, M. A. (2010, Spring). What makes for an ideal principal? A framework for leadership development and organizational success as perceived by lead teachers. *Leadership in Focus, 19,* 46–49.

Sorenson, R. D., & Goldsmith, L. M. (2006). *The principal's guide to school budgeting.* Thousand Oaks, CA: Corwin.

Sorenson, R. D., & Goldsmith, L. M. (2009). *The principal's guide to managing school personnel.* Thousand Oaks, CA: Corwin.

Sousa, D. (2009). Brain friendly learning for teachers. *Educational Leadership* [Electronic version], *66,* 1–6.

Sparks, D. (2005). Leading for transformation in teaching, learning, and relationships. In R. DuFour, R. Eaker, & R. DuFour (Eds.), *On common ground: The power of professional learning communities* (pp. 155–175). Bloomington, IN: Solution Tree.

Steffy, B. E., Wolfe, M. P., Pasch, S. H., & Enz, B. J. (Eds.). (2000). *Life cycle of the career teacher.* Thousand Oaks, CA: Corwin.

Stenhouse, L. (1988). Case study methods. In J. P. Keeves (Ed.), *Educational research, methodology, and measurement: An international handbook.* New York: Pergamon Press.

Stewart, V. (2009). A classroom as wide as the world. In H. Jacobs (Ed.), *Curriculum 21: Essential education for a changing world* (pp. 97–114). Alexandria, VA: Association for Supervision and Curriculum Development.

Strand, R., & Ewing, B. (2006). *Living by design: Discovering the spirit, soul and body connection.* Rapid City, SD: Real Life Press.

Taba, H. (1962). *Curriculum development: Theory and practice.* New York: Harcourt, Brace & World.

Tanner, D., & Tanner, L. (2006). *Curriculum development: Theory into practice.* Englewood Cliffs, NJ: Prentice-Hall.

Tapscott, D. (2009). *Growing up digital: How the net generation is changing your world.* New York: McGraw Hill.

Teachingvalues.com. (2010). *The golden rule in world religions.* Retrieved March 23, 2010, from http://www.teachingvalues.com/goldenrule.html

Texas Association of School Administrators. (2008). *Creating a new vision for public education in Texas: A work in progress for further development.* Austin, TX: Author.

ThinkExist.com Quotations. (2010). Lao Tzu quotes. Retrieve October 11, 2010, from http://thinkexist.com/quotation/a_leader_is_best_when_people_barely_know_he/214091.html

Tobias, S. (1994). Interest, prior knowledge, and learning. *Review of Educational Research, 64,* 37–54.

Tomlinson, C. A. (2005). *How to differentiate instruction in mixed-ability classrooms* (2nd ed.). Upper Saddle River, NJ: Pearson Education.

Tomlinson, C. A., & McTighe, J. (2006). *Integrating differentiated instruction and understanding by design: Connecting content and kids.* Alexandria, VA: Association for Supervision and Curriculum Development (ASCD).

Tomlinson, C. A., et al. (2004). Differentiating instruction in response to student readiness, interest, and learning profile in academically diverse classrooms: A review of the literature. *Journal for the Education of the Gifted, 27,* 119–145.

Turville, J. (2007). *Differentiating by student interest: Practical lessons and strategies.* Larchmont, NY: Eye on Education.

Ubben, G. C., Hughes, L. W., & Norris, C. J. (2007). *The principal: Creative leadership for excellence in schools.* Upper Saddle River, NJ: Pearson Education.

U.S. Department of Education. (1998). *Preventing bullying: A manual for schools and communities.* (Publication No. EQ0118B). Washington, DC: Author.

Vaill, P. B. (1989). *Managing as a performing art: New ideas for a world of chaotic change.* San Francisco: Jossey-Bass.

Vaill, P. B. (1996). *Learning as a way of being: Strategies for survival in a world of permanent white water.* San Francisco: Jossey-Bass.

Vars, G. F. (1991). Integrated curriculum in historical perspective. *Educational Leadership, 49*(2), 14–15.

Vars, G. F. (2001). Can curriculum integration survive in an era of high-stakes testing? *Middle School Journal, 33*(2), 7–17.

Von Frank, V. (2009). Teacher learning turns school from F to A in one year. *The Learning Principal, 4*(6), 2–3.

Waddell, G. (2009). Who's that teacher? *Journal of Staff Development, 30*(3), 10–16.

Walker, D. F. (1971). A naturalist model of curriculum development. *School Review, 80*(1), 51–65.

Walker, D. F., & Soltis, J. F. (1997). *Curriculum and aims.* New York: Teachers College Press.

Wasley, P., Hampel, R., & Clark, R. (1996). *The puzzle of whole school change.* Providence, RI: Coalition of Essential Schools, Brown University.

Waxman, A. (2009). TAKS testing heaps stress on students. *El Paso Times*. Retrieved March 23, 2009, from http://www.elpasotimes.com/ci_11880998?IADID=Search-www.elpasotimes.com-www.elpasotimes.com

Webb, L. D. (2006). *The history of American education: A great American experience*. Upper Saddle River, NJ: Pearson Education.

Wei, R. C., Darling-Hammond, L., Andree, A., Richardson, N., Orphanos, S. (2009). *Professional learning in the learning profession: A status report on teacher development in the United States and abroad*. Dallas, TX: National Staff Development Council.

Weick, K. E. (1976). Educational organizations as loosely coupled systems. *Administrative Science Quarterly, 21*, 1–19.

Weiner, E. S. C., & Simpson, J. A. (2009). *The Oxford English dictionary*. Oxford, England: Oxford University Press.

Wenglinsky, H. (2005). *Using technology wisely: The keys to success in schools*. New York: Teachers College Press.

Whitaker, T. (2003). *What great principals do differently: Fifteen things that matter most*. Larchmont, NY: Eye on Education.

Whitehead, A. F. (1929). *The aims of education*. New York: Macmillan.

Wiggins, G. A. (1999). *Assessing student performance: Exploring the purpose and limits of testing*. San Francisco: Jossey-Bass.

Wiles, J. (2009). *Leading curriculum development*. Thousand Oaks, CA: Corwin.

Williams, M. (2007, September 21). Father, forgive them. *Our Daily Bread*. Retrieved December 15, 2009, from http://odb.or/2007/09/21/father-forgive-them

Wineburg, S. (2006). A sobering big idea. *Phi Delta Kappan, 87*(5), 401–401.

Wolper, D., & Stuart, M. (1971). *Willy Wonka & the chocolate factory* [Motion picture]. Warner Bros.

Words of wisdom. (1995). Time now for a little inspiration. Retrieved February 10, 2009, from http://www.waterbirthinfo.com/wisdom.html

Yukl, G. A. (2001). *Leadership in organizations*. Englewood Cliffs, NJ: Prentice-Hall.

Zemke, R., Raines, C., & Filipczak, B. (2000). *Generations at work*. New York: American Management Association.

Index

CORWIN

A SAGE Company

The Corwin logo—a raven striding across an open book—represents the union of courage and learning. Corwin is committed to improving education for all learners by publishing books and other professional development resources for those serving the field of PreK–12 education. By providing practical, hands-on materials, Corwin continues to carry out the promise of its motto: **"Helping Educators Do Their Work Better."**